SECOND EDITION

The Action Research Guidebook

SECOND EDITION

The Action Research Guidebook

A Four-Stage Process for Educators and School Teams

RICHARD SAGOR

CORWIN
A SAGE Company

For information:

Corwin
A SAGE Company
2455 Teller Road
Thousand Oaks, California 91320
(800) 233-9936
Fax: (800) 417-2466
www.corwin.com

SAGE India Pvt. Ltd.
B 1/I 1 Mohan Cooperative
   Industrial Area
Mathura Road, New Delhi 110 044
India

SAGE Ltd.
1 Oliver's Yard
55 City Road
London EC1Y 1SP
United Kingdom

SAGE Asia-Pacific Pte. Ltd.
33 Pekin Street #02-01
Far East Square
Singapore 048763

Printed in the United States of America

Library of Congress Cataloging-in-Publication Data

Sagor, Richard.
The action research guidebook : a four-stage process for educators and school teams / Richard Sagor. — 2nd ed.
      p. cm.
Includes bibliographical references and index.
ISBN 978-1-4129-8128-6 (pbk.)
   1. Action research in education. 2. Teachers—In-service training. I. Title.

LB1028.24.S33 2011
370.72—dc22   2010037396

This book is printed on acid-free paper.

10   11   12   13   14   10 9 8 7 6 5 4 3 2 1

Acquisitions Editor:	Arnis Burvikovs
Associate Editor:	Desirée A. Bartlett
Editorial Assistant:	Kimberly Greenberg
Permissions Editor:	Karen Ehrmann
Production Editor:	Jane Haenel
Copy Editor:	Nancy Conger
Typesetter:	C&M Digitals (P) Ltd.
Proofreader:	Ellen Howard
Indexer:	Rick Hurd
Cover and Graphic Designer:	Michael Dubowe

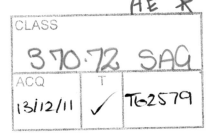

Contents

Preface to the 2nd Edition   viii

Publisher's Acknowledgments   xv

About the Author   xvi

1. Introduction to Action Research   1
   Why Conduct Action Research?   1
   The Complexity of Routine Instructional Decisions   2
   Key Terms and Concepts   5
   Universal Student Success   11

2. Finding a Focus   12
   Zeroing in on Your Priorities   12
   Using Reflective Writing to Find a Focus   13
   Performance, Process, and Program Targets and
      Action Research by School Leaders   20
   Using a Journal to Identify Action Research Foci   20
   Reflective Interviews   25
   Reflective Interviewing and the Problem of Isolation   25
   Analytic Discourse   26
   Team Reflection   27

3. Refining the Focus   30
   Visualizing Success   31
   Doing an Instructional Postmortem   32
   Taking Stock of One's Recent Leadership Experience   35
   Comparing Your Experience With the Experience of Others   35
   Developing Criteria to Measure Changes With Priority
      Achievement Targets   41
   Creating Performance Rating Scales   43
   Rating Scales and Program Action Research   47
   The Special Problem of Long-Range Goals   49
   Assessing Rate of Growth   50
   Determining Adequate Yearly Progress in Real Time   50
   Producing Your Own Rate-of-Growth Charts   53
   Ascertaining Rate of Growth in Leadership Projects   54

4.	**Articulating a Theory of Action**	**56**
	If Not Us, Who?	57
	An Adequate Knowledge Base Already Exists	58
	Going Beyond Proven Practices:	
	Building a Theory of Action	58
	Two Kinds of Variables	61
	Creating Mileposts on the Route to Mastery	62
	Inferring Independent Variables	62
	Using the Priority Pie to Identify, Clarify, and	
	Weigh Independent Variables	63
	Using the Priority Pie With Descriptive Research	68
5.	**Drawing a Theory of Action**	**70**
	Why a Map?	71
	Building a Graphic Reconstruction	73
	Graphic Reconstructions for Quasi-Experimental Research	74
	Graphic Reconstructions With Descriptive Research	76
	Proofing a Theory of Action-Leadership Projects	85
6.	**Determining the Research Questions**	**87**
	Three Generic Action Research Questions	88
	Developing Your Own Research Questions	96
	Two-Step Walk-Through	97
	Drafting the Questions	101
	Surfacing Research Questions for Leadership Projects	104
7.	**Building a Data-Collection Plan**	**105**
	Data Collection and the	
	Competing Demands for Your Time	106
	What Qualifies as Teaching?	106
	What Qualifies as Data?	107
	Data in Descriptive Research	107
	Data in Quasi-Experimental Research	108
	Data Collection and Concerns About Precision	108
	Fishing in a Sea of Data	110
	Securing Research Assistants	110
	Building a Triangulated Data-Collection Plan	112
	Data-Collection Planning for Leadership Projects	115
	Integrating Efficiencies Into Your Data-Collection Work	115
	Using Technology to Compile and	
	Assemble Action Research Data	124
	Keeping a Researcher's Journal	125
8.	**Analyzing the Data**	**126**
	Trend Analysis	127
	Organizing Data to Help Answer the	
	Three Generic Questions	129
	ACR Question 1: What Did We Do?	130
	ACR Question 2: What Changes	
	Occurred Regarding the Achievement Targets?	138

ACR Question 3: What Was the
Relationship Between Actions Taken and
Any Changes in Performance on the Targets?   143
Drawing Tentative Assertions   148
Using Member Checking to Add
Credibility to the Tentative Assertions   149
Additional Tools for Qualitative Data Analysis   151
Qualitative Data Analysis Using Bins and a Matrix   153
Low-Tech Strategies for Bins and Matrixes   155
Using a Computer for Bins and Matrixes   157

9. Turning Findings Into Action Plans   **163**
Modifying Your Theory of Action   163
Data-Based Decision Making   167
Turning Your Findings Into Ed Specs   171
Solicit and Brainstorm Action Alternatives   172
Using Ed Specs to Evaluate Action Alternatives   174
Using Ed Specs to Evaluate Action
Alternatives for Schoolwide Projects   177
Completing the Cycle: Revised Theory of Action 2   177

10. Reporting and Sharing Action Research   **179**
Common Issues   180
Formats for Reporting   184
Creating a Bank of Abstracts   186
Creating a District Archive   189

11. Conclusion: The School as a Learning Organization   **191**
The Two Keys: Coherence and Congruence   192
Putting the Pieces Together   193

**Resource A: How to Use the
Feedback Forms and Summary Reports**   **196**

**Resource B: Five Characteristics
of a Quality Action Research Project**   **198**

Resource C: Applications for Leadership Projects   **202**

Glossary   **214**

References   **217**

Index   **219**

Preface to the 2nd Edition

As I approached the writing of the second edition of *The Action Research Guidebook: A Four-Stage Process for Educators and School Teams*, I spent considerable time reflecting on two questions.

1. What have I learned about the conduct of action research since the publication of the first edition? and

2. How had the context of education changed during this time?

My answer to the first question can be found in numerous subtle ways throughout this book. My experience working with educators over the past seven years has reinforced my view about the centrality of the four stages of the action research process: *Stage 1: Clarifying Vision and Targets; Stage 2: Articulating Theory; Stage 3: Implementing Action and Collecting Data; and Stage 4: Reflecting on Data and Planning Informed Action*. For that reason, the second edition, like the first edition, is organized around those four sequential stages. However, to reduce confusion for the reader, I have provided more examples and, in several cases, elaborated on and clarified instructions for the strategies presented.

While my beliefs regarding the basic process of action research haven't changed that much over the years, I have been impressed and pleased with the evolution of the professional environment where most educators do their work. Increasingly it is expected that our schools will be collaborative workplaces marked by school improvement initiatives driven by collegial teams. More and more I hear schools describing themselves as professional learning communities. This is a significant change. It wasn't that many years ago that Roland Barth (*Run School Run*, 1980) referred to the typical elementary school as a string of one-room schoolhouses connected by a corridor. It is now far more common to see groups of teachers collaborating as a grade level or through vertical teaming in an effort to discover answers to perplexing issues of practice.

The Action Research Guidebook: A Four-Stage Process for Educators and School Teams, 2nd Edition, is premised on a belief that all readers (in fact all educators) share the same ultimate vision: fostering universal student success. It is unlikely that any of us will ever consider our work complete until every student is accomplishing everything he or she is capable of accomplishing. Realizing that vision will require attention to three categories of action: changes in our students' and our own *performance*, changes in the *processes* we utilize, and changes in the *programs* we offer. In this book these three categories of action are called *performance targets*, *process targets*, and *program targets*. While it is possible for individual educators to utilize the action research process to succeed with projects focused on any of these areas, it is becoming increasingly the norm to find teams pursuing this work collaboratively. If you engage in action research collaboratively, you will experience several benefits. For starters, the product of multiple minds is inevitably better than one. Therefore, the very act of including more people and more perspectives in a study will make it more likely that the study will be insightful and robust.

Another benefit of working as a team is that it reduces professional isolation. Some years ago a long-term study was funded with the goal of tracking a cohort of new teachers as they progressed through their careers (Schlecty & Vance, 1983). The subjects in this study were the most academically able graduates of a prestigious university. These were young people who had an academic pedigree that would have enabled them to pursue any career they chose. They could easily have been accepted into law school, medical school, business school, or engineering. But this group was so motivated by a desire to help young people that they chose a career in education. Sadly, the study was brought to a premature halt because after a few years, virtually every one of these young people had left teaching. Why did this happen? When the researchers checked, they found out it had nothing to do with the remuneration teachers receive, and they found these young people were as concerned about students and their futures as they had been when they entered the classroom. It was the day-to-day work of teaching that drove them away. But what aspect of the day-to-day work was so problematic for these young people? As it turned out, they didn't find the work to be boring, routine, or easy. Quite the opposite, they found classroom teaching to be incredibly challenging and complex. What caused them to leave teaching for easier work in other "more prestigious" professions was the loneliness and isolation of teaching. This group of bright and creative young people understood that the challenges faced routinely by classroom teachers are simply too intellectually and emotionally challenging to be solved by any one person working in isolation.

There are several ways you may want to approach conducting action research collaboratively. However, it is strongly suggested that you find a method of collaboration that will work for you. The three most common forms of collaboration with educational action research are indicated by this continuum.

Type 1 Collaboration	Type 2 Collaboration	Type 3 Collaboration
Same four-stage process Same focus Same questions Same theory of action Same methods	Same four-stage process Same focus Same questions Different theories of action Same methods	Same four-stage process Different foci Different questions Different theories of action Different methods

Type 1 collaboration is where the researchers are conducting their action research as a team. The team shares the same theory of action and research questions, collects the same data, analyzes it as a group, and produces a single report. An example might be a team of teachers at the same grade level investigating the impact of a new textbook adoption on student concept acquisition.

Type 2 collaboration is where the researchers share an interest in pursuing answers to the same question. For example, they might all be members of a Language Arts department trying to increase student proficiency with expository writing. This is a very common approach for teachers who work together on professional learning community (PLC) teams. What makes Type 2 different from Type 1 is that in this case, while the members of the team are pursuing the same goal (greater writing proficiency), it is assumed that they hold different perspectives on the best way to realize their shared goal. Therefore, while they share the same vision and will use the same criteria and data sources to measure their students' success, they may be attempting fundamentally different interventions. Elsewhere (Sagor, 2010), I have referred to this as the competing pilot projects model. The wonderful thing about Type 2 collaboration is that colleagues are empowered to be creative in their pursuit of common goals, yet everyone can learn from their teammates' unique experiences.

Type 3 collaboration operates much like an action research support group. Each participant is involved in a project of unique and personal passionate concern. In all likelihood he or she is the only one in the building pursuing action research on that particular topic. There is no question that it is invigorating and exciting to pursue an investigation into a project that you deeply care about. However, it can also be lonely if you have no one to discuss your ideas with. Finding a group of colleagues (perhaps classmates in a graduate class) to meet with on a bi-weekly basis for the sole purpose of sharing what you are doing and what you are learning can be incredibly reinforcing.

A second positive trend I've noticed in school environments in the years since the publication of the first edition is a positive flattening of the organizational structure of the schoolhouse. Opportunities for teacher leadership are expanding at an incredible rate (Reeves 2008). Initiatives that once were routinely created and directed by administrators are now frequently collaborative ventures or even entirely managed by teacher leaders. In the revisions for the second edition, I have attempted to provide examples of work at each of the four stages and with each technique (where relevant) for both classroom teachers and school leaders. The reader will notice that the term used is "leader" or "school leadership" not school administrator. This choice in language was quite deliberate. Hopefully, school administrators reading this book will find the leadership examples helpful and relevant to the action research they will be conducting on their administrative work. In fact, one of the cases that will be followed throughout the book is a project conducted by a principal about her efforts to enhance faculty collaboration. However, her example wasn't included only for administrators. School leadership teams (made up of administrators and teachers) and teacher leaders working by themselves will find these strategies particularly helpful when pursuing process or program achievement targets.

As we look at the four-stage process, the discussion and procedures will address both classroom and leadership projects. Where I found it necessary to maintain the flow of the text and maintain continuity and felt there was only space for a single example, I provided a classroom application of the concept. I then followed that example with a comment pertaining to a leadership application and supporting materials in Resource C.

THE NEED FOR CREATIVE PROBLEM SOLVERS

Another significant change to the educational landscape since the publication of the first edition is the widespread acceptance of standards. Not only does it now seem that educators are largely in agreement that students should be expected to demonstrate proficiency on established standards of performance, but it now appears we may be reaching a national consensus on exactly what those standards should be. But knowing what we want our students to know, what skills we want them to attain, and what attributes we would like to see them acquire is only the starting point for school improvement.

While there may be increased acceptance of standards, professional educators are rightfully wary of standardization. I applaud this resistance to a "one size fits all" approach to instruction. Sadly there are some policy makers who continue to argue for the mandating of instructional and educational practices. As a school improvement strategy, educators are frequently told to implement "scientifically proven practices" and do so with "fidelity." Sadly, that approach is built on a myth. The myth being that one approach has ever or could ever be proven to work effectively for every student and every teacher in every classroom and every school. To understand the relevance of this issue, I find it helpful to use an analogy.

In all modern societies, there are legally binding construction standards. For purposes of safety and consumer protection, it is understood that all buildings, bridges, and infrastructures be built to withstand unforeseen threats such as fires, floods, and earthquakes. Yet no one would ever suggest that there is only one appropriate design for each category of building or bridge. Not only would such a position produce an aesthetically appalling result, but it would result in the construction of many inappropriate projects. This is why our society needs architects. An architect is a professional who understands building standards and knows how to determine if a design meets those standards. But that's not all. More importantly, the architect is capable of creatively and artistically adapting everything that is known about civil engineering to the uniqueness of the site and the needs of the client.

I have begun thinking of the professional educator as an educational architect. While technical drawing is the major tool for the architect, action research is the essential tool for the educational architect. Our goal is to creatively design classroom interventions and school programs that will enable our students to demonstrate proficiency with standards. But, just as with our peers in the construction business, that will take more than knowledge of the standards and how to assess them. This challenge calls for all our creative insights in adapting what we have learned about the principles of teaching and learning to the unique characteristics of our current students, our classes, and our schools.

This book was written to serve as guide for the next generation of educational architects. More than anything, I believe that the practice of education is a thoughtful and creative endeavor. The tool of action research is a flexible and pliable tool toward that end. There is no one approach for engaging in this process, hence I organized this book around the following four stages:

1. Clarifying vision and targets

2. Articulating theory

3. Implementing action and collecting data

4. Reflecting on data and planning informed action

My principal reason for using this organizational strategy was to create a handbook that would provide a busy educator wanting to experience the action research process with an easy-to-follow template, one that could be readily adapted to a variety of professional interests and foci. I hope I succeeded in accomplishing that goal. In writing this book, my goal was to provide the reader with two things:

1. Examples and step-by-step instructions for carrying out the action research process

2. A discussion of the rationale for and function of each of the components that make up the action research process

If you are new to action research, I hope the step-by-step instructions will enable you to have a productive and professionally fulfilling first-time experience with practitioner research. Furthermore, I hope the discussion of the rationale for these procedures will help you creatively incorporate each of the four stages of the process into the particular context of your work and adapt them to your own priorities. Later, as you become a more experienced action researcher, you will undoubtedly choose to modify and customize the strategies presented here, as well as invent new ones, as you use the four stages of the action research process to realize your own professional goals.

If you are already an experienced action researcher, I encourage you to look at the activities provided in this book as illustrative suggestions from a fellow educator. Use this book as a potpourri of ideas, which you might choose to try out as written or use to stimulate alternative creative approaches that support your search for answers to the perplexing questions of practice that you are struggling with.

As a handbook, this text was written to be used *while* you are working your way through the action research process. I don't recommend that you sit down and read through the entire book at once. Rather, I envision you reading through a section as you are preparing to work through that stage of your action research project. The intent of each chapter is to provide concrete strategies for immediate use.

Consequently, the book has been organized sequentially, and each activity as well as each discussion is conceptually built on what has gone before. If you are using the handbook in this way—as a personal guidebook to provide guidance as you work your way through an action research project—it likely means that there may be several days, weeks, or even months between the reading of chapters. For this reason, most chapters start with a brief review of previous material to provide continuity.

One of the wonderful things about the action research process is that it is relevant to all professionals, not just educators, who wish to improve their practices. I have attempted to capture the range of educational applications for action research. In the pages that follow, you will meet a teacher attempting to improve student reading skills, a fifth-grade teacher struggling with an ADHD student, a principal trying to transform a school into a more collegial workplace, as well as a middle school language arts teacher attempting to improve his students' proficiency writing five-paragraph persuasive essays.

In each of these examples, the researchers use the same four-stage process; however, you will see them using it in a manner that fits their particular priorities. Each example has been drawn from the work of real educators whom I've had the pleasure of working with or have observed while they conducted their action research projects. I have turned these folks into hypothetical examples by liberally combining bits and pieces of different projects to better illustrate each concept.

As you proceed through the book, you will see that while action research can be undertaken by everyone—teachers, administrators, counselors, and specialists, from people with building responsibilities to those with district duties—their fundamental rationale for engaging in this work may differ on one dimension. There are two principal categories of action research: *descriptive research,* studies whose purpose is to illuminate what is occurring in a particular setting; and *quasi-experimental research,* inquiries designed to test a hypothesis or examine a chosen innovation being implemented by the practitioner. This is another case where my goal as the author was to be inclusive. I attempted to address both types of action research, as much as space permitted.

Considering all the pressure today's educators face, it would be nice if they could call a time-out in order to get definitive answers to all their perplexing problems. But since that isn't possible, they are frequently obliged to simply go with what seems best. As a result, when most educators first engage in action research, their goal is to determine if the actions they have decided to take (their hypotheses) are working as they had hoped, which explains why most action research ends up being quasi-experimental. For this reason, I will introduce each topic in terms of how it applies to quasi-experimental research and then follow with examples of how it can be used with descriptive research, should the process be different.

Hopefully, conducting action research will help you better understand the efficacy of your practice as you document the impact of your work on the variety of learners with whom you work. Every day, you receive feedback through the dynamic relationship of teacher and learner, and that feedback fuels growth.

I, too, have a need to grow professionally and would very much appreciate your feedback on the effectiveness of this handbook. As I wrote it, I imagined myself interacting with each of you. So, as you explore the ideas in this book, I would love to know about your experiences. Please write and share your ideas, your experience, and your wisdom.

In closing, I want to extend to each of you my very best wishes. I hope you find action research to be as enriching as I have. I hope this book proves helpful as you explore and enrich your work and endeavor to enrich the lives of those you work with. But most of all, I hope your work provides you every ounce of joy, fulfillment, and satisfaction that is humanly possible.

Publisher's Acknowledgments

Corwin gratefully acknowledges the contributions of the following individuals:

Carrie Carpenter, Principal
Deschutes Edge Charter School
Redmond, OR

Deborah Court, Professor
Bar-ilan University, School of Education
Ramat-Gan, Israel

Dean Fink
Educational Development Consultant
Ancaster, ON, Canada

Steve Hutton, School Improvement Consultant
Kentucky Department of Education—Highly Skilled Educator Program
Villa Hills, KY

Frankie Rabon, Associate Professor
Grambling State University
Grambling, LA

Diane Smith, Counselor
Smethport Area SD
Smethport, PA

About the Author

 **Richard Sagor** recently retired from his position as professor and director of the Educational Leadership Program at Lewis & Clark College. In 1997 he founded ISIE (pronounced "I see"), the Institute for the Study of Inquiry in Education, to work with schools and educational organizations on the use of action research and data-based school improvement while he was a professor of educational leadership at Washington State University (WSU).

Prior to his work at the university level, Sagor had 14 years of public school administrative experience, including service as an assistant superintendent, high school principal, instruction vice principal, disciplinary vice principal, and alternative school head teacher. He has taught the entire range of students, from the gifted to the learning disabled, in the areas of social studies, reading, and written composition.

Educated in the public schools of New York, Sagor received his BA from New York University and two MA degrees as well as a PhD in Curriculum and Instruction from the University of Oregon.

Beyond his work as a teacher and administrator, Sagor has had extensive international consulting experience. He served as a site visitor for the United States Department of Education's Secondary School Recognition Program and has worked with the Department of Defense's overseas schools, numerous state departments of education, and over 200 separate school districts across North America. His consulting has focused primarily on leadership development, the use of data with standards-based school improvement, collaborative action research, teacher motivation, and teaching at-risk youth.

His articles on school reform and action research have received awards from the National Association of Secondary School Principals and the Educational Press Association of America. Sagor's books include *The TQE Principal: A Transformed Leader; At-Risk Students: Reaching and Teaching Them; How To Conduct Collaborative Action Research; Local Control and*

Accountability: How to Get It, Keep It, and Improve School Performance; Guiding School Improvement With Action Research; Motivating Students and Teachers in an Era of Standards; and *Collaborative Action Research for Professional Learning Communities.*

Sagor can be contacted at the Institute for the Study of Inquiry in Education, 16420 SE McGillivray, Suite 103–239, Vancouver, WA 98683, or by e-mail at rdsagor@isie.org.

This book is dedicated with love
to Tanis Knight, the best educator I've ever known.

Introduction to Action Research

Action research: "A disciplined process of inquiry conducted by and for those taking the action. The primary reason for engaging in action research is to assist the actor in improving or refining his or her actions."

—Sagor (2000)

WHY CONDUCT ACTION RESEARCH?

Listening to politicians and policy makers, one might conclude that the consumers of education—parents, students, and their future employers—are those most passionate about school improvement. While the general public is clearly interested in school reform, no group of people are more emotional and passionate about promoting universal student success than classroom teachers. Most days, even the most celebrated teachers, who are teaching the highest-achieving students, leave their classrooms frustrated, feeling that despite their best efforts, each individual student didn't progress as far as he or she might. The ritual is replayed on a regular basis; exhausted teachers driving home every day wondering why things hadn't gone better and then hoping against hope that tomorrow would be a better day.

I've yet to meet the teacher who didn't enter the profession with a commitment to helping every one of their students prosper. Andy Hargreaves (1991) has insightfully pointed out that the greatest emotional turmoil faced by contemporary teachers is guilt. This guilt grows from the realization that they seem unable to generate the level of student success they desire. It is clear to anyone familiar with today's schools that this guilt syndrome, the debilitating experience of continually falling short of your own high expectations, isn't the result of a lack of commitment, caring, or intellect.

Several things conspire to keep educators in this chronic state of falling short. One is the high expectations that teachers, parents, and society set. There is no question that the higher the bar, the greater the pressure. But no one who cares about youth would want to set the bar lower. Nevertheless, while we pursue high expectations, we should acknowledge that the goal of universal student success, a dream held by most educators and an expectation now codified through state and federal regulations, has never been realized on a large scale. To my knowledge, in the history of humankind, no community has ever succeeded in getting *all* its children to high levels of performance on meaningful standards—which is the current expectation throughout North America. Therefore, not only are today's educators pursuing lofty goals, but they are being pushed to travel where no one has traveled before. And many of them feel they have been abandoned in this wilderness without a guidebook, a map, or a recipe.

Besides having to meet their own and society's high expectations, there are two other significant factors that contribute to chronic educator frustration:

- The complexity of teaching and learning
- The way teacher work is organized

The good news is that both of these contributing factors can be addressed while we advance on the goal of universal student success.

THE COMPLEXITY OF ROUTINE INSTRUCTIONAL DECISIONS

Any problem, be it personal, social, or scientific, can be expressed in the form of a mathematical equation. Arriving at a solution requires giving consideration to all potential possibilities and probabilities. Every variable (factor) involved in the decision needs to be considered in light of (and multiplied by) each of the other variables. For example, when I am deciding what I should wear to work on Thursday, the decision-making equation that expresses this problem is

$$(A) \times (B) \times (C) \times (D) = X$$

A = Shirt choices

B = Pants choices

C = Tie choices

D = Shoe choices

The problem confronted at least 12 times per day by the elementary teacher and minimally 5 times daily by the secondary teacher is determining the best answer to the question

What is the most appropriate strategy for teaching this content to this particular group of learners?

Coming up with a viable answer requires the teacher's consideration of a multitude of variables. To illustrate, let's assume I am a middle school math teacher who is preparing a lesson where I will introduce the concept of signed numbers. The variables that I must take into account begin with the relevant affective factors. For example, I will need to consider how each one of my students feels about me, about math, about themselves as math learners, about our classroom, and so forth. Then I will need to multiply these variables by 30, assuming that is the number of students I'm assigned and my goal is to meet each of their needs. If this sounds complex, just wait; this is only the beginning.

Of course, I must also take into account the cognitive characteristics of each learner. For example, what prerequisite skills does each student possess or what skills is the student missing? Where is this student developmentally? What is her strongest learning style? And what conceptual understandings is she bringing to this math concept?

That's a lot to take into account, but simply knowing the affective and cognitive characteristics of each one of my students is only one aspect of the equation. Even if I understand each student perfectly, that still won't tell me how to teach them. There are at least two other sets of factors that I must consider when designing a lesson. Being a professional, I will want to consider the knowledge base on pedagogy (methods of teaching) and choose the most appropriate method. For example, I could elect to teach this content using direct instruction. Or I could use individually guided instruction, cooperative learning, modeling, and so on. As complex as all this is, just considering the affective, cognitive, and pedagogical factors won't solve this equation. For meaningful learning to occur, my lesson plans need also be grounded in a thoughtful understanding of the discipline itself. Specifically, what is the purpose for teaching this particular piece of content (in this case, signed numbers)? How does this concept fit with previously taught content and how does it relate to the upcoming material? What are the specific skills I want my students to gain from the study of this material?

Without belaboring the statistical aspect of this decision-making equation, it should now be clear that each and every lesson-planning decision made by a professional teacher requires the consideration and integration of a multitude of factors. In reality, designing appropriate lessons for a class of public school students is one of the most complex tasks any contemporary professional is ever asked to face.

The Way Teacher Work Is Organized

But the complexity of the decision making is only part of the problem. After all, in many fields, being expected to creatively solve complex problems is not a source of frustration or dissatisfaction. In fact for many professionals, engaging in problem solving is the very thing that makes the work fun and motivating. Even as complex as teaching is, we aren't the only practitioners that are expected to grapple with perplexing, mind-numbing problems on a daily basis. So why does the complexity of designing innovative solutions to persistent problems prove more frustrating for educators than for many professionals in other fields?

To answer that question, we need to take a look at the second problematic issue: the work context for most teachers. Even if the issues that a professional must overcome are complex, when the working conditions are such that the practitioner has reason to believe there is a decent chance of prevailing, there is justification for optimism. Unfortunately, the reverse is also true: If the conditions of work are such that it is unreasonable for a person to expect success, then pessimism, alienation, and burnout should be expected.

In other fields where practitioners are expected to prevail over unique and complex problems, two types of support are usually present: planning time and support staff. Unfortunately, neither adequate planning time nor support staff are provided for today's educators. These are critical working conditions that will need to be addressed, and, hopefully, one day we will secure the political will necessary to provide these resources for all classroom teachers. Realistically, however, this isn't likely to occur in the near future. On the positive side, there are other things that can be done to address the conditions of work in the short run. This is where this book fits in.

Action research is a small idea. It involves examining data on your work to help improve your performance. Although there isn't agreement on a single set of processes or steps that constitute action research, as presented here, it is a straightforward four-stage process. The four stages of action research are as follows:

1. Clarifying vision and targets

2. Articulating theory

3. Implementing action and collecting data

4. Reflecting on data and planning informed action

These four stages help bring to the surface the critical knowledge and insights we need to improve our practice and move ever closer to the goal of universal student success. As with many simple ideas, the ramifications can be huge. The greatest virtue of action research is its potential for radically transforming some of the most critical working conditions of the classroom teacher, specifically those conditions that when left unaddressed, will frustrate and burn out our best and brightest. The cultural norms and organizational practices that support professional inquiry have an impact on student performance (Reeves, 2010). In schools where the ethic of action research has been institutionalized, teachers routinely experience success, as demonstrated by continually improving student performance and a reduction in achievement gaps (Little, 1982; Rosenholtz, 1985; Hattie, 2008). Better yet, in these settings, teachers find their work more satisfying, more energizing, and less guilt producing (Nir & Bogler, 2008).

In the chapters that follow, we will explore numerous strategies used by teachers as they work though the four stages of the action research process. As you read through this text you will encounter specific examples of teachers working through each of the four stages and explore the strategies they employed. Each example is followed by step-by-step instructions and sample materials for your use or for you to adapt for use with your own action research. As we wind our way through the four-stage process, we will constantly return to the issues of teacher working conditions (complexity of the challenges, limitations on time, and support) and explore how incorporating the habits of action research into your work can help you improve the conditions of your own work.

KEY TERMS AND CONCEPTS

Action Research

At the start of this chapter, we offered a definition of action research that said action research was any investigation conducted *by the person or the people empowered to take action concerning their own actions, for the purpose of improving their future actions.* At this point it would be helpful to expand on that definition so that we can clearly distinguish *action* research from other forms of scientific or educational research. The best way to decide if an inquiry qualifies as action research is to ask three questions about the proposed study. If the answer to all three questions is "yes," then the inquiry justifiably fits under an action research umbrella. If the answer to any of the questions is "no," then while it might be an area worth investigating, action research probably isn't the appropriate approach. The questions are as follows:

1. Is the Focus on **Your** Professional Action?

If you are studying your own work, then the answer to this question is clearly "yes." In addition, if you are studying an issue that you are considering making part of your work in the future, then the answer can also be "yes." According to Kemmis and McTaggart (1988), there are three types of action that can legitimately serve as foci for action research:

Research of Action (Past Action): In this case, the action being studied has been completed (such as an evaluation study).

Research in Action (Present Action): In this case, the action is underway (as in a monitoring study).

Research for Action (Future Action): In this case, the action will occur in the near future (for example, evaluating materials for adoption).

2. Are You *Empowered to Adjust Future Action* Based on the Results?

This question pertains to your sphere of influence. Most teachers are free to adjust their instructional strategies as they deem appropriate. Therefore, a proposed investigation into a new instructional strategy probably merits a "yes" to this question. This is because most teacher-researchers are free to adjust their teaching based on the data they collect in the classroom. Likewise, the members of a school's improvement team who were examining a schoolwide issue and felt that they were empowered to institute changes for implementation in their building would answer this question with a "yes." If, however, circumstances will prevent you from implementing changes, regardless of the data assembled, then you will have to answer "no" to this question.

3. Is *Improvement* Possible?

Although we all know that research for its own sake is a worthy pursuit, the only justification for practicing K–12 educators to invest their finite time in research is if the particular inquiry holds promise for increasing the success of their teaching or learning in their schools. If you hold serious doubts that performance can be improved in a particular area, then you would be wise to avoid action research concerning it.

To recap, an investigation qualifies as action research if it pertains to one's professional action, focuses on an aspect of one's work where one has a significant degree of control, and focuses on a particular area where (with enough information) improvement can be expected to occur.

The Four Stages

As you pursue the action research process through its four sequential stages, you will find that each stage is designed to help you answer a key question.

Stage 1: Clarifying Vision and Targets

Key Question: What do I want to accomplish?

In Stage 1, action researchers clearly enunciate their goals, clarify each of the subskills or attributes that contribute to success for each goal, and identify specific criteria that can be used with validity and reliability to document changes in performance. Ways to accomplish the tasks of Stage 1 and answer its question are the focus of Chapters 2 and 3.

Stage 2: Articulating Theory

Key Question: What approach do I believe has the greatest potential for helping me to realize my goal(s)?

In this stage, the action researcher articulates a detailed rationale for proceeding in a particular fashion. Earlier we talked about the many factors that need to be considered when making a lesson-planning decision. When there is no proven best way to accomplish a goal, professionals may elect to pursue alternative strategies that seem theoretically sound. It is in Stage 2 where the action researchers engage in a deliberate planning process that involves examining and incorporating all the dynamic relationships and interactions they believe exist between the relevant factors that might influence their success in realizing their vision or the performance targets identified in Stage 1. We will work through several processes for articulating your theory of action and answering Stage 2's key question in Chapters 4 and 5.

Stage 3: Implementing Action and Collecting Data

Key Question: What data will I need to collect if I am to understand the effectiveness of my theory of action?

This is the portion of the action research process that takes place while we work, that is, while we take our professional action. It is here that we carry through on our theory of action while systematically compiling information (data) to help us understand what is going on, both above and below the surface. This is where we determine what is being accomplished and the relationship between the actions being taken and the results being obtained. Our work on Stage 3 will begin in Chapter 6, where you will learn how to generate a set of research questions to guide your study. Then in Chapter 7, you will develop a viable data-collection plan designed to produce valid and reliable answers for your research questions.

Stage 4: Reflecting on the Data and Planning Informed Action

Key Question: Based on this data, how should I adjust my future actions (teaching)?

Stage 4 is where we complete the first lap around the action research cycle. It is here that action researchers return and revisit their visions or targets (Stage 1) as well as their previous thinking on the best way to realize that vision (Stage 2). Then, based on data regarding the impact of their actions (Stage 3) and an analysis of those data, action researchers produce a revised theory of action, which becomes the basis for future action. Figure 1.1 illustrates the cyclical nature of the work accomplished through the four stages.

The Two Categories of Action Research

Action research, like most types of inquiry, is generally undertaken for one of two fundamental purposes:

1. To determine what is currently occurring

2. To test a hypothesis (theory)

When researchers seek to understand what is occurring, they are engaging in what is called *descriptive research*. When the research is primarily concerned with testing a hypothesis, the inquiry is called *quasi-experimental research*. (The qualifier "quasi" is used here because in the social sciences, it is both ethically and practically impossible to implement

Figure 1.1 Action Research Cycle

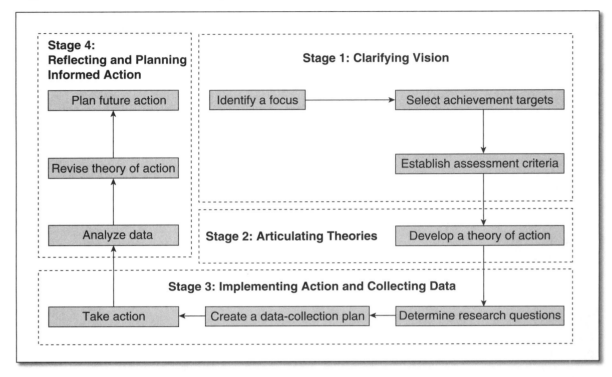

a classic experimental design, since that would require a control group. Research that seeks to test a hypothesis without a control group is classified as quasi-experimental.)

Quasi-Experimental Research

As teachers, we are frequently involved in quasi-experimental research, although most of us haven't been in the habit of documenting our studies. Every day, teachers make use of the best approaches they know. Yet it is a very rare day when all the students in a class accomplish everything they possibly could. More often than not, when we reflect on why a student or group of students hasn't succeeded, it triggers some creative thinking. We find ourselves asking, "What if . . . ?" When we are pondering the what-ifs, we are considering ideas or hypotheses that we might investigate. If we decide to attempt something new, we are saying that we believe this approach is likely to produce superior outcomes than the ones we had obtained before. When you decide to focus on the use of a new or modified idea, your research becomes a quasi-experimental study of the adequacy of that idea or, what is called in this text, your *theory of action*. Because of the dynamic and ever-changing nature of teaching, it shouldn't be surprising that this is the most common form of action research one sees undertaken in schools.

Descriptive Research

There are many times when we find ourselves concerned about something occurring in our classrooms, with our kids, or in our schools. We know that we want to do something about the problem, but we don't feel we currently understand the issue in the context of our school or classroom well enough to design an effective strategy for improvement. When this occurs, our long-term goal is no different than that of educators who have decided to conduct quasi-experimental research. In both cases, the desire is to learn what we need to know to improve performance; it is only the immediate focus that is different. While the lens of the quasi-experimental researcher is trained on the efficacy of a particular innovation (the theory of action) and its impact, the lens of the descriptive researcher is on the system or approach that is currently in place (the *operative* theory of action) and trying to understand its workings. Whatever the focus of your study, be it your theory or the operative theory, at Stage 4, all action researchers end up doing the same thing: they produce a plan for future action based on valid and reliable data regarding what has occurred. Figure 1.2 contrasts these two types of research across the four stages of the action research process.

It is worth noting that these two categories of research (quasi-experimental and descriptive) are not mutually exclusive. Sometimes they can occur simultaneously. In Chapters 7 and 8 we will explore an example of action research being conducted by a hypothetical fifth-grade teacher, Ms. Pioneer. She is implementing a theory of her own design. Her theory of action involves making use of cooperative learning and multimedia technology in her teaching of social studies content. The major thrust of her study is quasi-experimental, as she wants to understand if and how her theory of action is succeeding in furthering her goals for cooperative learning. But at the same time, she will be conducting a study within a study. This is because she has a particular student in class, Joann Heathrow, who is a real handful. Joann hasn't experienced much success in Ms. Pioneer's class, nor has she been successful in any other teacher's classroom. Ms. Pioneer would like to see Joann doing better but has been unable to develop confidence that any specific strategy will help this ADHD child succeed with her curriculum. She is interested in examining Joann's experience in her class (a descriptive action research study), not primarily to understand her program but to better understand how the instructional environment and Joann interact with each other. Ms. Pioneer's hope is that after gathering more data on Joann's experience, she will be better able to develop a theory of action for helping Joann achieve success within her classroom.

It should be noted that *descriptive* and *quasi-experimental* are not simply synonyms for *qualitative* and *quantitative* research. While qualitative research methods are used to paint a robust picture of a phenomenon, they are also frequently used by action researchers conducting quasi-experimental studies. For example, if I were trying to determine the impact of a new innovative reading program (a quasi-experimental study), I might want to use qualitative data drawn from student reading journals and observational notes to illuminate the phenomena under study. Likewise, a team conducting a descriptive study aimed at understanding the climate at their school might use a numerical survey, where students and teachers rate attributes of the school on a 10-point scale (a qualitative method). In reality, most action

Figure 1.2   Comparison of Four-Stage Action Research Process Between Quasi-Experimental and Descriptive Research

Stage	Quasi-Experimental Research	Descriptive Research
1: Clarifying vision and targets	The researchers draw clear and robust pictures of the desired outcomes. An attempt is made to visualize and imagine success in as much detail as possible.	Same as quasi-experimental
	The researchers identify the subcomponents of their vision. For each critical component, they decide on criteria to assess changes occurring with that component.	
2: Articulating theory	The researchers consider their own experience as well as the experience of others attempting to realize the vision and its components.	The researchers consider their own experience as well as the experience of others attempting to realize the vision and its components.
	Based on this examination, the researchers develop a new theory of action that involves a modification of past practice and holds promise for improving performance.	After reflecting on personal experience and the experience of others, the researchers conclude that more information (on what is occurring and how things are working) would be helpful.
	The new theory of action becomes the focus of study.	The researchers clarify the operative theory of action (what is now being done), which becomes the focus of their study.
3: Implementing action, collecting data	The researchers examine the new theory of action and determine a set of questions that they need or want to have answered.	The researchers examine the operative theory of action, looking for aspects of the theory (strategies, materials, outcomes, and so on) whose effects need to be better understood.
	The researchers develop a viable plan for collecting the necessary data.	The researchers develop a viable plan for collecting the data needed to illuminate the implementation of the operative theory.
	The researchers implement the new theory of action and collect the data as outlined in their plan.	The researchers collect the data as indicated in their plan.
4: Reflecting on data, planning informed action	The researchers compile and summarize the data collected in Step 3 and generate a list of findings.	Same as quasi-experimental
	Using these findings, the researchers summarize any insights gained regarding the realization of the vision.	
	The researchers develop a revised theory of action, incorporating new and relevant insights.	
	The researchers make plans to implement the revised theory of action.	

research studies end up making use of both qualitative and quantitative data-collection methods.

UNIVERSAL STUDENT SUCCESS

As mentioned earlier, most teachers approach their work with very high expectations. Ultimately, our goal is to have all students doing their very best work and becoming as skillful as possible. This is not unlike physicians approaching their work with the goal of curing *every* condition and helping *every* patient live a long and vigorous life.

Realistically, we know that this can't and won't happen all at once. Rome wasn't built in a day, and all human illness will not be eradicated in one fell swoop. Likewise, figuring out how to assist all learners to realize their potential will take time. But as inquiring professionals, we want to be continuously advancing our wisdom on what it will take to realize a vision of universal success. In the next chapter, we begin working on Stage 1, where you will be asked to take stock of your personal vision of success. To do this, you will articulate a picture of truly outstanding performance that will be detailed enough to enable you to incrementally measure your success as you move ever closer to assisting every student in achieving proficiency. When we use the term *universal student success,* that is precisely what we mean. It is that Promised Land that we are constantly reaching for, that wondrous time and place where all of us educators are in possession of all that we need know to maximize the learning of all of our students.

With this as our goal, it is likely that this collective search for answers to the perplexing problems of teaching, learning, and school organization will keep us occupied for the rest of our careers. However, as long as we are purposefully engaged in the action research process and possess evidence that we are continuing to learn our way forward along the road to universal student success, we can anticipate a career of repeated celebrations, times when we can stop and collectively acknowledge each and every breakthrough we are making along the way.

2

Finding a Focus

Every educator and any parent with his or her eyes open can see how demanding teaching has become. There simply aren't enough hours in the day for teachers to accomplish all the things on their plates, much less attend to their families, their mental health, and the everyday chores of modern life. But even with all that is required of them, teachers regularly volunteer to abuse themselves, put in countless hours, and burn an infinite number of calories trying to generate improved performance in areas that have emerged as personal priorities. Consider, for example, the time spent by English teachers responding individually to student work or the time coaches spend analyzing game film in preparation for the next contest. When educators have reason to believe that their efforts will produce a payoff in student performance, they willingly and excitedly invest whatever it takes to make success a reality.

Action research has been proven to be a productive strategy for improving teaching and learning (Fishman, Marx, Best, & Tal, 2003; Brown & Macatangay, 2002; Hord, 1997; Joyce & Calhoun, 1996). Furthermore, educators have found conducting action research to be enjoyable and rewarding (Caro-Bruce & Zeichner, 1998). While this is most often the case, these positive outcomes aren't guaranteed.

ZEROING IN ON YOUR PRIORITIES

Research has demonstrated clearly that the intellectual and affective benefits of action research correspond directly to the focus of the research conducted (Sagor & Curley, 1991). If a teacher's action research addresses an issue of significant personal and professional importance, then, invariably, the time they invest conducting the research will be considered well spent. However, if the issue under investigation turns out to be peripheral to the central concerns of the researcher, then even the smallest investment of energy is resented. This is completely logical. With time in short supply, any time spent on one endeavor is time that is not available for other things. Inviting educators to pursue anything they lack passion for is encouraging them to invest in frustration and guilt.

For this reason, the selection of a focus for one's action research is a step that mustn't be taken lightly. Prematurely rushing to a research focus may be the single worst thing a prospective action researcher can do. While there is no one best way to choose a focus for inquiry, there are a number of strategies that have proven helpful. We will explore a few of these approaches as we get started on *Stage 1: Clarifying the Vision and Targets* of the action research process.

The remainder of this chapter will be devoted to five specific strategies that have assisted educational action researchers in identifying high-priority, meaningful topics for study. The strategies we will explore are *reflective writing, journaling, reflective interviewing, analytic discourse,* and *team reflection.* It is suggested that you read through the entire chapter and then decide which of these approaches, which combination of approaches, or what approach of your own design would work best for you; then use that process to narrow your focus before proceeding to Chapter 3.

USING REFLECTIVE WRITING TO FIND A FOCUS

Most educators find their daily to-do list is huge. The have-to's are often-times so numerous that they frequently crowd out the want-to's. Worse, the absence of time for meaningful reflection often results in busy educators losing touch with their own priority want-to's. Occasionally, it has been such a long time since educators have had the luxury of reflecting on what really matters to them that matters of professional passion can no longer be found on their to-do lists.

If you are to enjoy your work as an action researcher, you will be well served to call a timeout at this point precisely so you can reconnect with your professional priorities. While most everyone agrees with the need for and value of reflection, the pace of school life leaves little opportunity to engage in purposeful reflection. I have found that to accomplish this I must find a way to temporarily shut out all other distractions and create a time and space for the quality reflection necessary for zeroing in on a meaningful topic for action research.

Creating a time and space for private thought is the primary virtue of the *reflective writing* process. The cognitive process of composing our thoughts and producing a written narrative necessarily consumes all of one's available intellectual energy (even if just for a few minutes), and consequently it provides us with the concentration necessary for reflecting on a potential action research focus.

While no one questions the writing process as a marvelous way to become focused, it is frequently difficult to overcome writer's block and get started. Many teachers who have used the writing process with their students have found that an effective way of helping someone overcome negative inertia is through the use of prewriting exercises. It is not uncommon for teachers to invest several class periods just helping their students get ready to write. This isn't just a problem for novice writers. Many professional authors spend days, weeks, or even months reflecting and mentally working over an issue before they feel ready to approach the keyboard.

Since it can be difficult to get started with reflective writing and since time is usually in short supply, it is a good idea to create boundaries prior to starting. Boundaries help with concentration and jumpstart the process. An effective way to create boundaries for reflective writing is through the use of a prompt. Any prompt that helps you focus on your professional priorities will work.

The prompts that I've found most helpful are ones that have me engaging in an imaginary conversation with a significant other. I suspect there are several reasons why imagination and fantasy are so helpful in stimulating my reflections. The most important is that sometimes, especially when I am feeling depressed or worn down, I find I begin losing confidence. But as long as I'm breathing, I will never lose my innate human capacity to dream. There is, however, another more important reason why the use of imagination and fantasy is productive for an action researcher. When I free myself to imagine and dream, I am no longer limited by the constraints of what is realistic; instead, I get a chance to dwell, at least momentarily, on the fantastic.

One writing prompt that I have found particularly helpful is the following:

Writing Prompt

Imagine it is the close of this school year. The year that just concluded has been, without a doubt, the most satisfying of your entire career. It has been so good that you are actually feeling depressed that you won't get a chance to return to school for nearly three months! You leave school on that last day positively glowing. You are practically walking two feet off the ground, feeling terrific about your work, about the profession you are a part of, and about the impact your work is having on your students.

Returning home, you find yourself talking on the phone with an old friend. Your friend asks how the year went. You reply that it was unequivocally the best school year ever, exceeding even your wildest expectations! Your friend then asks, what specifically did you and your students do and what was accomplished that made this such a wonderful year?

What do you hear yourself saying in return?

Write your answer in as much detail as possible. Write in the same conversational voice you would likely use with a friend (when we avoid professional language and jargon, most of us tend to become more creative and our ideas tend to flow more easily).

Let's now imagine that I am a middle school social studies teacher who has just written in response to that prompt. I might well have written something like this:

Prompt Response

Teaching social studies to eighth graders had become such a battle for me. Over the years, I became used to seeing the same pattern: My students came to class on Day 1 expecting to hate it. They saw no purpose in studying government and were sure that this was going to be the most boring material they would ever have to endure. Truthfully, I was starting to dread the start of each new class. I once read where at the beginning of each term, the students and the teacher negotiate a treaty. In essence, the kids offer to trade their cooperation and positive behavior in exchange for lower expectations from the teacher. Each year I was seeing myself giving away more and more in these exchanges. It had actually gotten to the point that sometimes I wasn't quite sure why I was teaching this stuff at all, as it seemed the less I covered, the happier it made the kids.

What was even worse was dealing with their cynicism. Heck, the reason I majored in political science and decided to teach social studies was because I love our political system and believe deeply in the democratic process. For the past few years, the message I've been receiving from my students was that I was just another adult, "preaching this nonsense"! In every way possible, from their behavior to the things they said in class and wrote in their papers, they consistently told me that they believed you couldn't fight city hall. In their minds, those in power, be it their parents, the school administration, or the holders of political office, would continue to do just as they pleased. The only choice they felt they had now or, for that matter, would have in the future was to avoid making waves or to get their needs met by cheating or conniving. I'm telling you, it was getting so depressing to hear such fatalism from the lips of thirteen-year-olds that I was seriously thinking of giving up teaching.

Well, last summer, not knowing what else to do, I decided to try something radical. It seemed that every book I'd read said that middle school students thrive when doing hands-on activities. All the consultants say that kids learn best and enjoy it most when they are actively involved. It all sounded good, but it seemed irrelevant to my subject. According to the state regulations, my kids had to learn about the United States Constitution, the separation of powers, and the three levels of government. What was I going to do, put them in a time capsule and ship them back to 1776?

As nothing else was working, I decided to throw caution to the wind and do just that. Well, almost. Since we couldn't do time travel, I did the next best thing. I told them that if they felt oppressed by the current system, they were in the same boat as the colonists. Once they secured their independence from the British Crown, the colonists faced another problem: figuring out an effective way to govern themselves. At that point, the ball was in the colonists' court. Could the founders actually create something superior to the one they so detested? This was when I took my big-time risk. I granted them their independence.

I told them, "I surrender. Your revolution has succeeded; you are now free from my expectations, my curriculum, and my system! It's now up to you to decide how to take care of the business of eighth-grade government!" Of course, I also reminded them that if they didn't pass the district social studies level test, they would have to deal with the consequences. But I told them, as free citizens, this was now their responsibility.

(Continued)

(Continued)

Well, after a few awkward days, all five of my eighth-grade civics classes asked me if I had any advice to give. Breathing a sigh of relief, I told them what the representatives of the thirteen original states had decided at this point: They committed themselves to the work of designing a constitution that laid out what they wanted to accomplish and the processes they would use to get things done.

To make a long story short, the kids took the bait. They asked me what a constitution was, how it worked, and how one could be created. The next thing I knew, they were developing a parallel constitution for the eighth-grade civics classes. Each of my five classes became an independent state, and together they designed a constitution that governed "our" republic as well as preserved "states' rights" for each of the independent classes. Later, each class designed its own "state" constitution. Before I knew it, the kids had designed a system remarkably similar to the three-tiered U.S. system of government. We had three levels: Inside each class, cooperative learning teams worked like local governments, each class behaved like a state, and the United Classes of East-Side Middle School performed just like a federal government.

Well, the year seemed to fly by. The kids had a ball and worked harder than any group of kids I had ever had before. I stopped assigning readings from the textbook, although many times I noticed kids looking stuff up when they needed it to solve an emerging problem. Two weeks before the district exam, I provided a copy of the same study guide I had used in past years and left them on their own to prepare. I was amazed!! They did better than any group of students I'd had before. If you can believe it, my kids tied for the highest scores in the district.

Not only did they learn the material, but also they loved the class. The best part was that on my end-of-year questionnaire, 90% of my students said that social studies was their favorite subject.

I'm jazzed. This experience has given me a whole new lease on my teaching life. . . . I think I'll stick with it!!

Notice that I truly let my imagination flow. I didn't get bogged down in educational lingo or shorthand; I simply fantasized what heaven would look and feel like for me. Later you may want to try your hand with this same prompt. The Reflective Writing Worksheet (Figure 2.1) has been provided for your use when drafting your vision of the Promised Land.

Most state laws or district evaluation policies require educators to set goals at the start of each school year. While on the surface these policies appear rational, rarely do they result in the development of meaningful goals that hold emotional significance for the authors. This happens largely because the drafting of these goals occurs devoid of meaningful reflection. In all likelihood, the narrative you wrote (or will write) on Figure 2.1 will bring to the surface goals that matter more to you personally and professionally than the often perfunctory goals that you are required to generate as part of the evaluation process. Hopefully, your narrative brought to life things that *you* would really love to see accomplished. My narrative certainly did. It contained a vision that, if it were realized, would have made me a very happy and fulfilled educator.

While written narratives are helpful in illuminating an overall focus, they are often too general. One way to sharpen your focus and to gain the

Figure 2.1 Reflective Writing Worksheet

Imagine it is the end of the next school year. The past year has been, without a doubt, the most satisfying of your entire career. You left school glowing with good feelings about your work, your profession, and about the impact your work is having on students.

A close friend has just asked you how your year went, and you reply that it was the best ever. When your friend asks you to share what specifically occurred that made you feel this way, what do you reply?

_____

_____

_____

_____

_____

_____

_____

_____

_____

_____

_____

_____

_____

_____

_____

_____

_____

_____

_____

_____

_____

_____

_____

precision that will be needed for your action research is to systematically dissect your reflective writing. This is done by looking at the big picture contained in your narrative and then identifying the specific outcomes that contributed to the realization of the overall vision. From this point on, we will refer to these specific outcomes as your *priority achievement targets*. The range of potential achievement targets is quite broad. However, I have found that priority achievement targets inevitably fit into one of three categories:

1. Performance targets

2. Process targets

3. Program targets

Performance targets relate to what students are expected to gain from our actions. There are many synonyms for *performance targets:* Sometimes they are called content standards, essential learnings, curriculum goals, and so on. A well-stated performance target can help us focus on what students should know, should be able to do and/or choose to do, and may even cause us to look for changes in how students should feel if our instruction is successful. There are four major categories of performance targets:

1. *Cognitive:* What students know

2. *Demonstrative:* What students can do

3. *Behavioral:* What they choose to do

4. *Affective:* How they feel about themselves and the situation they are in

Process targets relate to techniques or strategies that we want to be part of our teaching or professional repertoire. While performance targets refer to what students can do (or will be able to do better), process targets focus on specific improvements that we would like to see in ourselves (such as our teaching skills, communication skills). For example, I might want to improve my ability to conduct classroom discussions or become better at modeling problem-solving strategies.

Program targets focus on outcomes for an entire classroom or school as an organization. In many ways, program targets are similar to performance targets, but with program targets, we are primarily concerned with the impact on the group or the organization as opposed to the impact on any one individual participant. For example, a program target might refer to the impact a new initiative will have on school climate, faculty morale, or parental involvement.

The Target Identification Form (Figure 2.2) is designed to help you identify your priority achievement targets through a review of your reflective narrative. Use this form to locate and synthesize the specific targets (components or outcomes) that, when taken together, contributed to your imaginary most satisfying year. For example, the priority achievement targets that contributed to my great year are shown in Figure 2.3.

Figure 2.2 Target Identification Form

Reread your report or your journal or review your interview, asking the following questions (write your responses under each one):

What specific accomplishments were made by the people whose work you are facilitating (such as taking greater personal responsibility, more precision in their writing, improved thinking skills)? These are *performance targets.*

_____

_____

_____

_____

_____

What specific changes did you observe in your teaching or leadership behavior (more use of project-based learning, improved questioning skills, more personalized instruction, more interactive faculty meetings)? These are *process targets.*

_____

_____

_____

_____

_____

What specific changes did you observe in your classroom or school (greater sense of community, higher levels of on-task behavior, less misbehavior)? These are *program targets.*

_____

_____

_____

_____

_____

_____

Figure 2.3 My Great Year: Priority Achievement Targets

- Higher scores on district social studies exam (performance target)
- Conceptual understanding of separation of powers (performance target)
- Conceptual understanding of levels of government (performance target)
- Enjoyment of social studies (performance target)
- Positive classroom behavior (performance target)
- Increased skills in managing hands-on learning (process target)
- Increased skills in facilitating rather than directing learning (process target)
- Improved classroom climate (program target)
- Increased students' liking of social studies (program target)

PERFORMANCE, PROCESS, AND PROGRAM TARGETS AND ACTION RESEARCH BY SCHOOL LEADERS

The same three categories of targets (performance, process, and program) apply when rather than being classroom-based, a school leader or teams of leaders are carrying out the action research. For example a principal, concerned about becoming a better instructional leader, might choose to pursue the *performance target* of providing high-quality formative feedback to the teachers she supervises. Or if the leader's goal were to improve the quality of collaboration at the school and she felt this could be advanced through changes in the way faculty meetings are conducted, she might find herself pursuing the *process target* of facilitating faculty meetings with greater amounts of engagement. Likewise, a school leader might want to investigate a *program target* such as an initiative to make "literacy development" the central focus of the school.

The Target Identification Form (Figure 2.2) should prove helpful when finding a focus for most action research. A slightly modified version of this form designed for those in leadership positions can be found in Resource C (Exhibit 1).

Once you have identified your priority achievement targets, you are getting closer to finding a focus for your action research. All you need to do is preface each of your bulleted targets with the phrase, "Investigating how to produce . . . ," and you will have a list of potentially meaningful foci for action research. What makes these good topics for action research is that they focus on the three essentials:

1. Your actions

2. Improving performance

3. An issue of significant concern for *you*

USING A JOURNAL TO IDENTIFY ACTION RESEARCH FOCI

Using a journal to find an action research focus has many of the same virtues as reflective writing. The major difference is that journaling spreads reflections over a period of time. What is so good about extending the time frame for reflection is that it allows us to observe patterns and trends in our thinking concerns and passions.

Some educators are already in the journaling habit. However, for many, keeping a journal is not part of a daily routine and probably isn't very likely to become so in the future. This is another instance when establishing boundaries is helpful for structuring work. If the discipline of journal writing isn't part of your nature, this is another occasion when boundary setting can limit the time needed for this exercise while not reducing its value.

Boundaries or guidelines that I have found useful when using a journal to pinpoint an action research focus include the following:

- Two weeks (maximum) of daily journal entries
- Approximately ten minutes of writing per day (fifteen-minute maximum)
- Respond to the same prompt each day

When using journal writing to find a research focus, it is wise to make use of a consistent prompt. Writing to the same topic each day creates boundaries and makes it much easier to analyze your reflections once you are finished. One versatile and productive prompt I have used appears in the boxed text:

Writing Prompt

What occurred today that was significant for me?

By *significant*, I mean what *went well*, what *went poorly*, what *surprised* me, and *what questions* did I end the day with?

The following hypothetical journal entry is from a fifth-grade teacher, written during the first two weeks of school.

Journal Entry

I felt a little guilty about today's science lesson. It being only the second week of school, I thought I should be presenting this material myself. Having the students learn the material through the jigsaw activity felt like I was cheating, taking the easy way out. But by not having the responsibility of directly teaching the material, I think I was more relaxed than I usually am when I have to teach science. And the fact that I wasn't stressed was a real plus. I moved around the room and interacted with a number of kids I hadn't spoken with much up until now. Maybe I'm trying to convince myself of something, but I think *my* being relaxed was contagious. It seemed to lighten the mood for everyone. I'll be curious to see if this same thing happens next time I have them doing group work.

This is a hypothetical journal entry from a school leader who was attempting to develop her questioning skills:

Journal Entry

I was really happy with my meeting with the intermediate grade teachers today on the new writing program. I sensed early on that they were looking for me to provide an answer to the "sloppiness" problem they had been grappling with. I used this as an opportunity to practice the new approach to questioning I have been working on. At first it felt a little awkward. There were many pregnant pauses when it seemed I was expected to provide the solution. However, in very little time everyone began contributing his or her ideas, and the quality of the discussion that ensued was simply incredible. The solution they designed for the "sloppiness" problem, the use of peer-editing groups, was not only well thought out but emerged with complete buy-in from all the participants.

Journaling is an especially good way to find a topic for a collaborative or team action research project. When using this process for this purpose, every member of the team should be expected to write in response to the same prompt over the same time period. Later, the team looks for patterns in the issues and concerns that came to light across the team members.

What I like most about the journal process is how much material is produced in so little time. After a mere two weeks, you will have produced ten separate journal entries. Now consider this: If you were planning on doing action research collaboratively (for example, with ten other teachers from your school), two weeks of journaling would have yielded 100 real-time teacher reflections.

In Chapter 7, journaling will be revisited as a data-collection strategy. Perhaps you can already see what a powerful data-gathering instrument a journal can be. One hundred individual journal entries generated by people working on a regular basis with the students attending a single school, each one focused on classroom issues that are significant to them, would constitute a goldmine of data. And collecting all that treasure would take just ten minutes per day.

Returning to our original purpose, which was using journals to identify a focus for research, your ten entries may appear, on the surface, to be creating too much material. However, once you spend a little bit of time analyzing the entries, you will easily be able to spot an issue or a few select issues with personal meaning that will be worth spending your time researching.

If you choose to use the journaling strategy, you will likely want to create forms like the Action Research Journal pages shown in Figure 2.4, to collect the journal entries that you and any other members of your action research team generate.

Once you have collected all of your journal entries, it is time to look for patterns. The questions found on the Journal Analysis Form (Figure 2.5) will help you identify recurrent themes that surfaced during the two-week writing period. Now, use the same process that was used with the narrative visions: Preface each of your items with the phrase, "Investigating how to produce . . . ." You now have a list of personally meaningful foci for action research.

Figure 2.4   Action Research Journal

Date: _____

Make ten copies of this sheet for your daily journal entries. Beginning on the agreed-on start date, keep a journal for ten consecutive days. Do your writing after the school day has ended and when you have fifteen minutes of uninterrupted quiet time.

Be sure to place the date on the top of the page, and write in response to the prompt decided on (for instance, *What went well, what went poorly, what surprised me, and what questions did I end today with?*).

_____
_____
_____
_____
_____
_____
_____
_____
_____
_____
_____
_____
_____
_____
_____
_____
_____
_____
_____
_____
_____
_____

Figure 2.5 Journal Analysis Form

Read through your ten journal entries in chronological order, with a pad of paper by your side. Whenever you come upon something that concerned you, pleased you, surprised you, or raised a question for you, write it down. If you see a reference to the same concern, satisfying experience, surprise, or question on another day, put a check mark by that item on your list.

Now prioritize the items on your list in descending order of how many times each showed up during your two weeks of journaling.

_____
_____
_____
_____
_____
_____
_____
_____

For each item, ask the following questions:

1. Does this item have an impact on a performance outcome that matters to me? (Keep in mind an outcome can be academic, behavioral, or affective.) List the items that you responded to with a *yes:*

_____
_____
_____
_____
_____
_____
_____
_____
_____

2. For each item listed in #1 (above), ask yourself, Do I understand this issue or phenomenon as well as I'd like to? List the items that you responded to with a *no:*

_____
_____
_____
_____
_____
_____
_____
_____

The items listed above may be good candidates for action research foci.

REFLECTIVE INTERVIEWS

Another approach for identifying a meaningful focus is the reflective interview, a process where we make use of the ear of a colleague as we verbally articulate our thinking on an issue or concern. Most often, the reflective interview is carried out in pairs. Participants take turns discussing a matter of personal concern regarding their work. Each person has a predetermined amount of time to talk about his or her issue. I like to allocate fifteen minutes per participant. This way, in a scheduled forty-five-minute meeting, each person can have a full fifteen minutes for his or her issue, with another fifteen minutes available for clarification and summarizing.

Reflective interviews give the action researchers a chance to hear their own ideas as they are spoken and as they are heard through the schooled ear of a colleague. It is important to understand that the reflective interview *is not a discussion.* If someone were to track the talking with a stopwatch during a reflective interview, the interviewee would be seen using at least ninety percent of the allocated airtime. The only occasion when an interviewer should be talking is when he or she is confused and needs clarification or if the interviewee seems to have run out of things to say. In such a case, the job of the interviewer is to say something to get the interviewee started again, for example by probing:

- Has this concerned you for a long time?
- What other things have you tried?
- What would you like to do about this?

Figure 2.6 shows an example of a meeting agenda designed for paired reflective interviewing.

To recap, the purpose of the reflective interview is the same as with reflective writing and journaling: to clarify a focus for research that is

1. of significant personal professional concern,

2. within the researcher's personal sphere of influence, and

3. in an area where improvement is possible.

Frequently, the single act of conducting a reflective interview followed by filling out the Target Identification Form (Figure 2.2) is all that is required to identify a focus for research. Other times, it is helpful to follow the reflective interview with a few minutes of reflective writing using a prompt like the one in Figure 2.1, and then proceeding to fill out the Target Identification Form.

REFLECTIVE INTERVIEWING AND THE PROBLEM OF ISOLATION

One of the negative by-products of working in a contemporary school is how lonely the work can become. This seems counterintuitive to many

Figure 2.6 Reflective Interview Meeting Agenda

0:00–0:15

Interview 1

The first person takes fifteen minutes to talk about a work issue. The issue discussed must meet the following criteria:

- It is matter of significant interest (something one is excited or concerned about).
- Performance in this area can be influenced by the work of the interviewee.
- Significant improvement could potentially be made in this area.

0:15–0:17

The interviewer takes two minutes to summarize what was heard. The interviewer prefaces the comments with, "I understood you to say . . ."

0:17–0:22

The interviewee and interviewer clarify their understanding of the interviewee's issue.

0:23–0:38

Interview 2

The second person takes fifteen minutes to talk about a work issue. The issue discussed must meet the following criteria:

- It is matter of significant interest (something one is excited or concerned about).
- Performance in this area can be influenced by the work of the interviewee.
- Significant improvement in this area could potentially be made.

0:38–0:40

The interviewer takes two minutes to summarize what was heard. The interviewer prefaces the comments with, "I understood you to say . . ."

0:40–0:45

The interviewee and interviewer clarify their understanding of the interviewee's issue.

noneducators. They wonder, "How could anyone be lonely working all day in a building with all those kids and all those other teachers?" Of course, the people asking that question have never worked in an environment where they weren't free to leave their workstation for a simple trip to the restroom, without worrying that they might be abrogating their responsibilities. The sad reality is that many teachers and school leaders go for weeks and months without the simple luxury of fifteen minutes to speak their mind and reflect on pressing issues in the presence of a caring and knowledgeable colleague. One of the particular virtues of the reflective interview process for the busy educator is that in addition to helping us isolate a focus for our research it creates islands of adult support in what can become a lonely workplace.

ANALYTIC DISCOURSE

The analytic discourse is a close cousin of the reflective interview. However, in this case, a panel of three to six colleagues conducts the interview, all of whom share an interest in or concern about the same general topic.

An analytic discourse generally follows the following format:

1. *Presentation of Issue.* The action researcher takes five minutes to outline an area of interest.

2. *Clarifying Questions.* Each panel member gets to ask for clarification of anything that is not clear.

3. *Probing Questions.* Panel members ask questions designed to push the researcher to explore and enunciate a deeper understanding of the area of concern. The types of questions asked can include things such as, *What do you think explains this? What things have been tried to address this in the past, here or elsewhere? What would you like to see happen?*

When conducting an analytic discourse, three ground rules must be followed by the interview panel. These rules are designed to ensure that the researcher/interviewee arrives at a deeper personal understanding of the issue. The ground rules are as follows:

1. *Questions only; no comments* (The goal is clarifying the researcher/interviewee's understanding of the issue.)

2. *No critical comments* (The purpose is not to debate but to enhance understanding.)

3. *No suggestions* (It is the job of the researcher/interviewee to make all proposals.)

At the conclusion of an analytic discourse, use the Target Identification Form (Figure 2.2) to fine-tune a potential focus or foci for action research.

TEAM REFLECTION

Many times, a work group (a PLC team, a grade level, a department, or a cross-district group) will want to work together on a collaborative action research project. One good strategy for finding a meaningful group topic combines the attributes of the reflective writing process and the reflective interview. The focus form (Figure 2.7) is a worksheet that has been designed for use by their grade-level and departmental teams when selecting a focus for collaborative action research.

The process begins with each person separately spending fifteen minutes answering the four questions on the focus form. After all have had a chance to do their own reflective writing, a one-hour team meeting is called. The first half of the meeting is spent with random pairs conducting reflective interviews built on the material they wrote on the focus form (Figure 2.7). Once every person has had a chance to verbally discuss his or her ideas with a peer, the entire group convenes and compiles any common issues, ideas, and targets that were identified in the multiple

Figure 2.7 Collaborative Action Research Group Focus Worksheet

Group: _____

Purpose: Conducting action research collaboratively has proven to be both rewarding and productive for teachers, *if* the focus for the research meets four conditions: it is sharply focused, pertains to the realization of a shared vision, focuses on an area where improvement could and should be made, and is situated within the group's sphere of influence. Using this form will help your group find a meaningful focus for group work.

Instructions: Find a time and place where you can allocate fifteen uninterrupted minutes for writing and reflecting on the work your group will be engaging in next year. Check the time and begin responding to the four questions on these sheets. Stick with the task until the full fifteen minutes are up. If your thinking stalls, continue to reflect on the issues, as new thoughts and ideas will likely emerge if you give it time. If you need more space, write on the back of these sheets or add paper as necessary—the more elaboration the better! After fifteen minutes of reflection and writing, your work is done.

Here are the questions:

1. What are the priority issues, projects, and programs that we should be working on collaboratively next year?

_____
_____
_____
_____
_____

2. Which of the listed issues, projects, or programs is the highest priority to you? Why? (Please expand your answer as much as possible.)

_____
_____
_____
_____
_____

3. If the group succeeded with this endeavor beyond our wildest expectations, what would the results look like? (Please be as specific as possible.)

_____
_____
_____
_____

4. In the past what factors, issues, or obstacles have gotten in the way of our achieving this extraordinary level of success (#3, above)?

_____
_____
_____
_____
_____

reflective interviews. Achievement targets that surfaced repeatedly in separate interviews become possible foci for a group (collaborative) action research project.

There is no one technique to choose a focus for action research. Any one of the strategies discussed in this chapter or a combination of them should help an educator select a direction for research that is worth his or her time. Whatever approach you decide to use, it is imperative to *stop before proceeding any farther* to ask yourself or your team, "Is this topic really worth an investment of my or our precious time and energy?" Put another way, you might want to ask,

> If time is spent pursuing improved action in the pursuit of this target or these targets, and, consequently, if insights are gained that enable more success, will this time have been well spent?

If you can answer that question with an emphatic "yes," you are ready to proceed.

3

Refining the Focus

Recreational travel to exotic and infrequently visited destinations can be exhilarating. The anticipation that builds for months before your departure can be nearly as much fun as the trip itself. While there is no question that planning a trip takes significant time, planning is frequently the single most important thing one can do to guarantee that the trip will end up a success.

One of the aspects of pre-travel planning that makes it so much fun is that there are few, if any, constraints on our imaginations. As we envision what it will be like to go where we have never gone before, we are free to fantasize what the trip might turn out to be. Because we are open to every possibility and potentiality, we can approach our adventure with both excitement and optimism. In the day-to-day world, we often find ourselves overwhelmed by what feels like an endless set of roadblocks lying between our goals and our current situation. Yet when we are anticipating a new adventure, anything seems possible.

At this point in the action research process, you are in the same position as a traveler who has just chosen a destination. In Chapter 2, when you identified potential research foci, you were, in effect, selecting the region you would be visiting.

However, as any seasoned traveler knows, choosing a destination is just the beginning. The savvy traveler doesn't stop there. Part of the ritual, as well as the fun, of trip preparation is pouring over maps, reading guidebooks, and speaking with others who have traveled to the same or similar places. It is those activities that help the traveler identify the cities, the sites, and the attractions he or she plans to visit and the experiences he or she hopes to have along the way. In Chapter 2, when you identified your priority achievement targets, you were identifying specific elements of your upcoming trip that you wanted to be sure not to miss.

VISUALIZING SUCCESS

As you daydreamed about your trip (through the reflective writing and reflective interviewing processes), you began visualizing what a perfect trip might look like. For the educator conducting action research, this amounts to imagining all the aspects of student, teaching, and program performance one would see when all of the priority achievement targets were being met in an excellent fashion.

Earlier it was said that achievement targets could be divided into performance, process, or program targets. If your focus is on a performance target, you should have started thinking of what you believe outstanding performance would look like, if and when it is achieved. For example, if I decided to focus on improving my students' writing, I would be visualizing what a truly outstanding piece of expository student writing would read like.

When action researchers are focused on process targets, they are attempting to envision just how things should appear once the chosen process or processes are working perfectly. For example, if I wanted to improve my ability to lead class discussions, I would try to visualize what my classroom would be like when productive and lively discussions have become standard practice.

And when the focus is on a program target, the action researcher will be envisioning all of the attributes of a truly outstanding program. For example, if we wanted to create a positive school climate, we would be asking ourselves what would one observe in a school where the climate was maximally supportive of child development.

Why Is Having a Clear Vision So Necessary?

It has been said, "If you don't know where you're going, any road will get you there." That is more than a clever play on words. When people are unsure of their destinations, they tend to take wrong turns, extend their trips with unnecessary detours, and potentially end up where they hadn't intended to go. In our classrooms and schools, this could mean using inappropriate strategies, going off on tangents, and coming to the end of the year and finding that our students still lack the skills we had hoped and intended for them to gain. Nothing feels worse for an educator. When this happens, we feel a sense of loss. This is because at school, time inevitably marches on. Opportunities rarely exist for going back and giving it a second try. This very real risk of losing our direction and failing to reach our desired destination should motivate us to be disciplined and deliberative when planning our action research, our planned exploration of a not-yet-visited destination.

Dedicated teachers don't need to be encouraged to plan. In fact, it is insulting to infer that teachers don't consistently engage in meaningful planning. When our students aren't performing at the level we want (such as failing to produce universally excellent work), it doesn't mean we didn't plan; nor does it mean we didn't follow our plans. In all likelihood, our plans had been grounded in the best information we had available, and we implemented them with all the energy and enthusiasm we could muster. Simply beseeching us to plan "more" or "better" is like trying to squeeze blood from a turnip. If we are already doing the best we know how and we are working as hard as we can, then what we are currently getting is likely the best we can expect—at least without a significant change in our approach.

DOING AN INSTRUCTIONAL POSTMORTEM

Let's return to the phrase, "If you don't know where you're going, any road will get you there," and think of a lesson, unit, or class you recently taught. Now cast yourself in a new role. You have now become your own personal teaching coach.

After a performance or a match, coaches often conduct postmortems on the recently completed action. They review everything that occurred, trying to learn as much as they can from their mistakes so they can avoid repeating them the next time. Now conduct an *instructional postmortem* on a class you just taught, in your role as teaching coach. Begin with an examination of the outcomes obtained, how your students ended up after instruction or, if your focus will be process or program targets, where you and/or your program ended up. For an athletic coach, these outcomes are the equivalent of the final score.

Following the travel metaphor, the first question your teaching coach should ask you to reflect on is

What roads did you travel on your way to where you are now?

This is a critical question since it is logical to assume that if you take the same road again, it will lead you to the same destination. If we want to end up at a different and better place, it will be necessary for us to take a different route. The instructional postmortem is a reflective strategy that helps us learn from our past experience so we can avoid repeating past mistakes.

A golfer trying to understand what led to his final score will mentally replay every hole, trying to recall each and every shot. When I do this in my role as my teaching coach, I try to review every lesson I taught and each assignment I made. Frequently, I begin this process by thinking of a particular student whose performance I wish to understand better. Most often, I find I am considering a student whose final performance disappointed me. Consequently, when I go over each activity engaged in by this student, I am not thinking of what I had hoped would have transpired (I hit the green with my second shot and two putt for par) but what actually occurred (I hit three balls into the woods, landed in a sand trap, and four putted for a quadruple bogey). The Instructional Postmortem Form (Figure 3.1) is designed to help you review a student's experience with a recently taught unit of instruction.

Figure 3.1   Instructional Postmortem Form

Briefly describe the lesson or instruction unit:

_____

_____

_____

_____

_____

_____

_____

_____

State the skill or outcome that you had expected students to gain from this instruction:

_____

_____

_____

_____

_____

_____

_____

_____

List the significant characteristics of a learner whose experience you will be tracing (such as English language learner, precocious, cooperative, disruptive, gifted, and so on):

_____

_____

_____

_____

_____

_____

_____

Describe the performance of this student following instruction:

_____

_____

_____

_____

_____

_____

_____

_____

(Continued)

Figure 3.1 (Continued)

Using the table provided, list in sequence all the significant instructional activities and the facilitation you provided during this unit or lesson and what the learner produced (grades, scores, products) or what you recall the learner doing in response to the activity:

Date	Activity	Performance, Comment

Use additional space if necessary.

TAKING STOCK OF ONE'S RECENT LEADERSHIP EXPERIENCE

Frequently, school leaders will find it helpful to deconstruct what has transpired with an initiative they had been leading in a similar way to how teachers deconstruct a lesson or unit they have just finished. You will find a modified version of the Instructional Postmortem Form (Figure 3.1) called the Post-Hoc Analysis of Leadership Form in Resource C, Exhibit 2. This form was created for use by school leaders who wish to conduct a disciplined review of their past leadership activity to understand how it was experienced by the lead.

Once we have reviewed the road we traveled to get to our current destination, our next step is comparing our experience with that of others.

COMPARING YOUR EXPERIENCE WITH THE EXPERIENCE OF OTHERS

Suppose you have spent the last three years saving for a European vacation. This promises to be a once-in-a-lifetime experience. You have arranged to spend as much time in Europe as possible, but alas, the time available will be far less than you had hoped. Considering the expense involved as well as your time constraints, you are motivated to do whatever planning is necessary to provide the best possible travel experience.

You have good reason to want to minimize mistakes, such as wasting time at attractions with little to offer, and to get the most out of each venue. Going into an adventure blindly might make sense—it could even make a trip more exciting— providing you had unlimited time and money. But, given your parameters, you want to engage in serious and focused planning. For most of us, this begins with research. Experienced travelers seek the insights of others who have taken similar trips. They want to learn from the successes, what was enjoyed most, as well as from the mistakes, the places to avoid. When collecting this information, the wise traveler has good reason to take note of where the advice is coming from. When weighing the opinions of others, it is always essential to consider the source. This caution is absolutely critical for our work as action researchers because this ensures that we are factoring in the variable of context—those unique aspects of the setting: the characteristics of the students, the teachers, and the group. When it comes to making decisions that will guide teaching and learning, understanding the context can be the most important factor and the one most frequently overlooked. We know this intuitively, but when adopting programs, we often fail to take this fact into account.

The people who develop and market commercially available instructional materials operate as though specific teaching and learning contexts are irrelevant. They presume that what was successful in one setting will work in any setting. While this may be a good marketing strategy, this posture denies what everyone who has managed a school or classroom knows through experience: No two students, no two teachers, and no two classes can ever be exactly alike.

Gathering Insights From Colleagues

There are two main places where travelers go for information prior to embarking on their journeys. If they know people who have recently made a similar trip, they will often contact them to arrange to hear about their experiences. Similarly, when we are about to engage in our action research, if we know of teachers who have been having success in our focus area, we would be wise to talk to them and hear about their experience. The eight questions in the Colleague Interview Guide (Figure 3.2) should prove helpful when asking professional colleagues about their experiences working in your focus area.

Many travelers also find it helpful to consult guidebooks written and published by reputable authorities. When consulting authorities, it is essential to consider the source. One way travelers do this is by paying attention to the publication date. This way, they can be sure they are using the most current information. Ultimately, these two sources of data (peer explorers and reputable authorities) are invaluable when planning an itinerary. While it was reasonable to rely on intuition and personal passion when selecting the destination (the focus for either action research or exotic travel), it is hard to overstate the prudence of consulting with experts before purchasing an expensive program or locking in a nonrefundable plane ticket.

For action researchers, the equivalent of consulting travel guides is conducting a review of the literature.

The Literature Review

While the phrase *literature review* is certainly clear and descriptive, it frequently carries negative connotations for individual teachers and teams of educators preparing to conduct action research. Every educator has experience conducting searches of the literature. For some, this last occurred when completing the requirements for a college degree. While some of us may have found our time in the library to be stimulating, many others will remember this part of the research process as unpleasant and time consuming.

It is our fear of the time involved that keeps many of us from going to the library and conducting a literature review prior to teaching a new unit, introducing a new program, or introducing a new concept. This is understandable, yet terribly unfortunate. We omit this step to save time. But, as a consequence, we often find ourselves going over terrain where others have gone before, yet we do so without the benefit of their counsel. Later if we encounter problems that could have been avoided with a little helpful advice, we become frustrated that we have wasted our valuable time and energy.

I am reminded of a commercial for automobile oil filters that aired several years ago. The company's goal was to encourage consumers to invest

Figure 3.2 Colleague Interview Guide

The following questions can help you assess the applicability of an instructional process or program. Prior to conducting the first interview, ask yourself Questions 1 to 4 regarding your school or classroom. At the start of the interview, share a summary of your answers with the person or persons being interviewed.

Date: _____ Program, site: _____

Person(s) interviewed: _____

_____

_____

Your Setting	*Interviewee's Setting*
1. Why are you interested in the use of this program or process?	1. Why did you develop or introduce this program or process?
2. In what ways, if any, are those who will be affected by this program unique or unusual?	2. In what ways, if any, are those who will be affected by this program unique or unusual?
3. What are the characteristics of the staff members who would be working with this program or process (such as certification, teaching assignment, other responsibilities)?	3. What are the characteristics of the staff members who have been working with this program or process (certification, teaching assignment, other responsibilities)?
4. What resources will be available to support the use of this program or process?	4. What resources are used to support the use of this program or process?

(Continued)

Figure 3.2 (Continued)

Your Setting	Interviewee's Setting
	5. What specific outcomes do you attribute to the use of this program or process?
	6. In your opinion, what other factors contributed to the achievement of those outcomes?
	7. What problems did you encounter when developing or introducing this program or process?
	8. What else do you think a teacher or a school should know before implementing this program or process?

a few dollars in their product and use it for routine maintenance. They sold this concept by contrasting the minor cost of an inexpensive oil filter with the far larger cost of a complete engine rebuild. The company's slogan was, "You can pay me now or pay me later!" At this point you may be saying, "Enough already! I don't need to be lectured on the value of standing on others' shoulders, but I still don't have the time to conduct lit reviews."

Fortunately, the Internet has made examining the professional knowledge base far easier than many of us recall from college, and continuous advances in search engine technology are making it more efficient all the time. The Literature Review Planning Form (Figure 3.3) was designed to help you structure and organize a literature review using the Internet.

Tips on Using the Internet for Research

When using the Internet for research, it is especially important to consider the source. The best method I've found to do this is to follow these two steps:

1. Look in the article for the identity of a school or district that is currently using the approach. If it is asserted that this is a promising practice, but you cannot find evidence of its use anywhere, this should raise a caution.

2. If an implementing school or district is identified, contact teachers or others at the site by phone or e-mail who are currently using the program/practice or have recently used it. Ask them about their experience while taking notes using the Colleague Interview Guide (Figure 3.2). When conducting your phone interview, pay particular attention to gleaning everything you can about the context of their site to determine how similar it is to your own school/classroom.

On occasion, after a literature review or an examination of commercially available materials, we will identify a comprehensive program that appears to be a good fit for our needs. When this happens, we instinctively recognize that the most efficient thing to do is to *adopt and implement* the program as it was designed and packaged. This is another occasion where the travel metaphor may prove helpful.

Adopting Commercial Programs

Many times, vacationers will sign up for an all-inclusive package tour. This is a sensible thing to do, especially if they know other people who have taken and enjoyed that same tour and it includes their choice of venues. This is often the wisest, safest, and most economical strategy to follow. For me as an individual classroom teacher or for us as a faculty team, this is analogous to identifying an approach that other teachers in similar contexts have used with students similar to ours and obtained results that we would like to obtain. Adopting such an approach or program makes a great deal of sense.

Figure 3.3   Literature Review Planning Form

Review the area you've selected as the focus for your action research and the achievement targets you hope to impact through your work. Then answer the following questions:

1. List all the priority achievement targets you hope to see impacted by your actions.

_____

_____

_____

_____

_____

2. List every strategy you are aware of that educators have used in their efforts to improve performance on the achievement targets listed.

_____

_____

_____

_____

_____

3. Go over your answers to Questions 1 and 2, highlighting every key word.

4. Do an Internet search following these steps:
   a. Place the keywords in order of importance.
   b. Do a search using all of your key words.
   c. Repeat the search, dropping the least important key word.
   d. Repeat the process, dropping a key word each time, until you feel you have acquired enough information.

   Note: If you are unhappy with the results obtained, repeat the process using a different search engine.

5. Review the material from your search using the following table to record the strategies that have been reported as successful, noting the context and impact:

Strategy	Impact	Context (Student and School)

6. Reorder the data from the table in order of the similarity of the reported context to your own school or classroom:

Strategy	Impact

The logic of this explains why adoption of commercially available programs is far and away the most widely used approach to educational program improvement. Finding what has worked for others in similar situations and then using it ourselves prevents us from having to reinvent the wheel. But while the decision to purchase someone else's theory of action may be a wise initial course of action, it does not relieve us of the need to determine whether it turns out to be a good fit for us in our context through our own action research. In Chapter 4, we will discuss a process to use when conducting action research on the commercially available programs you may be adopting.

Tip on Adopting a Commercial Program

If after conducting a review of the pertinent literature, you haven't been able to identify ideas, programs, or strategies that you believe are superior to what you have been doing, it might indicate that you would be well served by conducting a descriptive study on your current program rather than rushing to introduce an innovation.

An investigation of what is occurring now may help you identify specific aspects of your program that need to be modified to foster further improvement in performance on your priority achievement targets. Even so, you are encouraged to wait before deciding whether or not your research will be *quasi-experimental* or *descriptive* until after completing your work on *Stage 2: Articulating Your Theory* (see Chapters 4 and 5). Frequently, the activities engaged in as part of theory articulation will result in the generation of an innovative strategy that you will want to implement and investigate.

This is a good time to pause and review where we are with the action research process. By now you should have selected a focus area. You have visualized what excellence looks like and you have identified a set of critical sub-elements (priority achievement targets) that, when taken together, constitute excellent performance in your focus area. Last, you have reviewed the literature and considered the experience of others who have pursued improvement in the same focus area. This brings us to the last aspects of our work in *Stage 1: Clarifying Vision and Targets*—establishing clear and unambiguous criteria for use when determining if we are, in fact, producing improvements with our achievement targets.

DEVELOPING CRITERIA TO MEASURE CHANGES WITH PRIORITY ACHIEVEMENT TARGETS

Earlier, you identified areas of student or program performance, called priority achievement targets. The targets spelled out specifically what you hoped to see improved. Once again, it is worth emphasizing how wide a range of achievement targets can be pursued through action research. It was also stated that achievement targets could be divided into three categories: performance, process, and program. Those three categories cover a great deal of territory. Examples of the types of foci that come under each of these categories are listed in the box that follows.

Tips on Achievement Targets Foci

Performance targets can include foci such as

- Changes in student academic performance
  - Improved computation skills
  - Improved inferential comprehension
  - Expanded variety of voices in writing

- Changes in student behavior
  - Increased attention to high-quality finished products
  - Increased on-task behavior
  - Enhanced cooperation and collaboration

- Changes in student attitude/affect
  - Enthusiasm for learning
  - Appreciation of art
  - Willingness to engage in long-range planning

Process targets can include foci such as

- Changes we would like to see in our teaching skills and methods
  - Leading more invigorating discussions
  - Providing clearer explanations for complex topics
  - Providing timely feedback to students

- Changes in school procedures
  - Adult-student rapport
  - School rules
  - Parent involvement

Program targets include foci such as

- Changes in curriculum
  - Making the content more relevant for the students
  - Integrating concepts across disciplines
  - Incorporating more creative problem-solving opportunities

- Changes in offerings
  - Elective programs
  - Required classes and experiences
  - Co-curricular programs

Occasionally, educational action researchers feel they should restrict the focus of their inquiries to a limited and specific range of targets. That is unfortunate for a number of reasons. When we place arbitrary limits on the focus of our research, we risk working on issues that could actually be relatively low on our professional priority list. When this happens, our work may, in fact, produce positive changes, but produce an unintended side effect. If our finite energy was expended doing action research on a low-priority issue, we will be reluctant to engage in this work in the future. This is a reasonable decision, since the time and energy consumed conducting the research was time that could have been invested in pursuits that could have proven more personally and professionally satisfying.

When we limit our focus to low-priority objectives, it most often happens for one of two reasons. The first is because of a faulty premise that educators should only concern themselves with goals that are cognitive and academic— a stance reinforced by much contemporary political rhetoric. This is a misguided notion for several reasons. There isn't a parent or student who doesn't expect more from education than mere facts and isolated skills. Furthermore, that isn't why most of us went into education. If all we wanted to accomplish was the transmission of bits of information, we should have become computer programmers, not teachers. As was mentioned earlier and cannot be emphasized enough, an action researchers' focus should be his or her area of passion. For that reason, it is once again appropriate to pause and ask yourself,

> What matters so much to me that were I to spend my time pursuing improvement with it, I would deem my time as being well spent?

If your answer includes such issues as student motivation, behavior, attitudes, or affective outcomes, then those are perfectly legitimate foci for your action research.

There is a second reason why action researchers occasionally avoid the pursuit of high-priority yet nonacademic achievement targets: the concern that many priority nonacademic targets, even those with great transcendent value, cannot be effectively assessed. This is incorrect. Any target that can be articulated can be assessed and with a high degree of validity and reliability.

CREATING PERFORMANCE RATING SCALES

Every car comes equipped with a tool for measuring its progress. This instrument is called an odometer. The tool most frequently used by educational action researchers for monitoring progress when pursuing long-term or complex achievement targets is the performance rating scale. In recent years, educators started using the term *rubric* as a synonym for the performance rating scale. Before we leave Stage 1, it's a good idea to develop performance rating scales to measure growth on each of your priority achievement targets.

A relatively easy strategy for constructing a performance rating scale for action research is to follow the following three sequential steps:

1. Visualize excellent achievement.

2. Identify the component traits.

3. Create performance continua for each trait.

Step 1: Visualizing Excellent Achievement

At the start of this chapter, we discussed the importance of holding a clear vision of success. Now, as we are shifting our attention to measurement, it is a good time to return to that concept. For each of the priority achievement targets you want to see improved through your work, you should ask yourself this question:

> If performance on this target was just as I'd like it to be, what would it look like?

To illustrate, let's take the case of Dr. Hernandez, an elementary school principal who is interested in helping her school become a more collegial workplace, believing that this will positively influence student learning. To help her faculty reach this goal, she believes it will be a good idea to encourage collaborative planning.

Dr. Hernandez might summarize her vision as follows:

> I want to see a collegial workplace that is supportive of continuous progress toward universal excellence in student performance. I envision a professional work environment that is supportive of the needs of faculty and results in high levels of staff morale.
>
> I want all of our teachers to feel they are part of a supportive faculty team, so that whenever a student or program issue arises we are able to apply creative problem solving in an effective and timely fashion. Then, as our collegiality increases, I see a tighter and tighter alignment of curriculum, instruction, and assessment.

For a classroom example of visioning, we'll consider Mr. Collins, a fourth-grade teacher who hopes to see his students become highly proficient readers. He might describe his vision this way:

> I want to see my students become skillful readers who love reading. For me it isn't enough for them to simply gain the skills to comprehend grade-level material; I also want them to be able to read between the lines. I want them to understand what the author is saying, but also I want them to gain insights into the author's point of view. I want them to appreciate the versatility of the English language by understanding a variety of techniques that successful authors use to convey meaning and tone.

Both principal and teacher have expressed detailed visions, which helped them clarify their targets. The principal is working on a *program* target, the development of a more collegial school, while the teacher is in pursuit of a *performance* target, the creation of skillful readers.

Step 2: Identifying Traits

Frequently, significant targets such as these are made up of components (subskills) that I will refer to as *traits*. A trait is a specific quality that is characteristic of a performance, process, or program that is critical for hitting the achievement target.

In the case of the collegial school, we can identify the component traits by carefully reading through the principal's statement. I noted the following traits as characteristic of the school Dr. Hernandez envisioned:

- Universal excellence in student performance
- Excellent staff morale
- A collaborative team culture
- Staff as skilled problem solvers
- Alignment of curriculum, instruction, and assessment

Mr. Collins's goal of producing more skillful readers also contained several components:

- Ability to use grade-level material
- Enjoyment of reading
- Literal comprehension skills
- Inferential comprehension skills

In Chapter 7, when our focus shifts to the design of a comprehensive data-collection plan, we will examine how action researchers can make use of performance rating scales as instruments for data collection. However, at this point, these rating scales will serve two other immediate and important functions:

1. Help us to further clarify the priority achievement targets we are pursuing.

2. Provide us with confidence that we can effectively document changes in performance on our priority achievement targets.

Step 3: Creating Continua

Performance rating scales with an odd number of columns (scores) are highly recommended for action research purposes since they enable us to identify a clear midpoint. I operationally define the midpoint on a performance rating scale as "good performance" or "meeting expectations." Good performance, or a score "right in the middle," is where I would like all my students to be; functionally, it can be understood to mean "at grade level."

You can practice building a performance rating scale by using the Rating Scale Worksheet (Figure 3.4). Construction of the rating scale begins by listing the components (the traits) of your priority achievement target

Figure 3.4 Rating-Scale Worksheet

Trait	Emerging (1)	Basic (2)	Developing (3)	Proficient (4)	Fluent (5)

in the extreme left column (one per row). Then, in the middle column, in bulleted form, write your description of what would constitute *a good level of performance* for each trait. Mr. Collins, who is working on improving his students' reading proficiency, might have put these items in the middle column (3) for the trait of inferential comprehension:

1. The student can correctly state the main idea.

2. The student can articulate the author's thesis and back up the thesis statement with multiple details from the text.

Now ask, *What would be the minimum performance* one might observe that could still be called a demonstration of the trait? This is a level of performance that constitutes any sign of movement in the right direction, the tiniest baby step along the road to proficiency. For inferential comprehension, this could be something like, "being capable of making a reasoned guess at the author's main idea." In the column labeled *Emerging*, to the left of the middle column, write down those observable behaviors that you felt would constitute a minimum observable performance on each trait.

Last, ask what *a truly outstanding example of performance* on this trait looks like. Here you are being asked to envision near perfection. For inferential comprehension, Mr. Collins might list the following items:

1. The student can accurately retell and support the author's thesis with multiple details from the text.

2. The student can draw logical inferences about the author's point of view.

3. The student can persuasively support those inferences by referencing specific rhetorical techniques, language usage, and vocabulary employed by the author.

Figure 3.5 reflects Mr. Collins's rating scale partially filled in for the trait of inferential comprehension. Now, using copies of the rating-scale worksheet provided (Figure 3.4), build a five-point rating scale that you believe illustrates a continuum of performance for each of your priority achievement targets.

RATING SCALES AND PROGRAM ACTION RESEARCH

Often, people think of rating scales or rubrics as devices to be used exclusively for assessment of student performance. This is unfortunate, as the rating skill is a wonderful way to articulate a shared vision of program excellence and can prove to be a wonderful monitoring device when facilitating school or program improvement initiatives. In Resource C

Figure 3.5   Rating Scale of Reading Proficiency

Trait	Emerging (1)	Basic (2)	Developing (3)	Proficient (4)	Fluent (5)
1. Ability to read grade-level material					
2. Enjoyment of reading					
3. Literal comprehension					
4. Inferential comprehension	After reading a grade-level-appropriate essay, the student can make a reasonable guess at the author's main idea.	After reading a grade-level-appropriate essay, the student can accurately retell the author's thesis.	After reading a grade-level-appropriate essay, the student can accurately retell and support the author's thesis with multiple details from the text.	After reading a grade-level-appropriate essay, the student can accurately retell and support the author's thesis with multiple details from the text and can draw logical inferences about the author's point of view.	After reading a grade-level-appropriate essay, the student can accurately retell and support the author's thesis with multiple details from the text, can draw logical inferences about the author's point of view, and can persuasively support those inferences by referencing specific rhetorical techniques, language usage, and vocabulary used by the author.

Source: Adapted from Sagor (2000).

(Exhibit 3), you will find a copy of a rating scale Dr. Hernandez might use to articulate a vision of performance with the program goal of faculty collegiality.

Tip on Rating Scale

The more long term the achievement target, the more columns you may find you need for your rating scale. That is fine. However, be sure that the distinction between the performances that make up each step on the rating scale are clear, distinct from each other, and unambiguous.

THE SPECIAL PROBLEM OF LONG-RANGE GOALS

Both of the targets discussed in the previous section—building a collegial faculty and developing skillful readers—are significant goals. In all likelihood, it will take these educators considerable time to move performance to the top of the scale. Nevertheless, it is reasonable for a fourth-grade teacher or a principal to expect some improvement on these types of targets during the course of his or her initial research.

There are targets, be they academic or nonacademic, that educational action researchers often shy away from simply because they take so long to complete and people are often impatient for results. The long-term nature of the targets makes them appear nearly impossible to monitor in the short term. For example, it is common for educators to value long-term targets for their students such as

- developing lifelong learning skills,
- preparing for success in college or careers, and
- developing integrity.

Because it takes many years of concentrated effort to get students to success on those targets, many action researchers will elect to avoid them. That is unfortunate because, in this era of high-stakes testing, if we don't deliberately focus on something and measure our progress toward its attainment, it is unlikely to receive the attention it deserves.

To understand the challenge of assessing progress on long-term targets, I use the work of the U.S. Space Agency, NASA, as an analogy. As part of its interplanetary studies, NASA has sent several Cassini probes to make fly-bys of Saturn and Jupiter and relay data on those planets back to Earth.

These are long-range projects in two ways. First, it took years to develop the technologies needed to design spacecraft capable of performing these missions. Furthermore, once the probes were launched, it took several years to reach Saturn and Jupiter. Clearly, it would have been folly for NASA to bypass these projects simply because they were so long-term. After all, interplanetary studies are at the very core of its mission. But it would be equally wrong for NASA to have proceeded with such ambitious projects without a strategy to monitor short-term progress.

Consequently, the two key assessment questions for NASA became

1. How do we determine if our research and development efforts are proceeding on schedule?

2. Once a spacecraft has been launched, how can we determine if the spacecraft is on course to pass by Saturn and Jupiter as scheduled, although several years hence?

The issues those questions present for rocket scientists (aerospace action researchers) are not conceptually different from the ones confronting educational action researchers pursuing long-term learning or program goals. Keep in mind, it could be twenty-five years before anyone will know with certainty if any particular student has, in fact, become a lifelong learner. Likewise, character traits are not acquired overnight. The challenge for NASA and the educator is one and the same: creating systems that reliably assess incremental advances on targets that may not be fully realized for years to come.

ASSESSING RATE OF GROWTH

It usually isn't enough to simply know that progress is being made. Steady progress could be occurring but at such slow rates as to be functionally ineffective. Consequently, when working with long-range goals, the question that demands an answer is whether the rate of progress is satisfactory. When it comes to the achievement of academic objectives, most educators are familiar with the concept of *rate of growth*. In the common school vernacular, when a student continues to perform *at grade level*, we classify his or her rate of growth as appropriate. This translates as achieving *one year's growth in one year's time*.

When working on a five-year project, the appropriate rate of growth is progress at a rate that will result in completion of the project in sixty months' time. For every NASA mission, there is an expectation of when the launch should occur. Therefore, the acceptable rate of progress is one that will have everything in place and ready to go on or before the projected launch date.

Federal regulations in the United States have codified an acceptable rate of growth for students. The No Child Left Behind Act (2001) requires schools to demonstrate that individual students, groups of students, and entire student bodies achieve "adequate yearly progress" (AYP). The procedures for accomplishing this involve the use of annually administered tests designed to determine if the progress made by students during the past year was at a rate sufficient to get them to the targets on time. This annual monitoring system, even when accurate, is far from helpful for classroom teachers. The results of spring testing come too late for the teacher to make instructional modifications for a student or class. It is about as helpful as receiving feedback on the efficacy of a 365-day weight-loss program by weighing yourself only once and doing so at the end of the year.

DETERMINING ADEQUATE YEARLY PROGRESS IN REAL TIME

Let's assume I am a teacher who is deeply committed to helping each of my students make adequate yearly progress. And let's assume I have developed a very clear vision regarding the target performance that I am after. In most cases, this would be the skills that the testing program assumes my students will possess by the end of the year. Last, we'll assume I am unwilling to wait until June to determine if my hypothesis on the best way to prepare them is working as well as I had hoped (helping them progress at a rate of "one year's growth in one year's time").

In all likelihood, the type of rating scale discussed earlier in this chapter won't be satisfactory. As good as a five-, seven-, or nine-point rating scale may be, it's not likely to be sensitive enough to detect minor incremental developments. Using such a scale would be like assessing my weight reduction program by weighing myself every morning, but doing so with an industrial scale that reports weight in twenty-pound increments. While it might be a great scale, it won't provide me with feedback that is either sensitive or precise enough to meet my monitoring needs.

Figure 3.6 is a visual from NASA that illustrates the trajectory of a Cassini spacecraft as it completes its seven-year mission. By knowing the launch date and the current position of the spacecraft, the aerospace action researchers can use this diagram throughout the mission to determine if the vehicle is, in fact, proceeding appropriately—achieving its AYP.

Figure 3.6   Cassini Interplanetary Trajectory

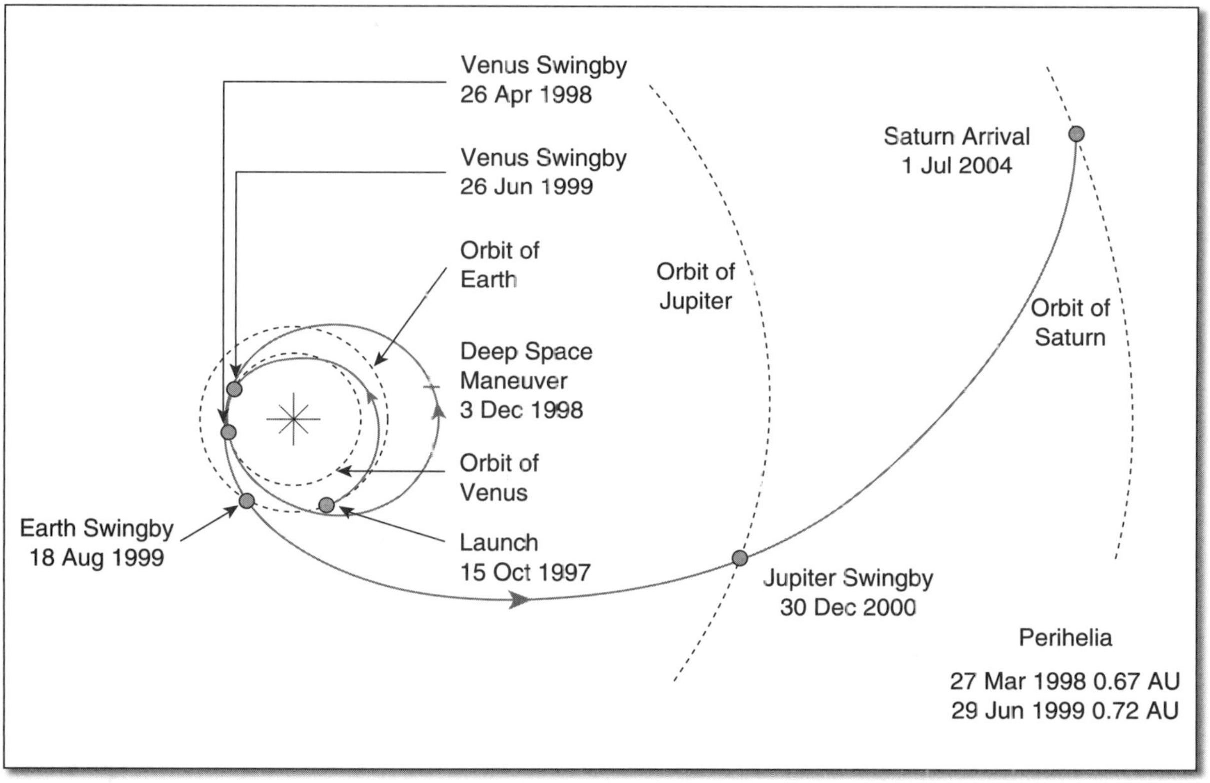

Source: http://saturn.jpl.nasa.gov

Let's now look at an academic example (see Figure 3.7). In this case, we will assume the goal is to have our students prepared to successfully enter advanced placement calculus once they finish eleventh grade. Let's also assume that at least some students entering kindergarten in our district aren't yet able to identify numerals correctly. Figure 3.7 illustrates the slope of the growth that needs to be demonstrated by a student entering school with zero math knowledge while staying on track to meet the goal of succeeding with AP calculus as a high school senior.

As teachers in pursuit of long-term objectives, we have a need to monitor our students' rates of growth by plotting their performance as they move up the grades. A quick look at a longitudinal graph will tell us if the slope of progress reflects a rate of growth that is

1. right on target (at AYP), enabling the student to take calculus as a senior;

2. faster than expected, and would enable the student to take calculus earlier (faster than AYP); and

3. below the expectation (slower than AYP), and not ready for calculus as a senior.

Figure 3.8 indicates the rate of growth of two students; one who is performing at a rate faster than AYP and one at a rate slower than AYP.

Figure 3.7   Rate-of-Growth Expectations

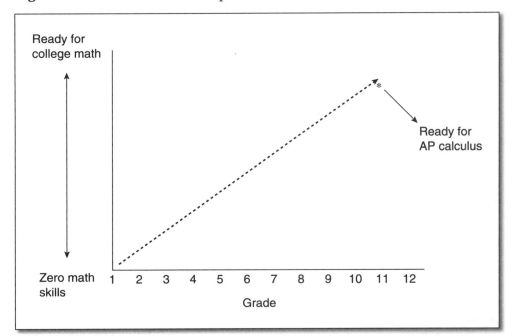

Figure 3.8 Rate-of-Growth Expectations: Two Students

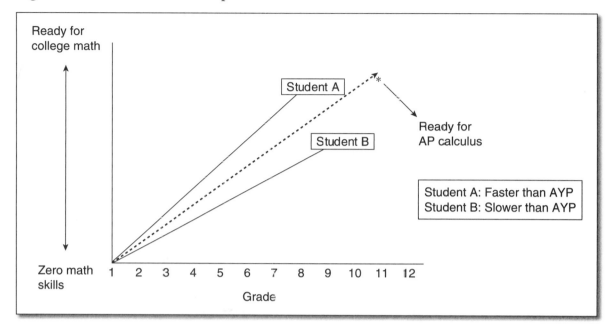

PRODUCING YOUR OWN RATE-OF-GROWTH CHARTS

There are seven steps you can follow to produce a rate-of-growth chart that can be used to track progress toward a long-term target. By using this strategy, you can meaningfully trace the efficacy of your work on a target, even when ultimate proficiency cannot be determined for several years to come.

Step 1. When pursuing a long-range, multiyear target, the first step is to place in sequence a list of the skills, backed up by an example of the type of work that is expected of students upon entrance into each grade, on this particular achievement target.

Step 2. Examine the list of skills to determine if it is logical, has any obvious gaps, and seems achievable.

Step 3. Now take a look at the examples of on-target work for a student entering the grade you will be teaching and for a student exiting your grade. Ask yourself or your team to brainstorm every single little baby step of a subskill that lies between the entry piece of work and the exit piece. Come up with as many subskills as possible.

Step 4. Make any adjustments to the sequence of skills or your list so it's as accurate and inclusive as possible. It's okay if the subskills on the list aren't sequential in nature, but to the best degree possible, place them in order.

Step 5. Now divide the list by the number of weeks in the school year (usually thirty-six). Let's assume that you identified seventy-two separate subskills. In such a case you would be able to say that a student who is acquiring skills at the rate of two per week is making AYP.

Step 6. Maintain a running record of each student's acquisition of the identified subskills. Periodically make a line graph with your running records to illustrate which students are demonstrating proficiency at an adequate pace, which are proceeding slower than a rate of "one year's growth in one year's time," and which are showing a rate of progress that is exceeding expectations.

Step 7. (Note: This step can only be done on a schoolwide or systemwide basis.) Place the listings of subskills on a continuum across all the grades served in your school. Then conduct an entry assessment for each child, either at the beginning of the school year or when he or she enters your room. Make plans to conduct an exit assessment of each student as well. With this type of assessment, you will be able to determine the rate of progress for each of the children during the time each of them spent in your class.

Keep in mind that what is AYP for any particular student is a value judgment. If I were teaching remedial students and I held high aspirations for each one of them, my goal might be to produce a rate of growth significantly in excess of one year's growth in one year's time, since that would be required if they were to catch up with their peers. But, regardless of how AYP is defined, a rate-of-growth chart will enable you to monitor and adjust in a timely fashion without having to wait for a year-end test or perhaps several years for evidence of achievement of a long-term goal.

ASCERTAINING RATE OF GROWTH IN LEADERSHIP PROJECTS

The importance of monitoring the adequacy of the rate of progress of an initiative is especially important for those engaged in school leadership. As was the case with the example of NASA's Cassini mission, whenever we are managing a long-term improvement effort we have a continuous need to know if we are falling behind, on schedule, or if we are likely to meet our goals on time.

There is a basic strategy school leaders can follow to track the rate of progress on their initiatives that is functionally similar to the rate-of-growth charting discussed for tracking student progress. The steps for following this process are detailed in Resource C (Exhibit 4). However, when leaders want to monitor the rate of progress of an initiative they are facilitating, it is best for them to have completed their *Stage 2: Theory Development* work before conducting this analysis. For this reason, leaders may wish to defer their work on rate-of-growth charting until after completing Chapter 5.

End of Stage 1

We have now finished our exploration of the first stage of the action research process, clarifying the vision and targets. To recap, at this point you have selected a focus for your research that relates to an area

- that you care deeply about,
- where performance could be improved, and
- where the actions needed to make changes in performance are within your sphere of authority.

In addition, you have identified a set of specific priority achievement targets where you hope to see demonstrable improvement. By now you should have consulted the literature and considered the experience of others who have worked at achieving success in the same focus area. Last, after reflecting on each of the traits or components of your target, you have identified a range of observable performance and a pace of development that you feel constitutes AYP.

You have now teased out and achieved some degree of precision on where you want to go, and you have sketched out a mechanism to measure your progress as you travel to the desired destination. You have closed your eyes and visualized the Promised Land as well as the mileposts you expect to pass along the way.

This brings us to the threshold of *Stage 2: Articulating a Theory of Action*. This is where you will engage in the rigorous but fun work of figuring out what route has the greatest potential for getting you closer to your vision.

4

Articulating a Theory of Action

In your work with Stage 1 of the action research process you identified your priority achievement targets and examined what you thought would constitute appropriate growth on those targets. You are now ready for the second stage of the action research process, articulating a theory of action. When we choose to become action researchers, *action* became more than just our first name. Our passion about providing the very best professional *action* is the rationale for investing our finite energy in this work. The products you've produced up until this point are very important; in fact, the work you have already accomplished in Stage 1 will prove essential to your ultimate success. But it is here at Stage 2 that the really creative intellectual work begins: It is with the work of theory development that you will be crafting original strategies and designing innovative techniques with promise for producing better results than you have been able to achieve in the past.

Action research, often referred to by other terms, is a key aspect of the systems approach to continuous improvement pioneered by W. Edwards Deming (1986/2000). Deming asserted that ninety-five percent of organizational performance could be attributed to the tactics, strategies, and processes used to accomplish the organization's work. Increasingly, research has shown that organizational success is not the result of the inherent goodness or badness of the personnel working there. Performance is not a factor of *who* is doing the work but, rather, how things are being done (Deming,

1986/2000; Senge, 1990). Consequently, when an improvement in performance occurs, the credit belongs to the theory of action that was developed and implemented by those carrying out the work. So if we find ourselves disappointed in student or program performance, it doesn't mean we are bad people or less-than-competent professionals. It indicates that our actions and the particular theories that informed those actions weren't adequate to the challenges we faced, and consequently those actions will need to be changed if we are to expect better results.

Action research is an empowering strategy. Exercising our control over the theory of action that informs our work is the most powerful thing a professional can do. But the idea of having educational practitioners take responsibility for the critique of their own practices and the design of innovative solutions for their own problems, while at the heart of this process, still generates some controversy. The two criticisms most often voiced against empowering educators with this authority are the following:

1. Full-time educators aren't able to focus on theory development and program design while attending to their other responsibilities.

2. An adequate professional knowledge base already exists, and educators ought to be expected to simply implement those practices with fidelity (Los Angeles Unified School District, 2010; Century, Freeman, Rudnick, & Leslie, 2008; O'Donnell, 2006) in their classrooms.

IF NOT US, WHO?

The first argument—that practicing educators aren't the ones who should be doing this work—flies in the face of a reality that educators face on a daily basis. All professional work is complex. And education is arguably the most complex, with hundreds of variables influencing each practitioner decision (see the discussion in Chapter 1). Due to the complexity involved in all professional decision making, the development and maintenance of each discipline's knowledge base has always been considered the responsibility of the profession itself. Furthermore, in most professions, the people who are taking the action are expected to be the ones designing the innovations, conducting the research, and consequently producing the evolving body of professional knowledge. This makes sense. After all, who is in a better position to identify the problems, understand the context, and integrate new insights into prevailing routines than those working on the front lines?

I have two dogs that I love dearly. Every time I take one of my retrievers to the vet, I am literally betting their lives on the treatment protocol that the veterinarian elects to follow. On these occasions I am comforted by the knowledge that it was veterinarians who conducted the research that informs the decisions of the veterinarian who is working with my dogs.

When tasks are simple and straightforward, it is often efficient to separate responsibility for the design and approval of implementation strategies from the actual conduct of the work. This is why supervisors are frequently hired to direct blue-collar work. However, when the work is complex, when it requires an understanding of nuance and idiosyncratic behavior and calls for constant assessment by a trained eye followed by continual adjustments in the operative theory of action, it must be informed by the insights of those taking the action: the practitioners themselves.

AN ADEQUATE KNOWLEDGE BASE ALREADY EXISTS

The second criticism leveled at practitioner research in education is a bit bizarre. For several years the stated goal of educational policy throughout most of North America has been getting every student to a high level of performance on a set of meaningful standards. If a knowledge base exists that documents how to accomplish this, why has this research been so widely ignored? Personally, I know of no evidence reporting the success of any city, state, or country in getting all of its children to high levels of performance on meaningful objectives. So unless there has been a worldwide and intergenerational conspiracy to deny the children of the world access to a good education, it would appear that the answers on how to accomplish universal student success have continued to elude the best and brightest throughout history. Therefore, it is safe to say that the current educational knowledge base is inadequate to get us to our shared goal of universal student success.

So, in the words of the Hebrew sage, Hillel,

> *If not us, who?*
>
> *If not here, where?*
>
> *If not now, when?*

GOING BEYOND PROVEN PRACTICES: BUILDING A THEORY OF ACTION

In Chapter 3's discussion of the literature review, a careful reader may have noticed that I avoided a phrase that has become part of the current school improvement vernacular: *scientifically proven practice*. It is a term that rolls nicely and easily off the tongue. The words *scientifically proven* deliver a good public relations punch, but shopping for and adopting those proven practices is a strategy that doesn't work nearly as well as its name might suggest.

Obviously, there is nothing wrong with making use of successful strategies. When a practice has been shown to work in a context similar to your own and the results that were obtained met your expectations, then adopting that practice for your school or classroom makes perfect sense.

External Pressure and Proven Practices

In a desire to encourage educators to make use of the best available practices, many government agencies and publicly supported programs now mandate the use of what have been labeled as scientifically proven practices. On the surface, policies like these seem quite rational. After all, if a strategy has been scientifically proven to be effective, it ought to be employed whenever and wherever appropriate. To ignore a proven practice would constitute educational malpractice, since it would mean denying a student a clearly beneficial educational experience. In other aspects of our lives, it is easy to think of proven practices that are always wise to follow, such as the following:

- File your taxes on or before April 15.
- When arguing a legal case, show respect for the presiding judge.
- Avoid contact with other people if you have a contagious disease.

Failing to adopt these proven practices would be irresponsible. In fact, not doing so could put you and/or others at risk.

But what of these so-called proven practices in teaching and learning? Repeatedly we hear of programs that were proven to be successful. Furthermore, when we examine data on these programs, we will frequently encounter impressive statistics, such as the following:

- With this program, attendance improved for eighty percent of the students.
- While using this program, seventy-five percent of the students posted gains in comprehension.

It is only right that we are impressed with gains like those. But simply adopting and faithfully implementing programs, even ones with such positive results, won't prove that satisfying for most educators in the long run. This is because in the opinion of most dedicated teachers, a seventy-five to eighty percent success rate simply isn't adequate. While at first blush those statistics might sound impressive, stated in another way, the same data says the following:

- Attendance showed no improvement for twenty percent of the students.
- While using this program, one out of four students showed no improvement in comprehension.

Logically, a faithfully adopted program can only be expected to work as well for others as it did where it was first proven successful. Therefore, the teacher or faculty adopting programs like these should expect to leave school every day knowing that twenty to twenty-five percent of their students won't likely be prospering. Few dedicated teachers will find this a very inviting prospect. Simply adopting a program that hasn't produced universal student success and then considering your school improvement work to be complete means accepting an intolerable degree of failure as inevitable. Having to go along with such an assumption is both emotionally and morally untenable for most educators.

This is not an argument against using or even adopting practices that have worked with many students. However, it does alert us to a set of critical questions that should be raised whenever a review of research or a reconsideration of a school policy directs us to implement a scientifically proven practice.

The first question is *With whom has this been proven to work?* As professionals concerned with promoting universal student success, we need to know about the characteristics of the groups who prospered as well as the characteristics of those who didn't. Were there patterns of performance that might help us to predict success or failure for some of our students? For example, did boys and girls succeed equally well in the past, or fail in equal proportions? Was this program successful with gifted students? How about kids with dyslexia?

If a proposed or adopted program appears to be beneficial for your students, then by all means, you ought to use it. However, if there is a type of student for whom the program has not succeeded in the past, and you have similar students in your classes, then you may have identified an excellent focus for your action research. Such an observation might cause you to investigate the question,

> What *alterations, modifications,* or *alternatives* to this program would make it likely that more students will succeed, especially those students that hadn't experienced success with this program elsewhere?

This question highlights the challenge for any inquiring educator who is hoping to isolate techniques with promise to increase the percentage of students experiencing success. There is no escaping the truth of the saying, "If we keep doing what we've been doing, we will keep getting what we've been getting."

Even if we were willing to accept the status quo as good enough, doing so now violates U.S. education policy. The No Child Left Behind Act (2001) requires that every identifiable subcategory of students in each school make AYP on their state's standards. Just obtaining the same level of success achieved the previous year is not enough. Students in each cohort need to be doing better than they were in past years.

Since continuing to get what we've been getting won't meet our own high expectations, and it will likely place our school outside of compliance with federal education regulations, we would be wise to turn that old saying around and restate it in reverse:

> If we want to get *more than* we've been getting, then we must figure out how to *do things differently* than we've been doing them in the past.

While this doesn't mean you will forever be engaged in conducting full-blown action research projects, it does mean that to some degree you will probably be involved with the four stages of the action research process—*envisioning success, clarifying a theory to get you there, collecting data while implementing your theory, and reflecting on the results obtained*—for as long as you are working in education.

One of the benefits of using the best practices developed by others is that it helps us construct boundaries around our inquiries. When we build a revised theory of action on top of an existing theory of action (one that has already succeeded with a significant number of students), we aren't trying to solve the entire riddle all by ourselves and we aren't starting from scratch.

Whether we are building on a strong program that has been implemented elsewhere or creating a brand new program, being *innovative* in the development of a theory of action isn't a choice; it is essential. Since things must be done differently than they were before, creativity will be required for us to figure out what needs to be changed. If the theory of action we develop is to succeed, it will need to take into account three factors:

1. What is known about the context where it will be implemented?

2. What is reported in the professional knowledge base?

3. What have we come to understand through the wisdom of practice, our professional experience?

TWO KINDS OF VARIABLES

In Chapter 3, you established success criteria and created rating scales for measuring changes in performance on your priority achievement targets. Researchers refer to a phenomenon they are trying to improve or change as their *dependent variable*. The word *dependent* is used because the researcher is positing that changes in performance will be *dependent* on something specific happening. When doing action research, we will consider the term priority achievement targets as synonymous with dependent variable. For example, if I desire to lose weight, my achievement target (dependent variable) is how much I weigh. The criteria I would establish to determine change on this target will be my weight in pounds and ounces as measured by my bathroom scale. Since I believe that changes in my weight will be dependent on my choices of behavior and diet, my weight is the dependent variable in my search for a lighter me.

The other category of variables researchers are concerned with have to do with those phenomena that the researcher suspects might influence changes in the dependent variable. These phenomena are called the *independent variables*. The term *independent* is used because the person carrying out the research is free to adjust the independent variables however he or she thinks best. Later the researcher will determine if those adjustments were shown to be worthwhile by looking for changes in measurements on the dependent variable. The independent variables that I might choose to adjust, in my investigation of weight loss, are my specific behavioral choices (what I eat and my exercise regime). This relationship is illustrated in the following table.

Choice of Independent Variables =	→	*Change* in the Dependent Variable
(our actions)		(achievement target)

The rating scales you have already developed will be used in your action research to measure changes in your dependent variables, your achievement targets. From this point on, we will use the terms *achievement target* and *dependent variable* interchangeably. Up until now, we have been concentrating on the dependent variables, your priority achievement targets. Now we will shift our focus and begin the process of identifying the critical independent variables that you have reason to believe hold the greatest potential for producing the positive changes you desire to see on your dependent variable.

CREATING MILEPOSTS ON THE ROUTE TO MASTERY

As we worked our way through Stage 1, we broke down our global visions into component parts that we called achievement targets. We moved from a general improvement focus to a defined vision of success on specific priority achievement targets. Then we broke down the achievement targets into subcomponents (traits) that could be effectively assessed. Now, as we develop a theory of action, we will engage in a similar sequential process but do so in reverse order. In constructing your theory of action, you will build a comprehensive theory by starting with the parts (like pieces of a puzzle) and then systematically assembling them to illustrate the big picture.

Discerning the components of your target (the traits) was important because performance on the target was defined as the sum of performance on its constituent traits. Likewise, when you have completed your theory of action, we will see that the efficacy of your comprehensive theory is the sum of a defined set of strategies and actions, the independent variables.

INFERRING INDEPENDENT VARIABLES

The first step in the process of building your theory will be to combine what you already understand from personal experience with what you've gathered from your review of the literature. The process begins by generating a list containing all the key factors (independent variables) you think will need to be addressed through your actions if significant improvement is to occur on the identified achievement target.

Let's put ourselves in the position of Dr. Hernandez, the elementary principal who was hoping to increase the problem-solving capacity of her faculty. Reflecting on the key variables that she could influence as the school's principal, she might well have generated a list like the following:

- Provide adequate time for teachers to meet.
- Provide faculty with easy access to pertinent data on student performance.
- Clarify and keep the faculty focused on our priority school goals.
- Be personally engaged with each faculty work group.

The identification of critical independent variables is an important step for action researchers like Dr. Hernandez, but it isn't enough to provide her with specific direction on the day-to-day actions she could or should take to achieve the desired results. In addition, this list wasn't prioritized, nor did it provide any insight into how these separate actions might influence each other. Consequently, Dr. Hernandez would have a hard time articulating a reasoned and coherent strategy for succeeding with her target without thinking through the answers to two additional questions:

- What is the relative importance of the identified independent variables?
- How do they relate and interact with each other?

In this and the next chapter, we examine two strategies that, when taken together, will allow you to respond to both of those questions. The first is a technique called the *priority pie*. The second technique, *the graphic reconstruction*, will be the focus of Chapter 5.

USING THE PRIORITY PIE TO IDENTIFY, CLARIFY, AND WEIGH INDEPENDENT VARIABLES

Thirty years of educational research have clearly established the relationship between time and learning. Both the allocation of time and the time spent on task have been shown to be key correlates of learning (Stanley, Spradlin, & Plucker, 2007; Aronson, Zimmerman, & Carlos, 1999). Time is, without a doubt, the most valuable resource under our control. And since class time is a zero-sum commodity, the decisions we make on how to spend this scarce resource are crucial. It isn't an overstatement to assert that in large measure, our effectiveness in hitting our targets is determined by the wisdom of our choices regarding the expenditure of the time and energy available to us. The priority pie is a simple strategy, one that will help you determine how you could most effectively allocate this critical resource.

To demonstrate the use of the *priority pie* strategy, let's follow two hypothetical action researchers as they work their way through the theory-building process. One is Dr. Hernandez, who is trying to enhance the problem-solving capacity of her faculty. Her target, changing the organizational approach to professional problem solving at her school, could be classified as a program target. The second project is the work of Mr. Seeker, a middle school English teacher who wants to increase his students' success with a specific academic performance target: He wants his eighth-grade students to develop the ability to write unified, sequential, and persuasive five-paragraph essays.

The priority pie process that they will be using has four steps:

1. Brainstorming

2. Summarizing

3. Evaluating

4. Graphing

Step 1: Brainstorming the Critical Independent Variables

If we are to succeed in improving performance on our priority achievement targets, we need to identify and attend to *each key independent variable.* The process of identification must occur consciously and deliberately because, should an essential variable be overlooked, it will have an impact on our ultimate success. Therefore, the first step is thinking through and answering the following question:

What are the issues, factors, programs, and processes that *must* be addressed to achieve success with this target (success meaning everyone performing at or above expectations)?

As you recall, Dr. Hernandez's four items were the following:

1. Provide adequate time for teachers to meet.

2. Provide faculty with easy access to pertinent data on student performance.

3. Clarify and keep the faculty focused on our priority school goals.

4. Be personally engaged with each faculty work group.

Mr. Seeker generated the following list of independent variables:

I need to provide both *instruction* and *feedback* for my students on the following skills:
- Organization
- Persuasive voice
- Editing
- Vocabulary
- Grammar and mechanics

Step 2: Summarizing the Independent Variables

Once action researchers feel confident that they have identified the key independent variables, they can begin to articulate an emerging theory of action. At this stage, Dr. Hernandez could articulate her theory as follows:

> For our faculty to succeed in becoming an effective problem-solving team, I need to ensure that adequate time is provided for teachers to meet and work collaboratively. I also need to make sure that they have access to all the pertinent data and information needed to make successful decisions. Since a sense of common purpose is essential, I need to take steps to achieve clarity on our school goals and to see to it that our collective attention stays focused on schoolwide priorities. To build support for this process, I must become a partner with each faculty work group as they work on addressing school goals.

Mr. Seeker might summarize his emerging theory this way:

> For my students to produce proficient, persuasive five-paragraph essays, they will need direct instruction and feedback from me. I must teach them how to develop their organizational skills, editing skills, word choice skills, skills in the use of mechanics and grammar, as well as a persuasive voice. And I need to provide them with timely feedback on their work in each of these areas.

Since time and energy are limited, both of these action researchers realize they need to apportion their limited time between each of the actions (independent variables) mentioned in their emerging theories. This brings them and us to Step 3.

Step 3: Conducting an Intuitive Regression Analysis

The next step in the priority pie process is determining the appropriate amount of attention to be paid to each identified factor. Determining the relative importance of each item (independent variable) on our lists is a judgment call, one that the action researcher will ultimately have to make for himself or herself. It is an informed judgment based on a combination of the review of the literature, past experience, and intuition.

One strategy to determine the relative importance of the independent variables is by dividing the time and energy available to be expended across the list of factors, based on the perceived importance of each factor to the realization of the whole—that is, excellent performance on the achievement target. This can be accomplished using the Intuitive Regression Analysis Worksheet, as shown in Figure 4.1. When using this worksheet, each item brainstormed in Step 1 is assigned a percentage based on how critical the researcher feels that item is to the achievement of

Figure 4.1   Intuitive Regression Analysis Worksheet

Using the following form, make a judgment regarding the relative importance of each of the factors that you had identified as critical to success on this achievement target. Use a separate form for each target being pursued.

Achievement Target: _____

List each factor deemed critical to fostering success with this achievement target	Importance of this factor (%)
	Total: 100%

the whole. There is no limit to the percentage that can be assigned to any one item; however, the total must equal one hundred percent.

Step 4: Graphically Displaying the Emerging Theory

Once you have completed your analysis using the Intuitive Regression Analysis Worksheet, you will be able to draw your emergent theory as a pie graph and write a summary paragraph explaining the reasoning behind your proposed allocation of resources. Figures 4.2 and 4.3 show Dr. Hernandez's and Mr. Seeker's graphs and narratives, respectively.

The development of a priority pie is an extremely important part of our work in Stage 2. It forces us to do the hard intellectual work of determining what we believe is of critical importance, and it also causes us to reflect on the relative importance of each piece of the puzzle. As important as this is, it still lacks the detail and precision necessary to provide adequate direction to our work. There are still several other crucial things that need to be considered before we could confidently declare our theory of action to be complete and proceed with implementing it. Even the best priority pie can't provide the clarity and direction needed to proceed to the

Figure 4.2   Enhancing Problem-Solving Capacity

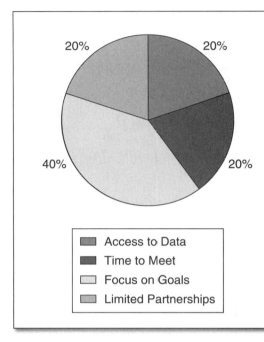

Access to Data
Time to Meet
Focus on Goals
Limited Partnerships

For the faculty to succeed in becoming an effective problem-solving team, I need to ensure that adequate time is provided for teachers to meet and work collaboratively. I also need to make sure that they have access to all the pertinent data and information needed to make successful decisions. Since a sense of common purpose is essential, I need to take steps to achieve clarity on our school goals and work at keeping our collective attention focused on schoolwide priorities. To build support for this process, I need to find a way to become a partner with each faculty work group as they work toward addressing a school goal.

I believe the most critical of all these actions will be my efforts to keep a clear and consistent focus on our school goals (forty percent). The three other critical factors that I must attend to as building principal are providing adequate and convenient times for problem-solving meetings (twenty percent), ready access to all the pertinent student and school data (twenty percent), and engaging every faculty work group as a limited partner (twenty percent).

Figure 4.3   Five-Paragraph Persuasive Essay

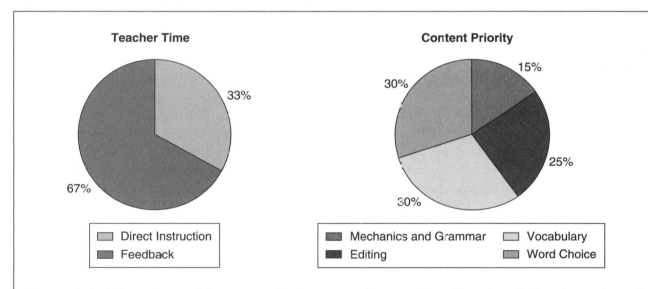

Teacher Time

Direct Instruction
Feedback

Content Priority

Mechanics and Grammar
Editing
Vocabulary
Word Choice

For my students to produce proficient, persuasive five-paragraph essays, they will need ample direct instruction and feedback from me as they develop their organizational skills, editing skills, facility with word choice, skills in the use of mechanics and grammar, and the skillful use of a persuasive voice.

I feel that the most critical of these skills is the development of voice and the related areas of word choice and vocabulary. Together, these elements account for sixty percent of the proficiency needed by my students. Proficiency with mechanics and grammar amount to fifteen percent, with editing skills being twenty-five percent of the equation. I believe that my students' success will be dependent on my providing appropriate direct instruction and feedback. Since I believe that becoming an effective writer requires practice, I suspect my students will need to spend two-thirds of their time and energy in the act of writing. For this reason, sixty-seven percent of my work will be devoted to providing students with feedback on their writing and thirty-three percent on the provision of direct skill instruction.

action phase. If we want to be confident of the likelihood that our "theory" will produce universal success, we will need to know and incorporate the following into our theory development:

- What specific actions are needed to satisfy each slice of the priority pie?
- Who is involved in each of these actions?
- When should those actions occur?
- Will multiple actions need to occur simultaneously?
- Is there a sequence of events that should be followed?
- If problems are encountered, what types of remedial steps should be undertaken?

When conducting scientific experiments as well as all other forms of exploration, it is necessary that the explorer work from as detailed a plan of action as possible. The process of clearly and unambiguously articulating one's plan of action serves several purposes:

- A detailed plan provides guidance and direction for the work.
- If and when success is achieved, the plan provides a road map that others can use as they attempt to reach the same destination.
- If and when the results aren't as expected, the plan can be meticulously retraced to find out where problems were encountered.

USING THE PRIORITY PIE WITH DESCRIPTIVE RESEARCH

When conducting *descriptive* action research, it is equally important to have clarity on the theories of action that are being observed and documented. The essential difference is that with descriptive research, the purpose is to clarify our understanding of the way things are currently being done—*the operant theory*—rather than to articulate a proposed theory of action.

It is hard to imagine an action occurring in the schoolhouse that isn't being done for a reason. But oftentimes, things have been done a certain way for so long that it has been years since anyone stopped to consider and reflect on the underlying rationale. To make these implicit theories of action explicit, action researchers who are conducting descriptive studies go through the same four-step process but do so in a slightly different manner.

Step 1: Brainstorming the Critical Independent Variables

Generate a list of independent variables by responding to the following question:

What issues, factors, programs, and processes are currently consuming most of our time and energy with this target?

Step 2: Summarizing the Independent Variables

Explain in a brief narrative statement the actions that are currently being taken in pursuit of the target.

Step 3: Conducting an Intuitive Regression Analysis

Ask how time is currently being spent. Look over the list of independent variables (Step 1) and the narrative statement (Step 2) for each target being investigated. Estimate the approximate percentage of the available time and energy that *is currently being devoted to* each variable. The total must equal one hundred percent.

Step 4: Graphically Displaying the Operant Theory

Draw the information from Step 3 in the form of a pie graph and do your best to explain the percentages. Be careful to avoid using interpretive language. Rather than saying, "We are spending an enormous amount of time on x" or "We are overly emphasizing the use of worksheets instead of teacher-generated examples," try to say it like this: "We are spending seventy-five percent of our time on x" or "Of the assignments used, eighty percent involve publisher-supplied worksheets while less than ten percent are teacher-developed assignments."

Occasionally, someone anticipates that he or she will be doing descriptive research, but then as the action researcher makes the operant theory explicit, he or she becomes so uncomfortable with the current state of affairs that he or she immediately decides that a better theory must exist or could easily be created. When this occurs, it is wise to go back and see if another priority pie can be created, one that will illustrate an improved and novel theory. To do this it is suggested that you use the Intuitive Regression Analysis Worksheet (Figure 4.1).

Whether you are doing descriptive or quasi-experimental research, you will need to use a second visual technique called the *graphic reconstruction* to assist you with the detailed action planning and clarification needed for articulating your emerging theory of action. In Chapter 5, we will explore the creation and use of this essential research and planning tool.

5

Drawing a Theory of Action

Let's expand the travel metaphor. As action researchers, we are traveling to distant lands, and in a larger sense, we are planning on exploring territory where in all likelihood no one has gone before, at least not successfully. This is not an exaggeration, nor is it self-congratulatory.

Clearly, if what you are hoping to accomplish had already been accomplished in a setting like yours, had been documented, and was well understood, it would be a waste of your time and energy to further document that it works. In all probability you are already using the best strategies and following the most promising practices known to you and your colleagues. In addition, you wouldn't be experimenting with something new or reexamining your current work were you not at least somewhat dissatisfied with the results you have been getting from your current practices. Perhaps, through your review of the literature (see Chapter 3), you have become inspired by the ideas and experiences of others. That inspiration may have lead you to reconsider your current practice, and consequently you may have decided to focus your action research on finding out if these promising ideas will succeed with your students and your classes. But even when you are attempting to replicate results produced elsewhere, you will still be exploring unexplored territory because, even if the promising practice had been documented, it could not have possibly been attempted in the precise manner you will be implementing it, in the precise context where you will be using it, or with students identical to yours.

In Chapter 4, the priority pie was used to help you identify some of the specific categories of action that should be addressed. You identified these by combining what you had learned from the wisdom of your practice with the experience of others, and you created a prioritized list of independent variables. In all likelihood, the list of variables you ended up with (your slices of pie) didn't depart radically from your current menu of action. Perhaps you added a slice or changed your views on the relative importance of a particular category of action. Nevertheless, regardless of how deeply you believe in the narrative statement you wrote to explain your pie, that statement alone won't be enough to convince you (or your students, their parents, or your colleagues) that you have discovered the "silver bullet," that one approach that will succeed where all others have failed. This brings us to the need for detailing a clear and comprehensive theory of action—what I often call an implementation road map. Geographic maps are used to illuminate the relationships among landforms. The maps we will be drawing have a slightly different purpose; they will illustrate the relationships between and among actions and variables.

WHY A MAP?

The map is the lifeline of the explorer. The route an explorer sets out to follow is informed by the best maps of others and the most detailed descriptions of the terrain ahead that could be gleaned from people with direct knowledge of the territory. On returning from their journeys, explorers share what they have learned by modifying and adjusting the best previous maps, augmented with their new knowledge. This is precisely what we shall do. We begin by developing an initial road map informed by a combination of our experience and the experience of others. The map we prepare will then become our guide as we travel to places where we haven't ventured before. To the degree that our maps are clear and appear accurate, containing what researchers call *face validity*, the greater the chance we will be able to approach our adventure with confidence and purpose.

Christopher Columbus: An Early Action Researcher

Action research is not a new idea. Occasionally, I have argued that one can trace action research back at least as far as the first voyage of Christopher Columbus. In my retelling of history, Christopher was an ambitious teacher, probably a high school marketing instructor. One morning he awoke with a terrific idea for a new course. He did a little library research and then developed what appeared to be a good hypothesis and emergent theory to share with his school administration:

> If I sail due west of Spain for approximately 4,000 miles, I will land on the East Coast of Cathay. I believe this to be the case for two reasons. I know the Earth is round [this was the view of most European

and Arab cartographers of the day], and I even know its circumference [also known through the use of celestial projection]. I then considered what we learned from Marco Polo. When Polo came back from Cathay with all that good stuff to sell, he told us how far he had traveled. So, I simply subtracted the distance he went from the circumference of the Earth and it became clear to me that 4,000 nautical miles will complete the circle.

So Chris went to his co-principals, Ferdinand and Isabella, and asked them to approve a budget for this new course proposal. Assuming that, as tight-fisted monarchs, they would want to examine the details of his proposal, I imagine they demanded that Columbus provide a graphic reconstruction before they would grant him permission to institute his new class. Recently, I did a literature review of my own to see if I could locate the type of graphic reconstruction Columbus might have used to illustrate his theory of action to his two authoritarian school administrators. Figure 5.1 is a map of the world produced by Henricus Martellus in 1489, a mere three years before Columbus's first voyage. As this was the most accurate map I could locate from a European cartographer of this time period, I assume that it is similar to one that Columbus might have used.

In my imagination, I see Columbus placing this map on an overhead projector, taking out a felt-tip marker, and illustrating his proposed route by inserting a line from the West Coast of Spain to the left-hand edge of the

Figure 5.1   Henricus Martellus's 1489 Map

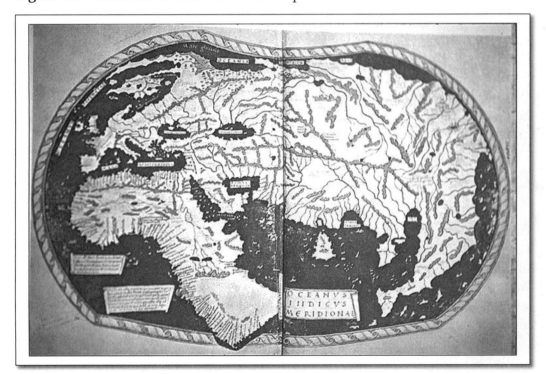

Source: http://www.henry-davis.com/MAPS/LMwebpages/256.html

map and another one from East Asia to the other edge of the map. Now that we've seen how well this process worked for Christopher Columbus, it is time for you to prepare a map for your journey to a new world of improved performance.

BUILDING A GRAPHIC RECONSTRUCTION

In Chapter 4, we looked at a priority pie prepared by a middle school English teacher, Mr. Seeker, to illustrate his view of the salience of the key independent variables that he theorized should be addressed if all his students were to become proficient writers of five-paragraph persuasive essays. To recap, these were the variables that Mr. Seeker believed would significantly influence his students' writing proficiency:

Direct instruction in

- Vocabulary, word choice
- Editing skill
- Voice
- Mechanics and grammar

Feedback on

- Vocabulary, word choice
- Editing skill
- Voice
- Mechanics and grammar

Now it's time to consider some additional questions, ones that might have been raised yet could not have been adequately answered through the priority pie process. For example, Mr. Seeker might have questions regarding the *sequence* of his actions:

- Should vocabulary be taught before introducing the concept of voice?
- Should he introduce the concept of voice prior to instruction in vocabulary?
- Should these two elements of writing be taught simultaneously?

There could also be questions regarding *instructional strategies*:

- Should students be provided with a vocabulary list?
- Should he have students identify and pull new vocabulary from their reading?
- How and when should he provide his students with feedback on their writing?

It is likely that he has many other questions about his emerging theory, for example:

- Who should be responsible for what?
    - Should he assume the role of editor of all student drafts?
    - Should he teach the students how to edit their own work and then make them responsible for editing their work?
    - Should he teach the students to edit cooperatively and revise their writing in peer editing groups?

While the priority pie was valuable in identifying the areas where Mr. Seeker needed to focus his energy, it couldn't provide him with adequate guidance on how to respond to these or other relevant procedural questions.

Whether your study is designed to be a quasi-experimental inquiry or a descriptive study, it is important that you go through a deliberate process designed to elicit and clarify in detail the full theory of action that is to be examined by your study, whether it is one you invented or one that is already in operation elsewhere.

GRAPHIC RECONSTRUCTIONS FOR QUASI-EXPERIMENTAL RESEARCH

When we are undertaking quasi-experimental research, it is essential for us to carefully articulate precisely what it is we are attempting and why we have chosen to do so in this particular way. In my revisionist history, Christopher Columbus was a quasi-experimental action researcher because he was testing out a new theory of action. In our work as quasi-experimental researchers we need to spell out our proposed actions for a number of reasons:

1. *To provide guidance to others who may follow us:* In Columbus's case, this would include future seafarers and explorers.

2. *To provide insights into the experimental process:* In Columbus's case, these insights would assist him in his future work as an explorer.

3. *To make our program clear to stakeholders:* In Columbus's case, this would be necessary to keep his benefactors happy and to keep his project funded.

To Provide Guidance to Others

When we engage in experimental or quasi-experimental research, we are, of course, hoping to find evidence that supports our hypotheses regarding the specific interventions we are attempting and their relationships to changes in our achievement targets. Should we be successful and the data confirms our hypotheses, it is to be expected that others will want to try to replicate our results. If those following in our footsteps are to have confidence in their ability to confirm our findings, they will need to clearly understand the specific procedures we followed.

To Provide Insights Into the Process

Even the most well thought-out interventions rarely work precisely as designed. Occasionally, this means that the theory of action was fatally flawed. More likely, it was because one or two relatively minor aspects of the plan didn't function as anticipated. Unless each and every aspect of a plan had been clearly documented, it will be impossible for anyone to determine where exactly the breakdown or breakdowns occurred. This is no small problem. In schools, this is often seen when adopted programs are evaluated, deemed ineffective, and tossed out. When these decisions repeatedly occur without serious reflection on the actual reasons for the lack of success (the source of the breakdown), it often seriously erodes staff commitment to the process of innovation.

In all likelihood, the adopted program arrived in a neat package without an explicit theory of action delineated by the developer or publisher. The district's justification for implementing the program was probably stated in educational shorthand, simply mentioning the name of the author or publisher. For example:

> After reviewing the available materials, we decided to teach reading with the Sagor reading program.

Such a theory could be depicted like this:

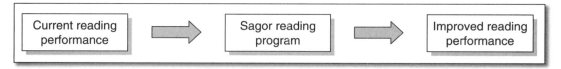

Current reading performance → Sagor reading program → Improved reading performance

Then, if performance didn't live up to the district's expectations, one would expect to hear the assertion, "The Sagor program didn't work." Consequently, the program would be abandoned, another one would be adopted, and the cycle would continue. Occasionally, throwing away complete programs that failed to live up to expectations is warranted; but often, it is not. Frequently, the program that was adopted was fundamentally sound. In all likelihood, the problem was simply that a few specific aspects of the program weren't adequate to meet the needs of the district's students. Certainly it would be more efficient as well as more intellectually honest to isolate the specific flawed parts of the program so they could be modified, adjusted, or supplemented, rather than to throw out the baby with the bathwater and start all over again.

However, if the interventions implemented are viewed as mysterious black boxes, when legitimate concerns arise it is impossible to determine which features of the operant theory need to be modified. When the process of adopt-evaluate-replace-adopt-evaluate-replace repeats itself over and over, it produces a syndrome of revolving-door programs that can lead a faculty to cynicism and defeatism. We can all agree that those two attitudes are destructive to a productive school culture.

The same thing applies to our action research. More likely than not, our well-conceived theories of action will be fundamentally sound. Yet, we still might not be obtaining the results we had hoped for. However, if we follow a detailed plan of action, we will be able to conduct a focused academic postmortem on our actions and use this to understand precisely where things went awry.

To Make the Program Clear to Stakeholders

When students, faculty, and families clearly understand the programs they are involved with and can see the rationale for the tasks they are being asked to complete, they are more likely to cooperate and put forth their best efforts. Conversely, when people feel they are being asked to do something new and out of the ordinary and aren't provided with any explanation as to the rationale, they can be expected to rebel or give the program something less than their best efforts. For this reason, I have made it a habit to share my graphic reconstructions and to explain my theories of action on the first day of class or at the launch of any program I'm facilitating. Figure 5.2 is a copy of a poster that I had prominently posted in the classroom for a graduate class I taught on action research.

GRAPHIC RECONSTRUCTIONS WITH DESCRIPTIVE RESEARCH

When engaging in descriptive research, our purpose is to develop a deeper and more profound understanding of what is actually going on here and now. If we are to succeed with this research, we need to be sure that we are looking in the right places to collect our data. The best way to do this is to invest some time at the outset, reflecting on the rationale for each of the principal actions (the operant theory) that are currently taking place, and use the results of that reflection to focus our data collection. Frequently, a careful review of the teacher's manual or curriculum guide is the best place to start. Those documents likely detail the actions that the program developers *expected* to occur.

Why Is It Important to Plan Visually?

When explaining something familiar, we often take intellectual short-cuts without even noticing them. For example, when outstanding teachers are asked to explain precisely what they do to produce the results they are obtaining, they are often at a loss to explain their accomplishments. It isn't

Figure 5.2 EDLL 706 Action Research and Inquiry "Theory of Action"

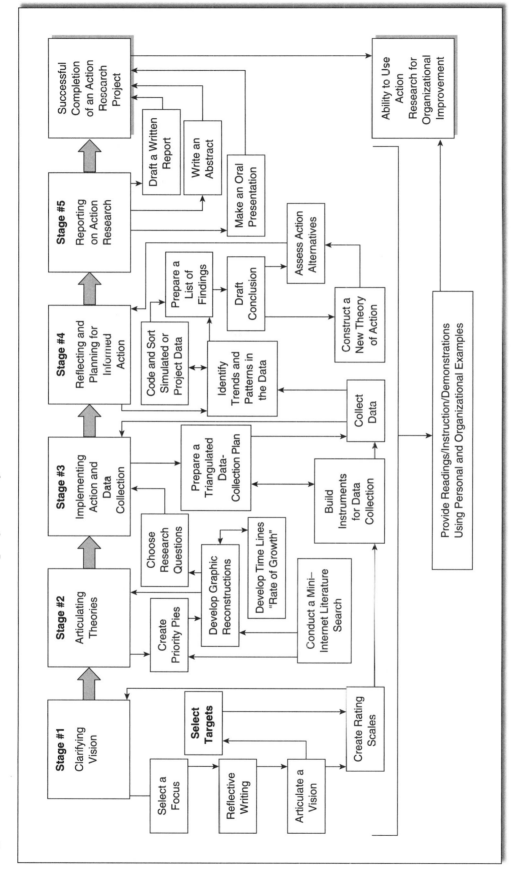

rare to hear an excellent teacher explain her success by saying, "This is just how my students perform." Of course, this is an inadequate explanation. Without question, there are specific actions this teacher consistently engages in that lead to positive results, but the actions have become so second nature that the teacher doesn't even recognize them as relevant.

Graphic reconstructions help us to flesh out and examine the details of our theories of action through the use of visualizations and pictures as opposed to words. The graphic reconstruction is a flow chart, a web that illustrates the dynamic relationships that exist between the various components of a theory of action. Figure 5.3 shows the graphic reconstruction produced by Mr. Seeker, illustrating his theory for improving his students' persuasive essays. Figure 5.4 reflects Dr. Hernandez's theory on enhancing the problem-solving capacity of her school's faculty.

There is no single way to build a graphic reconstruction, and there is no single format that will be effective in illustrating all our theories. It is suggested that as you create your first graphic reconstruction, you use the following five-step process. These sequential steps were designed to help you create a visual road map of whatever theory of action you wish to investigate.

1. Brainstorm variables, actions, and ideas.

2. Group and sort variables, actions, and ideas.

3. Put the parts into a sequence.

4. Proof the road map.

5. Review your final product.

Figure 5.3   Enhancing Student Persuasive Writing

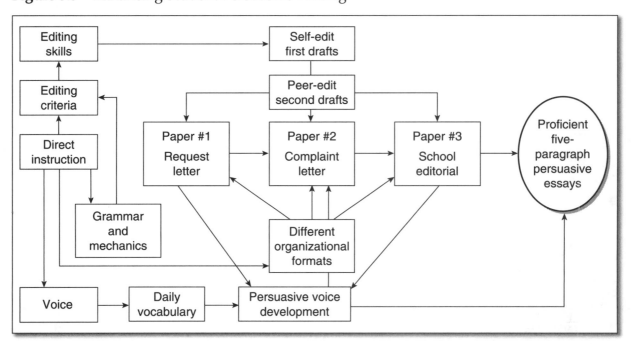

Figure 5.4 Enhancing Problem-Solving Capacity

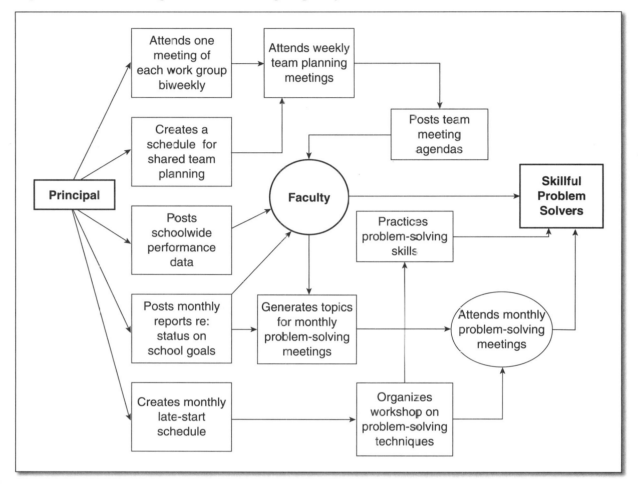

To demonstrate the use of these five steps, we will follow a hypothetical middle school faculty that is working collaboratively to develop a graphic reconstruction to clarify their theory for achieving success on a schoolwide program target: the improvement of student motivation. Figure 5.5 shows the priority pie and narrative created earlier by this faculty.

Keeping in mind their emergent theory (as illustrated by the pie and narrative), the faculty is ready to start building their graphic reconstruction.

Step 1: Brainstorm Variables, Actions, and Ideas

Using a pad of sticky notes, the action researchers brainstorm every factor, issue, phenomenon, program, and practice that they believe could have a bearing on the target being pursued. This includes ideas that surfaced during their literature review as well as items that showed up as separate slices of their priority pie. It is always important to be expansive when brainstorming. Action researchers are wise to include things they've discovered through personal experience as well as things gleaned from the

Figure 5.5 Building Motivated Learners

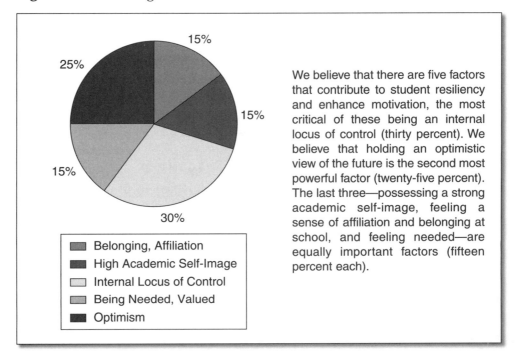

We believe that there are five factors that contribute to student resiliency and enhance motivation, the most critical of these being an internal locus of control (thirty percent). We believe that holding an optimistic view of the future is the second most powerful factor (twenty-five percent). The last three—possessing a strong academic self-image, feeling a sense of affiliation and belonging at school, and feeling needed—are equally important factors (fifteen percent each).

- Belonging, Affiliation
- High Academic Self-Image
- Internal Locus of Control
- Being Needed, Valued
- Optimism

literature. These are examples of some of the items that might have surfaced in the brainstorming of the middle school faculty regarding enhancing motivation:

- Cooperative learning
- Learning-style-friendly classes
- Feelings of competence
- External locus of control
- Teacher advisory program
- Problem-solving discipline practices
- Feelings of belonging
- Curricula emphasizing cause and effect
- Feelings of usefulness
- Internal locus of control
- Feelings of potency
- Service learning
- Project-based learning
- Feelings of alienation
- Feeling unneeded
- Mastery expectations

Step 2: Group and Sort the Variables, Actions, and Ideas

Once brainstorming is completed, it is time to spread the sticky notes (containing all the brainstormed items) on a table or onto a piece of chart paper and cluster them into related groups. Some of the categories that I often find helpful for initially sorting my brainstormed ideas are

- problems, interventions, and targets;
- things that occur prior to teaching, during teaching, and after teaching; and
- teacher actions, student actions, rules, and requirements.

Keep in mind there is no one approach for categorizing the items that surfaced during brainstorming. You should feel comfortable playing around with different categories until you find one that best helps you organize your ideas.

The team working on enhancing motivation decided to sort their items as *problems, interventions,* and *targets:*

Problems

- Low academic self-image
- Feelings of alienation
- Feeling unneeded
- External locus of control (feeling powerless)

Interventions

- Service learning
- Cooperative learning
- Mastery expectations
- Project-based learning
- Teacher advisory program
- Learning-style-friendly classes
- Problem-solving discipline
- Curricula emphasizing cause and effect

Targets

- Feeling useful
- Feeling optimistic
- Feelings of belonging
- Feeling potent (internal locus of control)
- Feeling competent

Step 3: Putting the Items in Sequence

In this step, the sticky notes are arranged on a large sheet of poster paper or a sheet of chart paper to illustrate all the key presumed relationships. When doing quasi-experimental research, I generally format my graphic this way: On the left-hand side, I group the items that describe the current situation or the problem my actions are designed to address. In the case of the student motivation project, the left side of the graphic would look like Figure 5.6.

Then on the right-hand side, I place my vision of success, or the Promised Land I am pursuing. Here I place descriptions of performance on the target that is at or above expected proficiency (the top of the rating

Figure 5.6 Building Motivated Learners: Problems

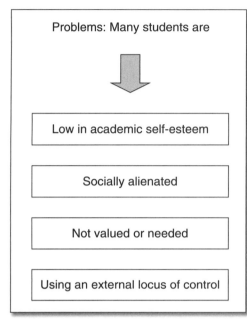

scales that were developed in Chapter 2). When those sticky notes are added to the enhancing motivation graphic, it would appear like Figure 5.7.

The last step is to arrange all the other items (that is, the variables or actions) in a manner that reflects the most logical and direct route that the action researcher sees the program or the learners traveling to get from the current situation to the target. Once the interventions have been added to the enhancing motivation graphic, the complete road map might look like Figure 5.8.

With quasi-experimental studies, researchers frequently assume that there is a defined sequence of actions and there are causal relationships between certain actions. For this reason it is often helpful to use lines or directional arrows to illustrate the way the different elements of the theory build upon or interact with each other. However, change doesn't always happen in a linear fashion. Particularly when working with early learners, instructional activities may be cyclical and repeated in a regular pattern. For this reason it is up to the researcher to determine if causal or sequential relationships should be indicated on the graphic or not.

The formatting of a graphic reconstruction for a descriptive study will often be idiosyncratic. It is, however, important that a graphic reconstruction that will be providing direction to a descriptive study illustrate each of the phenomena that the researcher believes are relevant to performance on the achievement target being studied and that could be observed in the

Figure 5.7 Building Motivated Learners: Targets

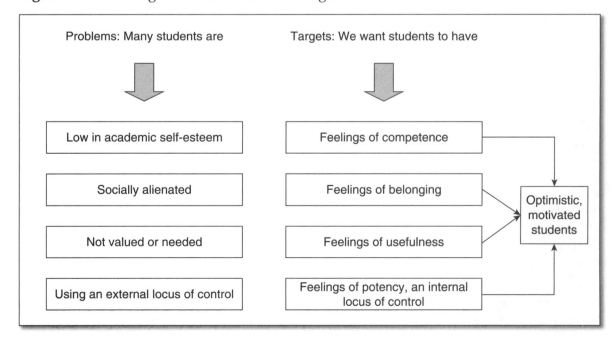

Figure 5.8   Building Motivated Learners: Complete

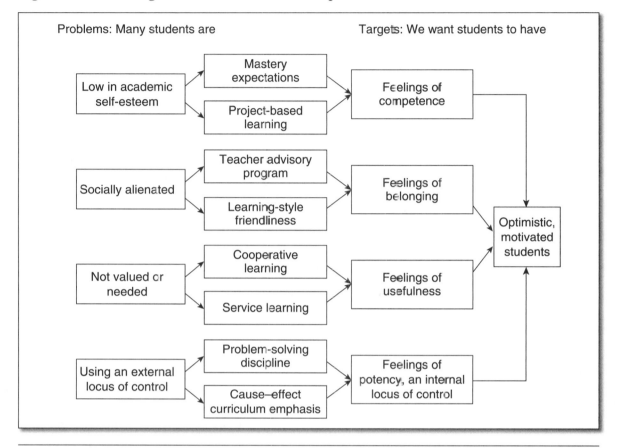

Source: Adapted from Sagor (1996), Figure 4.4.

environment under study. Therefore, it is critically important to identify these items at this point, since later they will become essential for the design of your data-collection plan.

> ### Tip on Drawing Graphic Reconstructions for Descriptive Research
>
> The locations where items are placed on a graphic reconstruction for descriptive research can be important, as they will help inform the researcher regarding when and where to look for data. Beyond that, however, determining the possible or probable relationships between items or variables is not that critical with a descriptive study.

This part of the process is complete when the researchers are able to step back and look at their graphic reconstruction and assert that it clearly and unambiguously illustrates their "current" understanding of the dynamics of the issue being studied, including all the independent variables (the actions to be taken) and the dependent variable (the achievement target being pursued).

When I think I am at this point, I imagine myself explaining my graphic to three audiences: my students, their parents, and a person new to our faculty. If my graphic is complete and clear when accompanied by a brief five-minute verbal explanation, my students should be able to understand what I am planning and will be able to demonstrate that understanding by restating my theory in their own words. Likewise, if after a five-minute explanation at an open house, the parents understand what I have planned and feel capable of explaining it to another parent, I would feel confident that my graphic had successfully communicated my theory. Last, if an educator new to our team could understand the program we have planned from my overview and would feel comfortable going ahead and implementing it, then I would feel I had illustrated my ideas with clarity. But if the graphic plus a short explanation didn't succeed in clarifying what was planned and the rationale for our actions, then we would need to assume that our theory of action was still too abstract or overly general. If in my imaginary presentations, the degree of clarity I was hoping for is not achieved, then I need to continue to refine my road map until it effectively communicates my intentions.

Step 4: Proofing the Graphic

Once Step 3 has been completed and I am confident that the graphic reconstruction does, in fact, successfully communicate my ideas, it is time for me to examine it for possible flaws or omissions. I conduct this examination by reviewing my theory through multiple perspectives. I begin by considering as diverse a range of students as I might ever have in class. Then I take several mental walks though my graphic as though it were a walking trail. Each time I walk the trail, I imagine myself as a particular category of student and imagine how one of these students would be experiencing the proposed program. As I take these walks, I try to identify any places where students such as these would likely encounter problems or lose their way. This is analogous to drawing a map to assist a person who will be making a first visit to your home. Prior to sending out your map, you will probably go over it one last time, looking for places where someone who is unfamiliar with your neighborhood might make a wrong turn.

When the teachers who were working on the motivation project did this proofing, they identified several problems. For example, their graphic (Figure 5.8) implied that requiring students to meet mastery expectations (academic credit only being awarded for grades of A or B) would lead to increased feelings of competence. But when they walked through their theory in the shoes of a student with a history of failure and defeatism, they realized that such a student might find the mastery requirement so intimidating that he might just give up—and consequently never hit the target of increased feelings of competence.

Another example involved the inferred relationship between the teacher advisory program and the development of feelings of belonging. The theory of action implied that the mere act of having a teacher advisor would increase a student's feelings of belonging at school. But when they engaged in the proofing exercise, the teachers identified many categories of students whom they feared wouldn't thrive in an advisory program. They were concerned that if the interpersonal chemistry wasn't exactly right between students and their advisors or between students and their peers in the advisory group, the advisory process actually could serve to make these students even more alienated than they were before.

If problems like these arise when you are proofing your graphic reconstruction, then you should reflect on the following question:

> How could this theory of action be modified to make universal success more likely?

After spending some time reflecting and deliberating on that question, it is time to for the action researcher(s) to work those modifications into the theory. In the case of the motivation project, the teachers decided to create an afterschool "academic coaching program" staffed with charismatic teachers and involving a great many fun activities as the venue for students who needed extra help on the way to mastery. In addition, they added a process where the school counselors played a prominent role in matching students to advisors and arbitrating advisor–advisee problems when and if they arose. Figure 5.9 shows the revised graphic after these modifications were added.

PROOFING A THEORY OF ACTION-LEADERSHIP PROJECTS

Often when school leaders are planning an initiative that involves other members of the professional staff, we subconsciously assume that our colleagues are similar to ourselves in both motivation and temperament.

Figure 5.9   Building Motivated Learners: After Proofing

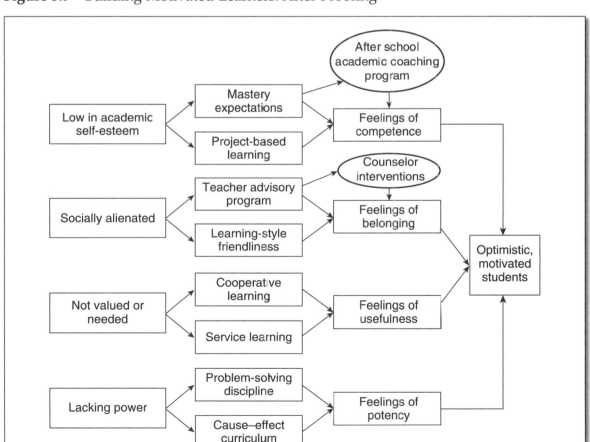

We tend to assume they share our concerns, are motivated by the same things, and share our understanding of the issue at hand. This is analogous to teachers planning their lessons under the assumption that all students share the same learning style. In many ways our colleagues can be as diverse as the students in our classes. Therefore, a program implementation strategy that may on the surface appear perfect might look so only because of how well it fits our own personality and perspective. For this reason, the act of proofing the initial graphic reconstruction of an initiative we are leading, by walking it in the shoes of different members of the faculty or staff, particularly ones who hold different perspectives and philosophies than our own, will alert us to issues that, left unaddressed, can cause an otherwise well-intentioned project to unravel.

Step 5: Finalizing the Graphic

For quasi-experimental research, the graphic reconstruction can be considered complete once the researchers can say with a degree of confidence, "We truly expect that every participant will experience success if this theory of action is implemented as displayed."

For descriptive research, the graphic can be considered complete when the researchers can say, "We truly believe that once we come to understand the manner in which all the variables displayed on this graphic interact with each other, we will understand why performance is as it is."

Tip on Creating Graphic Reconstructions for Descriptive Research

When doing descriptive research on a commercially produced program or the implementation of an adopted program, it is a good idea to follow the steps provided in this chapter to construct a graphic reconstruction of the theory of action *as you currently understand it.* Then, prior to commencing your study, it is suggested that you ask the developers of the program or their representatives to take a critical look at your graphic and provide you with feedback. Even if you have made a conscious choice to exclude some elements of the theory as the authors or developers in your classroom or program originally conceived it, understanding and acknowledging those differences in theoretical perspective will prove helpful later when you are engaged in data analysis.

When you have finished the creation of a graphic reconstruction that fully reflects your understanding of the issue under study, it is time to give yourself a deserved pat on the back. You have now completed *Stage 2: Articulating Your Theory*, and you are almost ready to move to the exciting implementation phase—the action part of the action research process.

6

Determining the Research Questions

Having completed a graphic reconstruction that clearly communicates your best and most current thinking on how to achieve success with your priority achievement targets, you have completed the second of the four stages of the action research process.

You have now arrived at the *action* portion, where you will be *implementing* and simultaneously *exploring* your theory of action. Two things will occur while you engage in your work during Stage 3:

1. Your theory of action will be implemented.

2. Data will be collected in response to a set of meaningful research questions.

The nature of the research questions influences both the types of data to be collected and the methods used to collect that data. So it is extremely important that care and thought be used in choosing the questions that will guide the inquiry. Just as it was important to choose a focus that was high on your personal priority list (Chapter 2), selecting the questions that will guide your inquiry must also be grounded in professional self-interest: A good action research question is one that leads to greater understanding of something you or you and your colleagues very much *need* or *want* to learn more about.

In this chapter, we will examine two alternative approaches to the selection of research questions. The first approach involves the use of a set of generic action research questions that can be applied to any issue you have chosen to study. The data produced in response to these three questions provides the type of information sought by most action researchers conducting quasi-experimental or descriptive studies. The second approach is a systematic process that asks you to analyze your theory of action and tease out a set of specific questions with potential for uncovering information you will find personally and professionally meaningful.

THREE GENERIC ACTION RESEARCH QUESTIONS

The range and scope of questions an action researcher might wish to pursue is unlimited. Nevertheless, there are three particular questions that when explored provide valuable professional insight for any project:

1. What did we actually *do*? (This focuses on action.)

2. What *changes* occurred regarding performance on the achievement targets? (This focuses on change.)

3. What were the *relationships,* if any, between the actions taken and any noted changes in performance? (This focuses on relationships.)

I refer to the three generic action research questions by the acronym ACR, which refers to their foci: "A" is for action, "C" is for change, and "R" is for relationships. Let's examine the ACR questions, one at a time, to determine if they have the potential to bring the answers and insights *you and your colleagues want and need* to the surface.

ACR Question 1: What Did I or What Did We Actually Do?

On the surface, this question seems so mundane that it is often overlooked, and the novice action researcher occasionally fails to collect the data needed to provide an adequate answer. Not knowing the answer to this question can create a significant problem during the final and perhaps most consequential part of the action research process (reflection and action planning). The essential rationale for probing and answering this question can be found in Newton's third law of motion:

For every action there is an equal or opposite reaction.

Whatever happens in our schools or classrooms was influenced by an earlier action or, more realistically, by a collection of actions. Knowing what precipitated an occurrence allows us to predict, with varying degrees of confidence, what might happen in the future. However, if we are unclear about the precipitating actions, our ability to predict an event or replicate results can be very difficult. This is not just an abstract or theoretical issue. It is a matter of real consequence.

In Chapter 5, we discussed the recurring problem of discontinuing fundamentally sound programs because of an initial failure to produce the anticipated results. These premature abandonments of fundamentally sound programs spring from a set of understandable circumstances. Individual teachers, schools, and districts adopt programs because they believe those programs hold promise for improving student performance. Then, after a year or two of implementation, the programs are frequently deemed failures and are discontinued. The justification for ending the programs is simple and straightforward: After implementation, the anticipated outcomes weren't realized. Such decisions seem perfectly reasonable, if one assumes the adopted program had been, in fact, implemented and implemented appropriately. Unfortunately, just because a program was adopted or was attempted doesn't necessarily mean it was implemented as intended or in accordance with the developer's theory of action.

This lesson was driven home for me a few years ago when a team of elementary school teachers attended an action research training program I was facilitating. Their superintendent had asked them to investigate the effectiveness of a very expensive and complex literacy program that had been adopted in their district three years earlier. The program had been brought in with much fanfare and with high expectations for spurring improvement in the district's reading performance. The program included texts, videos, workbooks, and a host of other supplemental materials. While expensive, the program appeared to be well worth the money considering its promise for improving reading scores. However, after three years of use there had been no evidence of gains in student performance on the state reading exam. It was no surprise that this team came to the action research training with a specific research question in hand. They wanted to know if their adopted program was worth the money. As much as it had cost to purchase the program materials, the superintendent was willing to admit the mistake, move on, and try another approach were it determined that the adoption was, indeed, a mistake.

As part of the data-collection plan they created to answer their question, these teacher researchers decided to develop and analyze teacher-developed *curriculum maps* (Jacobs, 1997; Hale, 2008). The data-collection process they used required every elementary teacher to record which portions of the program they had been using as well as the amount of time they devoted to the various program components. When this implementation data was laid out on a chart, the team noticed something right away.

Apparently, throughout the school the teachers had idiosyncratically been selecting which program components to use and, even more important, which components to ignore, based on personal biases or taste. Many teachers omitted entire portions of the program, while others gave some components minimal attention and spent considerable time with other parts. There were no discernable patterns of use, even across the same grade level and in the same school. As a consequence, in a typical class, a teacher could find some students who had considerable experience with certain portions of the program sitting right next to a classmate who never even encountered that aspect of the same program. Once this data was analyzed, it became clear that no teacher in the district could fairly assume that any two students had experienced the same scope and sequence.

When the superintendent asked the research team to report what they learned from their study, he expected one of two answers to his original question:

1. The program was shown to be a worthy one and had, in reality, succeeded in improving student reading performance.

2. The program had not delivered on its promise for improving reading performance.

But the research team determined that the data wouldn't support either of those conclusions and actually reported something quite different: *Few, if any, students had actually experienced the program as it was intended.* Therefore, they told the superintendent from the evidence collected they were unable to evaluate the program's effectiveness (the adequacy of the program's theory of action) because, in reality, it had never been properly implemented.

As this case demonstrated, neglecting to collect data to document what was actually implemented can prove costly in dollars, time, and missed opportunity costs.

In Chapters 4 and 5, we made our theories of action explicit by producing detailed graphic reconstructions and creating estimates of the amount of time and energy needed to realize success (our priority pies). Now that we have arrived at *Stage 3: Implementing Action and Collecting Data*, we will want to begin assembling the necessary data to allow us to draw conclusions about the adequacy of these theories. To do this, we will need to document all the critical actions that we took and the things that were experienced by our students. Fortunately, gathering this data is relatively easy.

Teachers develop and keep track of nearly everything they intend to teach and what they expect their students to experience in class. Our weekly lesson plans are repositories of all this data. However, a record of lesson plans (handwritten or electronic) alone is rarely adequate to provide accurate documentation to adequately answer ACR Question 1. Using myself as an example, it was the very rare week when the activities I anticipated doing and wrote out as lesson plans on Sunday night actually matched what I later taught and what my students experienced during the ensuing week. I make no apologies for this. Like most teachers, I willingly and readily adjusted my plans based on circumstances and student needs. I added additional time for work on skills that students were having difficulty with, and I omitted planned activities that later seemed redundant and appeared to be a waste of time. So although my weekly plans were written with sincerity and represented what I had thought I would do, they wouldn't provide an accurate record of what had actually transpired. This problem can be easily remedied. All that is required is allocating five minutes each Friday afternoon to go over the past week's plans and adjust them to reflect what actually transpired. Figure 6.1 is an illustration of a week's lesson plans annotated by the teacher to reflect what really happened.

By engaging in this one simple additional piece of record keeping, I can end each school year with a complete record of the actions that occurred on each of the 180 days in my classroom. Furthermore, by correlating this data with student attendance records, I can create an accurate report on the specific learning activities experienced by each of my individual students. Later, should I find myself pleased with the learning that occurred, I will be able to track the precise instructional activities that corresponded with the learning. Conversely, if I am disappointed with student performance, I will be in possession of an accurate record of which events coincided with the less-than-stellar results.

An additional record-keeping device that I have found helpful is the Time Priority Tracking Form (Figure 6.2). On this form, I write each category of action that appeared on my priority pie (see Chapter 4). Then, after reviewing my weekly activities, I write the approximate amount of time I devoted that week to each of these categories of action. Later, when analyzing my data, I am able to note how closely the percentages of time spent compared to what I had anticipated would be necessary.

ACR Question 2: What Changes Occurred Regarding Performance on the Achievement Targets?

If you were pleased with the rating scales and rate-of-growth charts you created in Chapter 3, you will probably want to use them to monitor ongoing changes in performance with your priority achievement targets. Even if you were delighted with the measuring tools you produced, you should still be suspicious of drawing conclusions regarding student performance using any single source of data. Putting that much weight on any single set of data is equivalent to a prosecutor, responsible for proving a case beyond a reasonable doubt, betting everything on the testimony of a single witness. Most trial lawyers would not rest a case after only one witness's testimony, regardless of how honorable and credible that witness might be. This is because they know that a jury, which might believe in the integrity of the witness, could still have justifiable concerns about the possibility that the witness was confused or otherwise mistaken. This is why lawyers always seek to present corroborating testimony. That is also a good approach for an action researcher. When we assemble data to answer

Figure 6.1 Lesson Plan for Week of October 15

Subject: Government				
Section: Sixth Period				
Monday	*Tuesday*	*Wednesday*	*Thursday*	*Friday*
• Write in current events journals (ten minutes). • Discuss initiative petition process. • Review arguments pro and con in voters' pamphlets. • Discuss initiatives #118, #217, and #482. • Homework: Read essay, "Direct versus Representative Democracy."	• Pop quiz on homework. • Class debate: Be it resolved that representative student government should be abolished. • Random assignment to teams, draw debaters from hat. Twenty minutes preparation. • Twenty-minute debate. • Homework: Reflection worksheet.	• Film: *The Founding Fathers: Why a Republic?*	• Direct democracy scavenger hunt. • In cooperative learning teams, allow twenty minutes to find direct democracy events in past two months from classroom media and Internet. • Compile team lists and submit by end of period.	• Write in current events journals (ten minutes). • Team presentations, ten minutes per team. • Work on problem-based-learning proposals.
Changes	*Changes*	*Changes*	*Changes*	*Changes*
• Didn't discuss initiative #482.	• Didn't do debate. • Didn't assign homework.	• Didn't show film. • Held twenty-minute debate (originally planned for Tuesday). • Homework: Reflection sheet.	• None.	• None.

Figure 6.2 Time Priority Tracking Form

Date: _____

Class: _____

Focus Area (from priority pie)	Approximate Class Time Spent (in minutes)	Comment

ACR Question 2: *What Changes Occurred Regarding Performance on the Achievement Targets?* it behooves us to look for multiple *separate* and *independent* sources of information on changes in performance on each achievement target under study.

Fortunately, locating multiple sources of data on performance isn't overly problematic. For example, if I want to know if my students have learned the proper use of writing conventions, I might assess this by having them edit a sample piece of work where they will be required to identify and correct common convention errors. However, if later I want to make assertions about their competence, I will need to corroborate those results with other sources of data. In all likelihood, the data required to do this already exists and are present in my classroom; therefore, no additional testing or data collection should be necessary. For instance, I could validate my initial findings with items found in their writing portfolios, where I could observe whether they have been using conventions correctly in their own writing. This process of using corroborating evidence to establish validity and reliability is what researchers call *triangulation*. In the next chapter (Chapter 7), you will receive guidance on developing a full-blown, triangulated data-collection plan to answer your research questions.

ACR Question 3: What Were the Relationships, if Any, Between the Actions Taken and the Changes in Performance?

Just because I can unequivocally report what I did and what my students experienced (ACR Question 1) and can establish with confidence what the students achieved (ACR Question 2), doesn't mean I can assert that there was a relationship between my actions and the documented changes in student performance.

Earlier, we discussed the relationship between dependent and independent variables, the dependent variable being those things we wanted to see changed and the independent variables being the actions we undertook to affect those changes. In the natural sciences, one observes the interaction of independent and dependent variables as a straightforward cause-and-effect relationship. Any changes observed in the dependent variable (the achievement target) can be unambiguously attributed to adjustments in the independent variables. Under experimental conditions in the natural sciences, these are justified conclusions because, in laboratory situations, it is possible for the researcher to fully control the environment.

However, when we are dealing with human behavior and with social interactions, things are never quite that simple and straightforward. For us to claim that "A" caused "B," we would have to be able to prove that *nothing* else could possibly have influenced the final result but "A." This is impossible to prove. Let's say my target is to have one of my students, Sam, become more diligent in editing his written work. I decide to accomplish this by providing my students with detailed teacher feedback after the first draft of each of their essays. As it turns out, the data I assembled reflects a clear pattern: The quality of the editing in Sam's final papers has improved considerably over the course of the term. The relationship seems clear to me, as illustrated in the following figure.

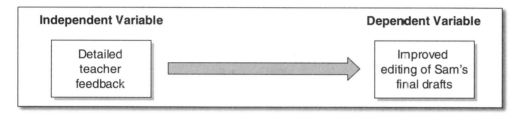

It seems apparent that when I changed my feedback process, Sam's editing improved. From this data, I started feeling confident in making the assertion that my actions had caused Sam's improvement.

But I didn't realize that at the same time that I began providing intensive feedback, other factors independent of my actions had also changed. Coincidental with my provision of intensive feedback, Sam's father began offering him a twenty-five dollar reward for every "A" he received on a major school project. Now that I am aware of this data, a new question has emerged: How might I determine if the improvement in Sam's work was due to my teaching or if it was the result of his father's bribe?

Two categories of factors can interfere with a direct relationship between dependent and independent variables. Researchers call these *extraneous* and *intervening* variables. An extraneous variable is something that has nothing to do with the phenomenon being studied (my teaching) but gets in the way in a manner that influences the result. The bribe provided by Sam's dad was separate and apart from the phenomenon I was studying (the relationship between my feedback and the quality of Sam's editing), but it influenced the dependent variable being measured (the quality of Sam's final papers).

An intervening variable is a phenomenon that is also influenced by an independent variable (my intervention) while having its own separate effect on the outcome (dependent variable). For example, let's say I'm a PE teacher who notices that students whose homes are located north of the river are better golfers than students living on the south side. I conclude that housing location improves one's golf game. The causal relationship might be illustrated this way:

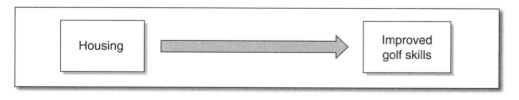

However, what I don't take into account is that the north end of town is where the more affluent families live, as well as where all the town's better golf courses are located. Consequently, the factor that may more powerfully influence students' skills with golf isn't their housing location; it may be the increased practice that results from access to golf courses and the financial ability to play the game. The influence of these extraneous variables are illustrated as follows:

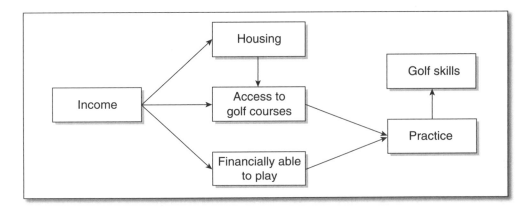

In the next chapter, where we will be working on developing valid and reliable data-collection plans, we will spend considerable time on strategies designed to enhance our confidence in the relationship between specific actions and documented outcomes. Having that confidence will be important as we plan revised actions based on our action research data.

DEVELOPING YOUR OWN RESEARCH QUESTIONS

In the last chapter, you worked through a set of processes designed to help you articulate your theory of action. You visually illustrated your theory with an implementation road map, a graphic reconstruction. Often our theories of action are robust. By this, we mean they involve dozens, sometimes even hundreds, of different assumptions. In human endeavors, nothing is ever certain. So, realistically, every item on your road map is an assumption: the role of each individual activity is an assumption, the way you sequenced the activities is based on assumptions, and the relationship of individual activities to each other and ultimately to the achievement of the priority achievement target are assumptions. As cynics like to point out, nothing in modern society is ever certain but death and taxes.

Some of the assumptions in your theory of action are right on the surface and easy to see. For example, a graphic reconstruction could contain a relationship as illustrated in the following figure.

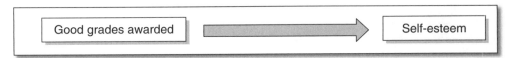

The connection between these variables is clear and direct; the action researcher is asserting a belief that there is a dynamic relationship between self-esteem and grades. But that is only the surface assumption. That same dynamic presumes numerous other underlying assumptions. For example, there are several implied assumptions in this relationship, including the following:

- Self-esteem is important.
- Good grades are valuable.
- Different grades are awarded to different students.
- Self-esteem is malleable.

As an inquiring educator, you may have an interest in investigating and developing a deeper understanding of some of those assumed relationships. But rarely is one person equally interested in or capable of exploring every one of the assumptions contained within his or her comprehensive theory of action. When one considers that there are literally hundreds of assumptions that could be investigated, the question for the part-time action researcher becomes this crucial one:

What are the specific assumptions that are worth spending my finite time and energy investigating?

We will now explore a systematic process designed to help you go about responding to that question.

TWO-STEP WALK-THROUGH

The last thing you did when completing your graphic reconstruction (implementation road map) was to proof your theory by walking through the road map in the shoes of different types of students/participants to see if you could identify obstacles or omissions and correct them. We are going to repeat the walk-through process once again, but this time you will be asking slightly different questions as you walk through your graphic reconstruction.

Hopefully, when you proofed your theory by walking through it and searching for problems, the process resulted in a final theory of action that represented your best thinking regarding a comprehensive strategy to get everyone to the desired destination. Now that you are ready to implement your theory and begin the action part of the process, there is another overriding issue you need to be concerned with: determining if your best thinking as represented in your theory of action was, in fact, adequate to produce success with your priority achievement target.

The role of the research questions is to help you accomplish that task. Earlier, we said that everything on your graphic reconstruction was an assumption and you could, if you had both the time and interest, go about systematically validating or refuting each one of those assumptions. Assuming that you do have a life outside of being an action researcher, you probably need to narrow the scope of your inquiry. This is done by focusing exclusively on those issues that you truly *need* or *want* to know more about.

You can find these issues by walking through your theory two more times. On each walk, you will be asking one of the following questions:

1. Is this factor, issue, variable, or relationship significant?

2. How confident am I regarding the workings of this factor, issue, variable, or relationship?

Based on your answers to these two questions, one or more meaningful action research questions should emerge.

Walk-Through 1: Determining Significance

Everything that makes up your theory of action is something you believe, and everything illustrated on your graphic reconstruction is something that, in your opinion, plays a role in realizing success on the achievement target. However, as we saw when developing the priority pies, everything involved in achieving success on our targets is probably not of equal importance.

On this first walk-through, you should question the relative importance of every single element of your theory. This includes every box, circle, square, arrow, line, and so forth that appears on your graphic reconstruction. Specifically, you should ask,

Is this factor, issue, variable, and/or relationship significant?

To be deemed significant for action research purposes, a factor or relationship needs to meet two qualifications. First, you must believe that this factor or relationship exercises a powerful influence over your ability to influence the phenomenon under study. For example, if your focus is on developing student self-esteem and you have an arrow that shows a relationship between "parenting skills" and "the level of self-esteem," one might conclude that you feel this relationship is significant, meaning you believe the relationship between parenting practices and a child's self-esteem is a powerful one. But that is only one aspect of significance for an action researcher.

The second aspect refers to whether you feel this factor can be significantly influenced by *your* actions. This is a good time to remind ourselves that action research should focus on investigations into the effect of *our* actions and not other concerns or phenomena, regardless of their importance, that fall outside our sphere of influence. While we may have deemed parenting to be a powerful factor in the development of a young person's self-esteem, we might also conclude that our ability to influence the parenting received by our students is quite limited. For our purpose as action researchers, we will only declare something to be significant if it qualifies under both aspects of this definition. Therefore, the relationship of parenting to self-esteem would not be classified as "significant" when using the two-step walk-through process.

Now let's imagine an arrow that reflects a relationship between grades received and self-esteem. In all likelihood, we would conclude that this relationship met both definitions of significance: it plays a powerful role in the development of self-esteem, and since grading is a practice we have control over, it is a factor that can be significantly influenced by our actions.

Figure 6.3 is a graphic reconstruction created by a hypothetical fifth-grade teacher, whom we shall call Ms. Pioneer. It illustrates her plan to use cooperative teaming to help her students achieve proficiency with two priority achievement targets: learning to contribute to meaningful cooperative work and producing quality multimedia projects. Those components of her theory that she deemed significant are indicated on her graphic with the letter "S." It isn't surprising that she identified fifteen of the *elements* and five of the *relationships* illustrated on her theory as significant. (We

Figure 6.3   Second-Quarter Group Projects: Social Studies—Walk-Through 1

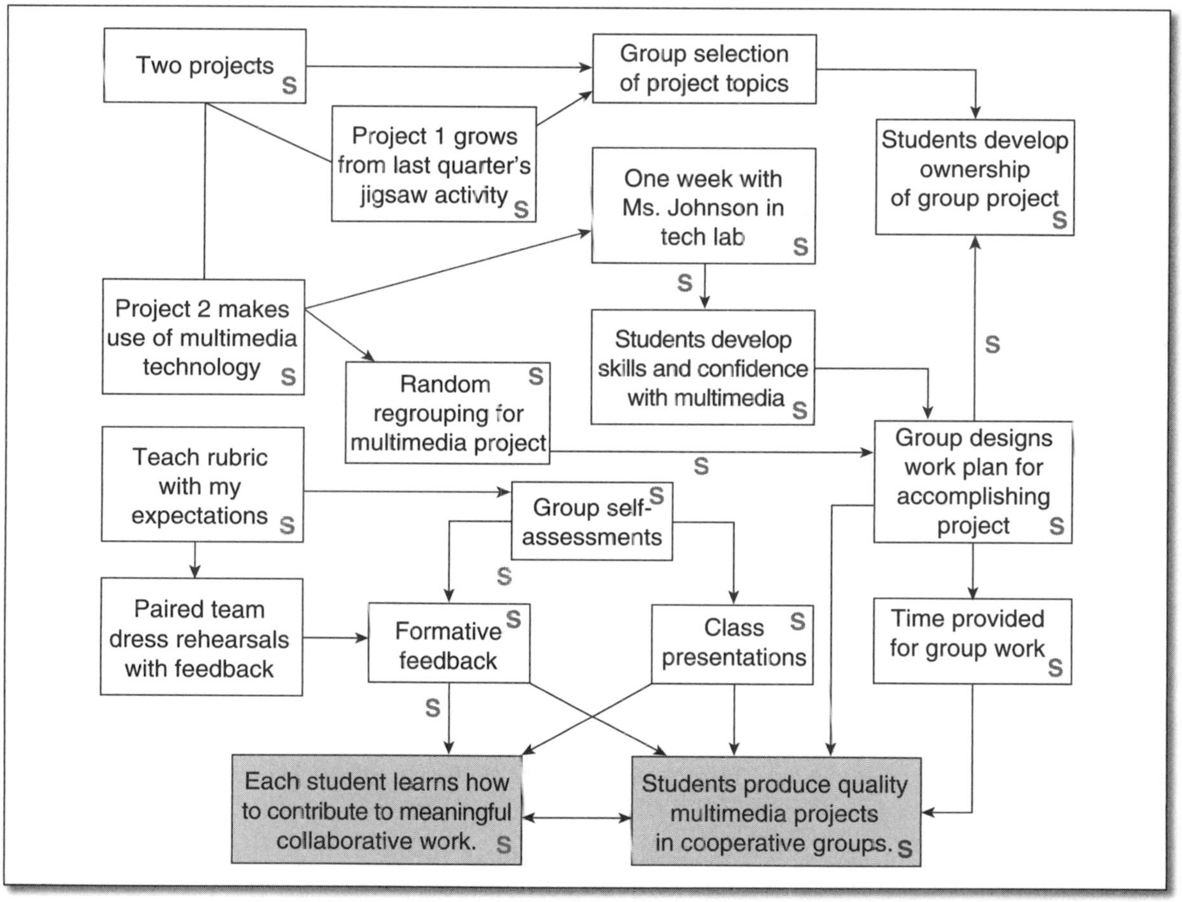

generally find significance in most components of a theory we authored since, intuitively, when designing our theory, we tended to focus on those issues we deem important.)

Your task now is to take out a copy of your graphic reconstruction and ask Question 1 of every single item (box, cluster of boxes, arrows, and so on) that makes up your theory. Then indicate your judgment on significance by writing an "S" by or on every item that meets the two-part definition.

Aspects of your theory that you designate as significant could very well be worth spending time investigating. Other aspects of the theory, those that didn't meet the definition of significance, shouldn't be dropped from the theory, and they should stay where they are on your graphic reconstruction; but in all likelihood, they won't justify any further investment of the finite time and energy available for data collection.

Walk-Through 2: Your Confidence in the Assumptions

Now walk through your theory a second time. However, this time, consider only those aspects of your theory that you deemed to be significant. The question you will be asking of these items is,

How confident am I about the workings of this factor, variable, or relationship?

No doubt there will be some factors or relationships about which you are quite confident, such as the earlier example of the relationship between self-esteem and grades. While you might have already decided that this is a significant relationship, you may also feel that you already have a pretty complete understanding of the way this phenomenon works. It is possible that you already possess a great deal of confidence in this assumption, and there are a number of things that could justify this confidence. For example, when you did your literature review, you may have read considerable research on the role of grades and self-esteem, or the source of your confidence could emanate from years of personal experience.

Alternatively, as you reflect on this question, you might conclude that, while you feel this is a matter of significance and you *believe* this assumption is correct, you recognize that it is still only a matter of conjecture and you might well be mistaken. When this is the case, indicate your uncertainty by placing the letter "U" next to the "S."

Once you've completed the second walk-through, your graphic reconstruction likely has several items marked with an "SU," factors that you have deemed *significant* and about which you are *relatively uncertain.* Figure 6.4 is Ms. Pioneer's graphic reconstruction after her second walk-through.

Significant issues that you are uncertain about are precisely the things that justify further investments of your finite professional time and energy. The one remaining task is to take the items that were flagged during the

Figure 6.4   Second-Quarter Group Projects: Social Studies—Walk-Through 2

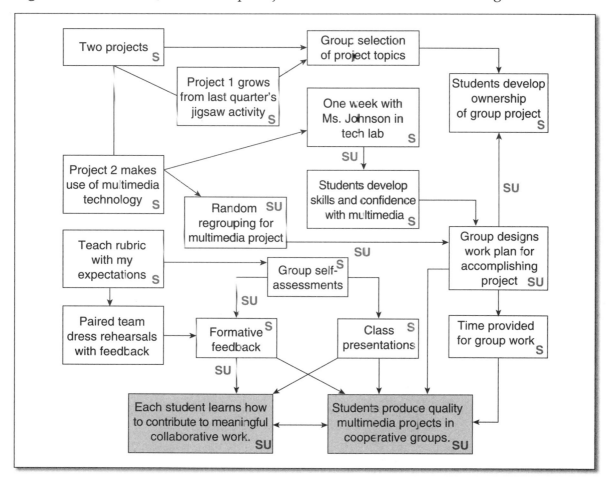

two-step walk-through and word them as action research questions. Figure 6.5 shows a list of thirteen elements and five relationships that Ms. Pioneer identified as *significant*. The elements and relationships in bold print are those that she deemed both *significant* and *uncertain* and consequently worthy of incorporating into research questions.

DRAFTING THE QUESTIONS

The way a research question is worded is not just a matter of semantics. Wording can make a big difference because the precise way a question is stated plays a major role in determining the nature of the data that will be required to provide an adequate answer. A set of guidelines follows, for your consideration while drafting your action research questions.

Avoid narrow questions that could be answered with a simple yes or no (such as, Does teacher feedback influence student motivation?). One way to determine if a question is too narrow is to ask yourself,

> Will a definitive answer to this question, in itself, provide helpful direction for further action?

Figure 6.5   Significant Aspects of Theory and Significant Relationships

Significant Aspects of Theory

1. That there be two projects
2. That Project 1 grows from the previous quarter's work
3. That Project 2 involves multimedia
4. That students develop ownership of projects
5. That students spend a week with Ms. Johnson
6. That students develop skills and confidence with multimedia
7. **That students be randomly regrouped**
8. **That each group designs its work plan**
9. That I teach the rubric
10. That the groups do self-assessments
11. That formative feedback occurs
12. That class presentations occur
13. That adequate time is provided for group work
14. **That students learn to be contributors to group work**
15. **That students produce quality multimedia projects**

Significant Relationships

1. **The relationship between one week with Ms. Johnson and the development of student skills and confidence with multimedia**
2. **The relationship between group design of the work plans and groups taking ownership of their topics**
3. **The relationship between random regrouping of the students and the development of each group's work plans**
4. **The relationship between group self-assessments and the provision of formative feedback**
5. **The relationship between formative feedback and learning how to contribute to meaningful cooperative work**

Let's assume the answer to the example given was,

Yes, teacher feedback influences student motivation.

Would you say that this answer provides enough direction for you to plan your next steps and it would inform your future professional action? Probably not. This is because the simple "yes" answer neither illustrated how and why teacher feedback influenced student motivation nor how different forms of feedback might have differentially influenced motivation.

Do ask open-ended questions, where a large number of potential answers may surface (such as, What are the relationships of different forms of feedback to changes in student performance?).

When this question is evaluated through the criteria of its *potential for informing future action,* we will be much happier with the result. This is because the data collected in answer to that question will undoubtedly provide insights into the specific nature of the feedback a teacher should consider using in an effort to enhance student motivation.

Avoid using causal language. Many beginning action researchers feel that conducting scientific research means uncovering definitive cause-and-effect relationships. This is understandable. Most of us learned about what constitutes research in our science classes. In the basic and natural sciences, it is actually possible to control for all relevant variables and consequently determine what causes what. However, in social science, this is never possible. When it comes to human behavior, results are influenced by such a wide array of variables that no one could ever control for every possible factor.

Fortunately, there are ways to enhance validity and reliability in social science research, and these will be elaborated on in the next chapter (Chapter 7).

Frame questions in a manner that is likely to highlight observable patterns and correlations between the strength of the independent variables and changes in the dependent variables. (For instance, what are the characteristics of teacher feedback that correspond to increases in the quality of student work?)

The answer to a question like this can help the action researcher recognize those specific teacher behaviors (feedback) that consistently accompany the student outcomes they were trying to influence.

Having completed the two-step walk-through of her theory, Ms. Pioneer was now ready to draft a set of research questions to guide her study. These questions will become the heart of her inquiry. Ms. Pioneer's questions were the following:

- What was the nature of student performance on my two-priority achievement targets? (This question focuses on the two significant elements rated SU: *That students learn to be contributors to group work,* and *that students produce quality multimedia projects.)*
- How did the week the students spent with the media specialist influence student development of skills and their confidence with the use of multimedia? (This question focuses on the first of the significant relationships rated SU: *The relationship of one week with Ms. Johnson and the development of student skills and confidence with multimedia.)*
- Which factors influenced the success of group work (assignment to groups, ownership of topic, quality of work plans, and so on), and in what ways did those factors influence academic performance? (This question focuses on two of the other significant relationships rated SU: *The relationship of group design of the work plan to group ownership of topic and the relationship of random regrouping to the development of group work plans.)*

- What was the nature of the formative feedback provided through group self-assessment, and in what ways did this feedback contribute to meaningful cooperative work? (This question focuses on the last two of the significant relationships rated SU: *The relationship of group self-assessments to the provision of formative feedback and the relationship of formative feedback to learning how to contribute to meaningful cooperative work.*)

It has often been noted that the most time-consuming aspect of the action research process is the work that leads up to the development of research questions (Hubbard & Powers, 1999). I have heard many first-time action researchers assert that it took them an entire year or more to come up with a really good question. Look how well you did; it only took you six chapters!

Sometimes we go through an extensive and lengthy process to find meaningful questions. However, if the questions that emerge end up guiding us to information that helps us move ahead with our priorities, then the time invested is time well spent.

Ms. Pioneer can now look forward to the rest of the action research process knowing that everything she engages in from here on will be focused on helping her to better illuminate answers to four very meaningful questions.

SURFACING RESEARCH QUESTIONS FOR LEADERSHIP PROJECTS

The two-step walk-through process for surfacing meaningful research questions works in precisely the same manner when the action research is focused on work being engaged in by a school leader. In the last chapter (Figure 5.4) you had a chance to review Dr. Hernandez's graphic reconstruction showing her theory for increasing faculty collaboration. In Resource C (Exhibit 5) you will find another copy of her theory of action with the results of her application of the two-step walk-through process and the research questions it generated.

7

Building a Data-Collection Plan

On the surface, no aspect of the action research process appears more daunting than data collection. While the planning you've engaged in thus far has been time consuming, there is nothing new about that. Teachers are accustomed to spending considerable time planning their instruction, units, and programs. While the work you've completed in Stages 1 and 2 of the action research process may be somewhat more extensive than what is required for other more routine types of planning, hopefully the additional clarity and focus that this deliberative planning process produced justified the extra expenditure of energy. However, at first glance, the time required for data collection often doesn't seem that worthwhile to a busy educator.

When anticipating the collection of data for action research, first-time researchers are often legitimately concerned about two things:

1. The time required

2. The need for precision

Because of the importance of these concerns, we will begin our discussion on data collection by addressing each one separately.

DATA COLLECTION AND THE COMPETING DEMANDS FOR YOUR TIME

If devoting time to data collection means using time that could be invested in other learning activities, the cost is greater than most dedicated educators are willing to pay. Fortunately, this is not a choice you have to make. These two categories of professional action appear to be in conflict only if one holds a limited view of what constitutes teaching and what qualifies as data.

WHAT QUALIFIES AS TEACHING?

As every teacher knows, there is more than one way to produce learning. One mechanism educators have historically used to stimulate student learning is direct instruction. This is the model where the teacher is positioned in front of the learner and is responsible for demonstrating or telling the student how to accomplish a task and providing the student with immediate feedback as he or she practices the new skill or recites the new information. There is much to commend this approach, especially when teaching certain types of straightforward basic skill content. And many teachers have found that the direct instruction model works well with learners who need consistent and immediate oversight. However, many teachers have also found that there are an even greater number of circumstances when direct instruction is not the only or even the best pedagogy. Many times, a reliance on direct instruction comes at a heavy cost: It is an all-consuming task, leaving teachers with little time and energy for monitoring, assessing, and adjusting.

Increasingly, teachers are finding out that we serve our students and ourselves best when we act as the *facilitators* of student learning. In this model, the students' role is transformed; they become what Ted Sizer (1984) defined as *knowledge workers*. Every day, the knowledge workers wake up and go to their workplace (your classroom) understanding that they will be expected to fulfill their job descriptions, which is to do that which is necessary to acquire new knowledge and develop greater skill. In this model, the teacher's role becomes analogous to the supervisor's function in the adult workplace. Our job becomes supplying whatever is needed to help the knowledge workers complete their job successfully—in this case, the acquisition of knowledge and the development of skills. In this relationship, the ultimate responsibility for learning becomes shared and no longer rests solely on the teacher's shoulders.

In the adult workplace, supervisors occasionally will demonstrate new techniques, but they spend far more time observing the workers and providing feedback. Supervisors also engage in planning, gathering data on worker productivity, and adjusting individual and group work plans accordingly. They attempt to monitor everything critical to the work being attempted so they can knowledgably and purposefully intervene when necessary. Last and most important, when the supervisors' goal is increasing worker productivity, they implement practices and procedures that result in the workers being motivated to put forth their very best efforts.

We need to approach data collection in the spirit of action researchers as learning supervisors. Most of the data-collection strategies presented here can occur during the workday, while your students are purposefully and actively engaged in their own learning. Properly implemented, most of the suggested strategies will also support achievement by providing encouragement, direction, and motivation for your learners.

WHAT QUALIFIES AS DATA?

If you think of data as something artificial, something that only comes into existence if and when we decide to solicit it, then generating and collecting data becomes a job unto itself. This isn't a productive way for an action researcher to view data collection.

As practitioner researchers, you are well served by applying a broad definition of data. Much action research methodology has been heavily influenced by anthropology. The primary work of anthropologists is observing, documenting, and attempting to understand human cultures that are different from their own. The strategy most often used by field anthropologists is direct immersion into the cultures they are studying. While doing their work, they try to take in everything encountered, from one-on-one discussions, to social activities, to local rituals. Even mundane activities, such as eating habits and home decor, are considered data. When all these observations are taken together and analyzed through a sensitive and thoughtful lens, these disparate bits of data can illuminate a complex culture that was the focus of the study.

DATA IN DESCRIPTIVE RESEARCH

When we are conducting descriptive research, our work is nearly identical to that of field anthropologists. Just as they hope to understand what is going on in other cultures by unearthing the meaning of the behavior, habits, and beliefs demonstrated by the members of that culture, the descriptive action researcher is trying to understand the particular circumstances, norms of behavior, and meanings attached to the behavior by the participants in a specific school, classroom, or academic setting. For this reason, when we are engaging in descriptive action research, nearly everything that occurs in the setting we're studying has the potential to be meaningful data for our understanding of the following questions:

- What is going on here?
- Why is it happening?
- What impact is it having?

DATA IN QUASI-EXPERIMENTAL RESEARCH

Action researchers conducting quasi-experimental studies will also be well served to view data collection through the anthropologists' lens. Undoubtedly, quasi-experimental researchers will want to monitor changes in performance on their priority achievement targets and, therefore, will almost always be using some quantitative methods. But that is only part of the process. The quasi-experimental action researcher needs to understand more than simply whether or not the priority targets were hit. It is equally, if not more important to understand the following as well:

- Why was the target hit or missed?
- How did various elements of the theory of action contribute to success or failure?
- What could be learned from this undertaking that might help illuminate other related aspects of the teaching–learning process?

To address these issues, the quasi-experimental researcher has the same need as the descriptive researcher to deeply understand the context and the nuances of the environment where the action took place.

I can hear some of you asking, "Is he crazy? Did he say I ought to be acting as an anthropologist and collecting data on *everything* going on in my school or classroom?"

Not to worry. While it is true that the range of things that you may want to document is vast, the good news is that much of the necessary data is already being and will continue to be collected, whether or not you had ever decided to conduct action research.

One of our primary tasks as action researchers is identifying *efficient* ways to collect and compile the data that already exists in our environment. But before we examine ways to accomplish this, we should spend a few minutes considering the other big concern regarding data collection: achieving adequate precision.

DATA COLLECTION AND CONCERNS ABOUT PRECISION

It is unwise to collect flawed data and even worse to make use of it. None of us wants physicians making treatment decisions based on faulty data, nor do we want to fly in aircraft designed by engineers who relied on imprecise data. Equally important, none of us wants our students to receive inadequate instruction simply because inaccurate data suggested an unwise strategy. Even those of us with the most minimal backgrounds in research and statistics probably recall from Ed Psych 101 the two key conditions that must be met if data is to be considered accurate: validity and reliability.

- *Validity* refers to whether the data actually reflect the phenomena they claim to. For example, we would all agree that a measuring tape is a valid way to measure height and a scale is a valid mechanism for determining weight.
- *Reliability* refers to the accuracy of data. For example, even though a scale is a valid way to measure weight, any particular scale could be broken and consequently provide an unreliable report on the weight of an object.

As professionals, we want the data that we use to influence our decisions on teaching and learning to be both valid and reliable. While there are a number of techniques researchers use to establish validity and reliability, the strategy used most frequently by action researchers is called *triangulation*. As pointed out earlier, triangulation is similar to the strategy used by trial lawyers to prove a case beyond a reasonable doubt. In planning their cases, lawyers strive to find corroboration for every bit of testimony or evidence. Corroboration is accomplished by offering additional independent pieces of evidence that lead to the same conclusion. While any single bit of evidence might be flawed or imprecise enough to raise suspicion, when enough separate and independent pieces of data all point in the same direction, the credibility of the conclusion becomes apparent. Figure 7.1 is a *triangulation matrix* for use with action research. The left column is where we list our research questions. Then, like a trial lawyer preparing a case, we consider all the independent sources of data (witnesses) that might be collected, consulted, and presented so that when taken together, they will provide a credible answer to the research question. Then the separate sources of data are listed in the row corresponding to the research question they will be addressing.

As we proceed through this chapter, it is suggested that you use the triangulation matrix to build a case worthy of your confidence. If you build a triangulated data-collection plan, it is likely that the findings and

Figure 7.1   Triangulation Matrix

Research Question	Data Source 1	Data Source 2	Data Source 3

Source: Reprinted with permission from Richard Sagor, *How to Conduct Collaborative Active Research* (Alexandria, VA: Association for Supervision and Curriculum Development, 1992).

conclusions that emerge from your research will possess both validity and reliability.

FISHING IN A SEA OF DATA

Schools and classrooms are data-rich environments. In any situation where life exists, data is continuously being created. Data represents what people choose to do and what they elect not to do. It involves who is doing an action, what they are doing, and their explanations for why they chose to engage in that action. In places where work is undertaken, such as schools, even more data is produced. Where people work, they produce products; those products are data. Here are just a few of the work products typically created in schools that you could use as sources of action research data:

Work Product	Data Regarding
Lesson plans	What I intend to teach
Grade book	The scores earned by my students
Attendance book	Who was and was not present
Faculty meeting agendas	The scope of a faculty business
PTA attendance	Parental interest in the PTA's work
Walk-through notes	Instructional activities in the building

Such a list could go on endlessly. The point is simply this: data is swirling around the schoolhouse, and this data relates to nearly everything that goes on inside. Collecting this data is much like catching fish with a net. If a fine enough net is cast, it will catch every living organism in the environment. Even if we could cast such a net in our classrooms and catch every minute thing that transpires inside, the time it would take to sift through all that data, separating that which is of value from that which is mostly irrelevant, would certainly take more time than we have available.

The fisherman solves this problem by designing a net that allows undesirable items to flow through and that hopefully retains only that which was intended. This is analogous to the task before us as we make our plans for data collection.

SECURING RESEARCH ASSISTANTS

This chapter began with a discussion regarding the time issue. Frequently, the way professors and other research scientists deal with limitations on their time is by employing research assistants, generally abbreviated as

RAs. In grant-supported research teams, the individual responsible for the study is known as the PI, or principal investigator. In most cases, RAs are highly motivated graduate students who willingly do much of the grunt work of data collection for the privilege of working alongside the PI. So, you might be asking, where are you, the poorly paid and overworked educator involved in the conduct of unfunded action research, going to find the motivated RAs to help you with your data collection? Fear not; the solution is nearer than you might think.

Earlier, we touched on the difference between providing direct instruction and facilitating learning. We mentioned that when the teacher becomes the facilitator of learning and the students perform as knowledge workers, they share the responsibility and accountability for the achievement of results.

Research in adult work settings has clearly established that when workers are involved in systematically monitoring their own progress and self-assessing their own work, performance improves (Depree, 1998; Hersey & Blanchard, 1993). This happens because when workers are delegated responsibility for monitoring their own work, they tend to hold themselves accountable to higher standards. Equally important, they tend to enjoy their work more and show more pride in their ultimate accomplishments. So when we ask our students to become the primary collectors of data (our research assistants) on their own learning and to document the activities they are engaged in, we are setting ourselves up for a classic win-win situation.

I would wager that you already know through personal experience that having students compile portfolios, self-assess their work, maintain logs and journals (on their learning activities), and prepare for student-led parent conferences is anything but a waste of time. By having the students monitor their own work, we are helping them learn and internalize what constitutes productive work as well as gain insight into how they learn best (the skill of metacognition).

It would be nice if I could say that by turning your students into RAs, you will free yourself from all data-collection responsibilities. But that isn't the case. Having RAs on staff doesn't eliminate the participation of the principal investigator in the data-collection process, but it does transform the work of the PI. As the lead researcher, the PI's job begins by fleshing out the theory (what you did in Chapters 4 and 5), determining the research questions (what you did in Chapter 6), and creating the research design: determining what data is to be collected, who will collect it, when it will be collected, and how it will be analyzed. Those are the tasks we will concern ourselves with for the remainder of this chapter. As you proceed to build your research design, our primary focus will be on strategies that

- emphasize the use of *available data,*
- emphasize data that can be collected *while you are facilitating learning,* and
- maximize the value for students of *monitoring their own performance.*

BUILDING A TRIANGULATED DATA-COLLECTION PLAN

There are no limits to the variety of things that qualify as data or the techniques that action researchers can use to collect data. There is, however, a limit to how much can be covered in one book. For this reason, we will work through the process of building a triangulated data-collection plan with a few sample strategies that are frequently used and can be efficiently implemented by school-based action researchers. To illustrate, we will return to Ms. Pioneer's action research project. As you recall, Ms. Pioneer was investigating the use of cooperative teaming as a mechanism to develop cooperative work habits as her students produced multimedia projects. While in the midst of this study, something occurred that motivated Ms. Pioneer to conduct a second descriptive action research study inside her quasi-experimental study.

During the first nine weeks of the school year, Ms. Pioneer became deeply concerned about a particular problematic student, Joann Heathrow. Joann was diagnosed as ADHD and had a history of low academic performance tracing back to her first years in school. Despite medication, her off-task behavior and academic problems continued unabated during the first quarter; and whenever the class engaged in cooperative activities, Ms. Pioneer noticed that Joann was off-task and frequently disruptive. Ms. Pioneer was at a loss as to what to do. She decided that since she didn't fully understand what was going on with Joann, she would conduct a descriptive action research study on Joann's experience in class. She chose social studies as the setting for her study, as the use of cooperative learning in this unit would likely prove problematic for Joann. She felt that if she could understand what was happening with Joann during second-quarter social studies, she might gain valuable insights on how to better meet her educational needs. She decided to frame her inquiry around the three ACR questions discussed in Chapter 6. Figure 7.2 is a triangulation matrix set up for use with the three ACR questions.

The process of constructing a data-collection plan begins by taking one research question at a time and then asking this question:

> What is a source of data that could be *efficiently* collected that would provide good information to illuminate the answer to this question?

After surfacing a first answer to that question, the process calls for continued brainstorming by repeatedly asking *what is another source? And then another? And then another?* This process continues until the action researcher believes that when taken together, the multiple sources of data identified will provide a comprehensive, credible, valid, and reliable answer to that research question.

Ms. Pioneer began this process with this paraphrased version of *ACR Question 1: What exactly did the class and Joann do?*

She started by considering sources of data that were already available. She recognized that her plan book, weekly annotated to reflect what she

Figure 7.2   Triangulation Matrix: Three ACR Questions

Research Question	Data Source 1	Data Source 2	Data Source 3
What did we actually do?			
What changes occurred with our priority achievement targets?			
What was the relationship between the actions taken and changes in performance on the achievement targets?			

actually taught, was one source of data. She realized that by cross-referencing Joann's *attendance records* with her plan book, she could determine what specific activities Joann experienced, and this could serve as a second data source. As her brainstorming continued, it occurred to her that since all of her students are required to keep their daily work in a portfolio, Joann's *daily work* could serve as a third source of data.

At this point she paused and asked herself, Will this be enough to create a credible report in answer to this question? She responded with a yes: A record of what was going on every day Joann was in attendance—as well as what she missed on the days she was absent—triangulated with the work she completed and failed to complete when she was there would provide adequate information to answer the first ACR question.

She then moved to *Question 2: What changes occurred on my priority achievement targets?* Once again Ms. Pioneer began her brainstorming with readily available information. The first thing that came to mind was her *grade book.* This is a treasure trove of data, as this is where she records grades on all assignments, quizzes, tests, projects, and student journals. She then added Joann's *daily work folder* to her list of data sources. (Note: A single data source may assist in answering multiple questions. For example, Joann's daily work folder can help answer both Questions 1 and 2.) Her thinking then shifted to include data she could collect during class while facilitating student learning. She remembered that she regularly carries a pad of paper and writes notes to herself while walking around the classroom.

She realized her *observational notes on Joann's behavior* would be data as well as the *narrative comments she wrote on Joann's assignments.* Remembering that she required all her students to *self-assess their major assignments,* she added that to her list of data sources. Last, since one of her priority achievement targets (for her quasi-experimental study) was increased productive engagement during group work, she had developed a rating scale for use each Friday for her to indicate a *teacher rating of engagement.* The students then used this same rating scale to create a *weekly student rating of engagement.*

Once again, it was time for Ms. Pioneer to stop and consider if, when taken together, the multiple sources of data she had just brainstormed would be adequate. She looked at her list asking, Will an examination of the information in my *grade book, Joann's daily work, my written notes on Joann's behavior, my comments on her papers, her self-assessments of her work,* and *weekly comparisons of Joann's and my engagement ratings* give me a good enough picture of any changes in Joann's performance? While one can always collect more information, Ms. Pioneer was satisfied that the picture that would likely emerge from this data would capture most of the pertinent changes occurring in Joann's performance.

Now she moved to the final action research question: What was the relationship between the actions taken and any changes noted in Joann's behavior?

It immediately struck her that the data she would be using to answer the first two questions would also assist her in answering this last question. Specifically, she realized that looking at the activities engaged in (her plan book and Joann's attendance) and comparing them to what was accomplished (Joann's work, her grade book, her written comments on Joann's work, Joann's self-assessments, her anecdotal notes, and both student and teacher engagement ratings) would enable her to identify any patterns that existed between specific classroom activities and Joann's performance. In the next chapter, when our focus will shift to analysis, additional processes for tracking the relationship between actions and outcomes will be discussed.

Figure 7.3 shows Ms. Pioneer's completed triangulation matrix for the descriptive study on Joann Heathrow's second-quarter experience in fifth-grade social studies.

Figure 7.3 Triangulation Matrix: Complete

Research Question	Data Source 1	Data Source 2	Data Source 3
What did we actually do?	• Lesson plan book	• Attendance record	• Joann's portfolio of daily work
What changes occurred with our priority achievement targets?	• Grade book (quizzes, homework, journals, reflection papers, projects, tests, weekly assessments)	• Teacher observations ○ Observation notes ○ Comments on tests and papers	• Joann's portfolio ○ Daily work ○ Self-assessments
What was the relationship between the actions taken and changes in performance on the achievement targets?	• Contrast lesson plans with performance data from grade book.	• Correlate lesson plans with observation notes and comments on papers.	• Correlate lesson plans with material in Joann's portfolio and Joann's self-assessments.

DATA-COLLECTION PLANNING FOR LEADERSHIP PROJECTS

While there are few places that are as rich in data as classrooms, when one is conducting a study pertaining to school leadership the process of planning for data collection should be governed by the same principles as with classroom research:

1. It is important that the data-collection plan utilize enough independent sources of data to produce both validity and reliability.

2. Data should be collected in an efficient manner.

As a rule, most members of a school staff will appreciate it when they see leaders collecting data on the impact of their leadership. Such behavior not only models a belief in the value of assessment, but when people see leaders acting on the data, it demonstrates the leader's commitment to the instructional ethic of "monitoring and adjusting." That being said, leaders need to be mindful of limitations on their own time as well as the time of those they are working with. Therefore, as much as possible data collection for leadership projects should be based on available and easy-to-collect data. In Resource C you will find two data-collection plans prepared by Dr. Hernandez: Exhibit 6 is a plan developed to answer the three ACR questions, and Exhibit 7 is a plan prepared on the assumption that she was pursuing the three questions that surfaced through her application of the two-step walk-through process.

Now it's your turn. Using the blank triangulation matrix (Figure 7.4), start developing a viable data-collection plan that you believe holds promise for producing the insights you will need to answer *your* action research questions.

Although each of the data-collection strategies Ms. Pioneer planned to use involve data that was either already being collected or could easily be collected while teaching, the amount of work involved in pulling all of this together could still prove significant. Earlier it was mentioned that one way to manage the data-collection workload is by enlisting your students as research assistants. That will certainly help. But there are other efficiencies (both electronic and manual) that can help one manage the work of data collection. We conclude this chapter and our work on *Stage 3: Implementing Action and Collecting Data* with a look at how classroom technology can help you manage your work while implementing your theory of action and collecting the data needed to answer your research questions.

INTEGRATING EFFICIENCIES INTO YOUR DATA-COLLECTION WORK

Ms. Pioneer's data-collection plan made use of several sources of written material that are routinely produced in classrooms:

- The comments she wrote on Joann's papers
- Notes she wrote to herself when walking around the classroom

Figure 7.4 Triangulation Worksheet

Research Question	Data Source 1	Data Source 2	Data Source 3

- Notes she might occasionally send to Joann's parents, the school's special ed teacher, and the school administration regarding Joann
- Joann's self-assessments

Compiling and organizing this data can become a project unto itself. However, I've had a great deal of success using a low-tech strategy to tackle this problem. My strategy involves the use of sets of carbonless paper.

Keeping File Copies of Narrative Data

Figure 7.5 is an example of a form I had printed on two-part carbonless paper (any school district or commercial print shop is able to print on carbonless paper).

Whenever I am writing something to a student, including comments I would normally have written on his or her tests or on an assignment prior to returning it, I do on the carbonless paper. I then give the top sheet to the student or staple it to the paper and keep the yellow copy for my own records. If I am writing a note regarding a student to a parent, to another teacher, or to myself, I will use the same paper. I maintain a folder for each student, and at the end of each day, I simply drop my yellow copies of the notes I've written into the appropriate folder, always making sure that each note is dated. If, as it turns out, I never have a reason to review these notes, nothing is lost. After all, it took hardly any time for me to file them. But should I ever need them as data for my action research, to prepare for a parent conference, or simply to refresh my memory regarding what transpired with a student, I can open the file, arrange the notes in chronological order, and quickly identify patterns in my comments or observations of a student's behavior or performance.

Keeping Running Records of Behavioral Ratings

In Chapter 3, we developed rating scales for measuring changes in performance on our achievement targets (the dependent variables). Earlier in this chapter, we discussed having students become RAs for our action research. Having your students keep running records on their performance as measured on your teacher-created rating scales is one excellent way to do this. This is an especially powerful strategy because of the motivational impact of having students monitor the direct relationship between their work and the results obtained. It is no surprise that fitness buffs, weight watchers, and bridge players all keep running records of their results. Observing patterns of improved behavior motivates people to keep trying, or, conversely, data that reflects stagnation or decline can provide motivation for changing old habits.

Action researchers can effectively and efficiently turn students into RAs by first teaching them the use of the appropriate rating scales. When working with younger children, this might mean translating the scales you developed in Chapter 3 into "kid language" and then providing each student with a copy of the scale or placing it on a poster on the wall of your room. With prereaders, teachers often do this by creating a scale with a range of

Figure 7.5 Carbonless Paper

A note from the teacher . . .

smiley to frowny faces. You recall that Ms. Pioneer was hoping to see increasing levels of engagement from her students, so she developed a rating scale (Figure 7.6) for use in assessing this performance. She also wanted her students to contribute meaningfully to group work, so she created another rating scale for use in assessing cooperation (Figure 7.7).

Then, on a weekly basis, she asked the students to rate themselves using these two scales. Had she wanted more sensitive tracking, she could have requested daily ratings. This is another instance where I have found carbonless paper to be extremely helpful. Figure 7.8 is an example of a form I have students use for recording their daily or weekly self-assessments. I have my students turn in the original and keep the carbonless copy in their portfolio. Ms. Pioneer could have had her students use forms such as those to make their weekly assessments.

By using the carbonless assessment forms I have a running record of how all of my students viewed their performances on my priority targets; and because these are dated, I will be able to correlate those perceptions to what was transpiring in class. (There will be more specificity on establishing the relationship between actions and performance in the next chapter, when we work on data analysis.)

After a period of time, usually a number of weeks, I provide my students with another set of carbonless forms (Figure 7.9), which they will use to produce line graphs reflecting their self-assessments over this time period. These line graphs provide me with trend data for each one of my students over an extended period. As a bonus, I can use these forms to effortlessly gather one additional piece of data. Once the students have graphed their performances, I will ask them, on the same form, to review the slope of their graphs and provide me with their explanations for any perceived patterns or trends.

By having the students keep the original rating forms in their portfolios they are able to compile these results. This way my RAs (my students) create the statistics and chart the trends in their own ratings, which saves me a great deal of time. More importantly, by doing it this way, I have provided them with a chance to take stock of, assume responsibility for, and justify to themselves their own choices of behavior.

To see the power and time saving of this one simple strategy, consider the following scenario. We'll assume I am doing action research with a class of thirty students, compiling daily ratings on two different scales over a three-week period. This amounts to thirty assessments per student, 900 assessments per class. Yet, if I provide my students with just one minute per day to jot down their daily ratings and then give them fifteen minutes to complete the summaries at the close of the three-week period, I will have had all this data compiled and summarized with an expenditure of a mere thirty minutes of class time. Most important, this meager time investment will have provided my students with an opportunity to take ownership of their own improvement. (Resource A contains detailed instructions on the use of carbonless reporting forms for collecting and analyzing data.)

Figure 7.6 Rating Scale: Engagement

Low	Basic	Developing	Meeting Expectations	Productive	High
The student didn't disrupt and interfere with others' learning.	The student did some of the assigned work. Worked productively for much of the period.	The student completed most of the assigned work. Worked productively for most of the period.	The student completed all of the assigned work. Was on task for the entire class period.	The student was on task for the entire period, completed all the assigned work, and went beyond expectations.	The student was on task the entire period and put forth a maximum effort.
1	2	3	4	5	6

Figure 7.7 Rating Scale: Cooperation

Low	Basic	Developing	Meeting Expectations	Productive	High
The student didn't disrupt and interfere with others' learning.	When prodded, the student made a contribution to group work.	The student contributed to group work. The student's labor moved the project forward.	The student made a unique, productive contribution to group work (something that would not have occurred if the student wasn't there).	The student took initiative to make the group more successful. Showed enthusiasm for the team and put forth a significant effort.	The student took initiative to make the group more successful. Showed enthusiasm for the team and put forth a significant effort. The student took affirmative steps to solicit and support the initiative of other group members.
1	2	3	4	5	6

Figure 7.8   Feedback Report

Name: _____

Date: _____

Scale 1

Today _____

1	2	3	4	5	6

Why?

Scale 2

Today _____

1	2	3	4	5	6

Why?

Figure 7.9   Feedback Summary

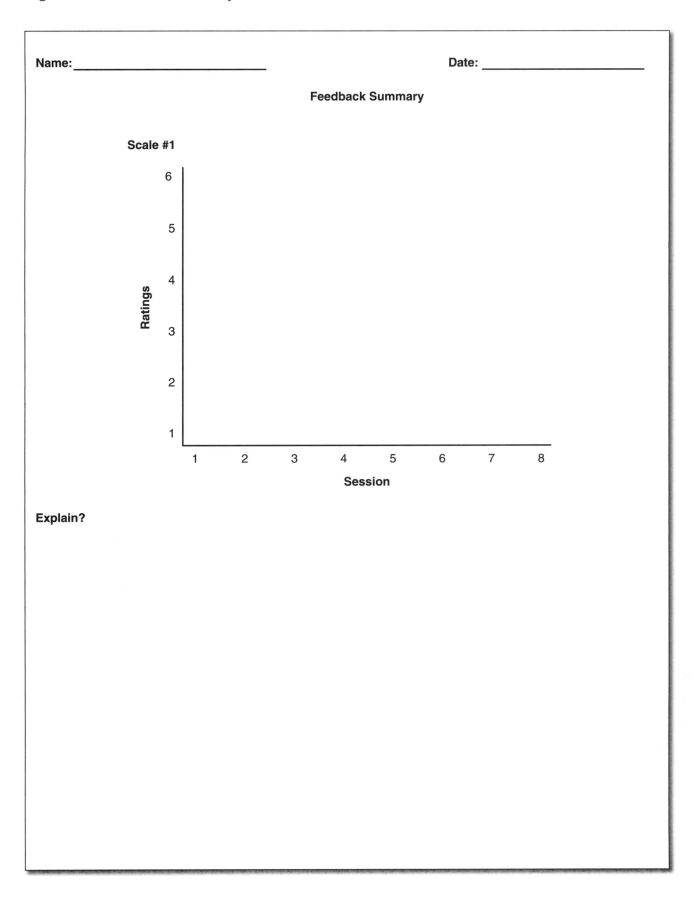

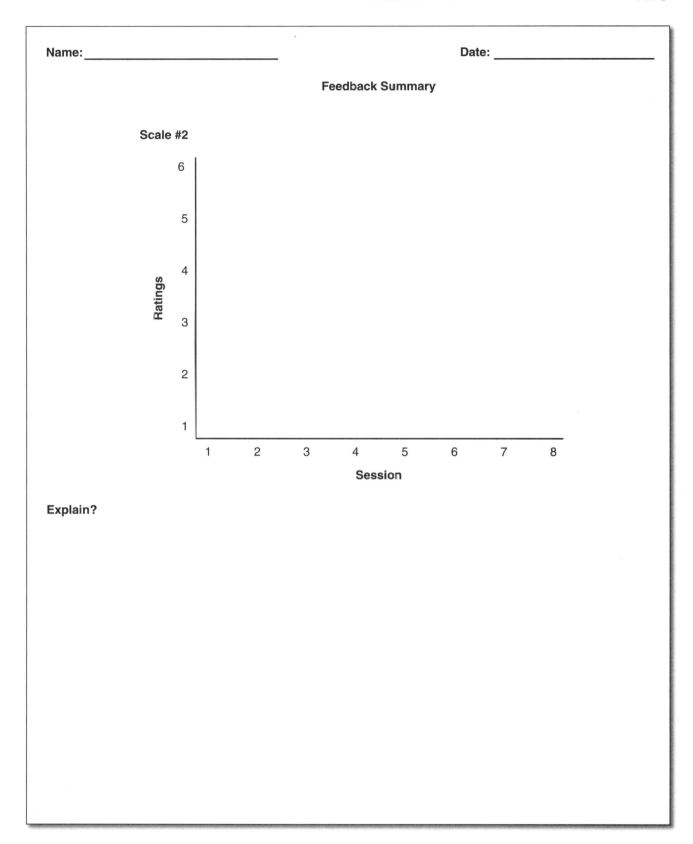

Name:_____   Date:_____

Feedback Summary

Scale #2

Explain?

USING TECHNOLOGY TO COMPILE AND ASSEMBLE ACTION RESEARCH DATA

The beauty of the time-honored teacher grade book is that in this one easy-to-maintain document, a host of different types of information regarding the performance of each of our students can be compiled. In one set of columns, we have attendance data; on another column we have a record of their homework as well as quiz grades and major assignments. And the list goes on. Data input is easy. When taking roll, we simply check if the student is present or absent, and before we return papers, we jot down the grade we assigned. Of course, pulling all this together (adding up each column and figuring the averages) can take considerable time at the end of the grading period. Fortunately, many school systems have moved to computerized grade books where the compilation of statistics and the graphing of trends in student performance is made much simpler.

Those readers who don't have access to computer grade books can accomplish many of the same things by using a spreadsheet on their computer. It is now commonplace for computers to be delivered with spreadsheet software preinstalled. If you don't own spreadsheet software, it is easy and inexpensive to acquire. Basically, a spreadsheet is no more than a grade book with an unlimited number of expandable columns. However, it is superior to a hardcopy grade book in three big ways:

1. It will automatically compile statistics (such as averaging the scores in each column), making end-of-term grading easier.

2. The cells of the spreadsheet can expand infinitely. In traditional grade books, each cell is just a fraction of an inch wide, not providing too much room for data. But in a spreadsheet you can enter an entire note or comment, even copy a photograph or a scanned image of student work into a cell.

3. Last, with a spreadsheet you can easily ask the computer to compute averages for subgroups, allowing for disaggregation by gender, ethnicity, past performance, and so forth, on virtually any assignment. This is extremely helpful when you are conducting data analysis, to be discussed in the next chapter.

One really good thing about using a spreadsheet as your electronic grade book is its portability. By using a handheld PDA, a Netbook, or a tablet computer, teachers can input data as they move around the room. Technologies such as PDAs, tablet computers, and computerized writing pads now enable teachers to write longhand notes or score student work and later have them automatically converted into print for placement in their computerized grade book. With voice recognition software, teachers are able even now to dictate notes into a digital recorder or microphone and have their comments turned into text.

What enables doctors to provide personalized treatment for each one of their diverse patients is the availability of an accessible running record of all the pertinent data on each patient's condition. Of course, the doctor has a support staff to transcribe the doctor's notes, input the lab data, and place the various items into the correct patient file. It is unlikely that we will see that type of support provided to teachers in the near future. But, fortunately, spreadsheets and portable computing technology increasingly can do nearly the same thing for the overworked educator.

This brings us nearly to the close of our discussion on Stage 3 of the action research process, *Implementing Action and Collecting Data*. It is now time for you, the action researcher, to begin the fun stuff: implementing your theory of action and collecting the data as indicated in your triangulated data-collection plan. There is only one little task that needs to be discussed before you commence action on your theory.

KEEPING A RESEARCHER'S JOURNAL

I strongly suggest that during this upcoming period of implementation, you keep a researcher's journal. Needless to say, the more observations you collect in your journal, the more information you will have available when you arrive at the final stage of the process, *Stage 4: Reflecting on Data and Planning Informed Action*. Even if your data-collection plan doesn't call for using information from a teacher's journal or if journaling isn't something you are comfortable doing, keeping a researcher's journal isn't a big commitment, and it takes very little time. In fact, you needn't even write in your researcher's journal on a regular basis. What is important, however, is that you make notes in your journal whenever you depart from the theory of action you articulated in *Stage 2: Articulating Theories of Action*. When this happens, in your notes you should indicate the date, the specific actions that differed from your original theory, and your rationale for making these adjustments.

As an educational action researcher, your first and most sacred duty is to the first part of your title, your work as *an educator*. Because that is your most important job, you should always feel comfortable deviating from your previously enunciated theory of action wherever and whenever you think it is in your students' or school's interest. However, later, when you put on your researcher hat, you will find it essential to document what actually transpired and the reasons why you may have felt it necessary to make adjustments to your theory of action. Unless you have an accurate record of what took place and why, you will be unable to learn from your experience.

Keep in mind, often the best learning comes from serendipity. You should stay open to letting this happen. Your researcher's journal will allow you to understand the significance of unanticipated events as well as enable you to share this learning with others.

Tip on Data Collection

The data-collection sources mentioned in this chapter are simply examples. You are encouraged to use them to stir your imagination, while keeping in mind that there exists a virtually unlimited universe of data-selection strategies for your use as a creative action researcher.

8

Analyzing the Data

We are now ready to begin our work on the final stage of the action research process, *Stage 4: Reflecting on Data and Planning Informed Action*. There are three distinct activities that occur during this stage:

1. Analyzing

2. Planning

3. Reporting

The process begins by *analyzing* the data that's been collected. Then the insights gained from that analysis are used to prepare a *plan of action*. This is followed by *reporting and sharing* what was learned with colleagues. In this chapter, we focus on the first of those activities, analyzing the action research data. In the next two chapters, the focus will shift to strategies for action planning and reporting.

Every action research project is a story of what transpired during the course of the research. As in the world of literature, each story has its own theme, plot, and set of characters. Our stories can range from a report on a single student's experience in class to the story of what was learned while teaching familiar content in a new way, or it could be the saga of a faculty and its attempt to become more collegial. Now that you have arrived at *Stage 4: Reflecting on Data and Planning Informed Action*, the events of your story have already occurred. Every element (the characters, conflicts, setting, and themes) can hopefully be understood through the data you collected. The task before you, when engaged in data analysis, is to figure out a way to liberate the story that is lying dormant inside your data and give it an opportunity to take form and reveal itself. In this chapter, we review several ways for accomplishing this.

Just as the nature of your research questions influenced the types of data collected, the nature of that data will influence the strategy you will use for analysis. When you prepared your research design (Chapter 7), we discussed the use of a set of three generic ACR research questions and saw how effective they could be with a wide range of research foci. We will now examine a few generic approaches to data analysis, all of which have the power to effectively bring to the surface the stories residing in most sets of school data. The first approach is called a *trend analysis*. This is a versatile strategy that can easily be modified and adjusted for use with an array of data sources and should help you answer a broad range of action research questions.

TREND ANALYSIS

Above all, education is about growth and development. Students, classes, and schools change over time. When things are proceeding as we'd like, the direction of those changes is positive. As educators, our hope and professional assumption is that the longer someone is engaged in the educational process, the greater will be his or her development. In this book, we framed the rationale for engaging in action research as a means to help us find the best routes for fostering that development and to assist us as professionals learning from our own experience as we travel ever closer to our vision of universal success.

The specific areas of development you will want to document are changes in performance on your priority achievement targets. When analyzing action research data, your goal is to accomplish two things:

1. Trace any and all changes in performance that occurred in the effort to reach your priority achievement targets.

2. Understand the pertinent factors or circumstances that contributed to those changes.

Conceptually, the way action researchers usually approach the analysis of data is very similar to the way historians and other reporters of naturally occurring events approach theirs. What first attracts the attention of a historian or a reporter is the awareness of a compelling event. Whether that event is a conflict, a discovery, a scandal, an accident, or an election, the analysis process begins with the reporter (that is, the historian or researcher) becoming aware that something has happened that he or she wants to know more about. Invariably, the aspect of the event that made it noteworthy was that it was unique or, at the very least, significantly different than what had gone before. After an event has been initially reported, the focus switches to understanding the event. After describing what occurred, historians train their eyes and ears backward, trying to understand what contributed to or otherwise influenced the event. The consuming questions at this point become the following:

- Why did this occur?
- Why did it occur here and not elsewhere?
- Why did it happen now and not at some other time?

The events we action researchers want to report on are changes in performance on our priority achievement targets. The circumstances that led up to the events are the things that transpired as the learner, the class, or the program developed to its current level of performance. Our job when conducting data analysis is to use the available data to deepen our understandings regarding which of all the infinite number of things that transpired (the potential independent variables) actually influenced the changes in performance we recorded on the dependent variable.

Since change occurs over time, we can pictorially illustrate the analysis process as a line graph, such as that shown in Figure 8.1. In Figure 8.1, the vertical axis represents performance on the achievement target and the horizontal axis represents the events that occurred over the term of the study.

Figure 8.2 is a graph representing the rates of highway fatalities in the United States from 1988 to 1998. An examination of this graph reveals something quite positive. Fatalities, per 100 million vehicle miles, dropped dramatically during this decade.

If you were working in the field of transportation safety and had selected as one of your priority achievement targets reducing highway

Figure 8.1   Trend Analysis

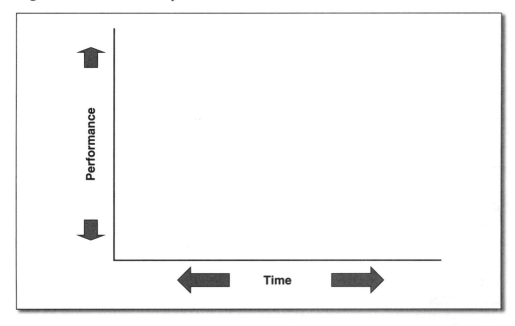

Figure 8.2   U.S. Highway Fatalities, 1988–1998

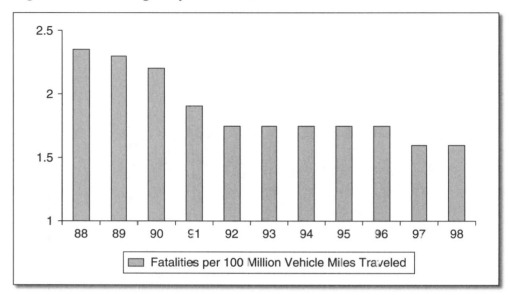

deaths, you would be delighted by this trend in performance. In all likelihood, you and your colleagues have been taking many different actions
designed to reduce the fatality rate. At this point, you would have significant interest in determining which of those actions, if any, contributed to
this positive change on your priority achievement target.

No doubt you and your colleagues have been collecting data on several aspects of driver behavior, and you would now be interested in seeing
if that data could help you understand what, if any, specific changes in
behavior corresponded to the drop in fatalities. One of the sets of data you
have happens to be annual reports on the use of seat belts. Wondering if
there might be a relationship between seat belt use and highway fatalities,
you decide to contrast seat belt use from 1988 to 1998 with the fatality data.
Figure 8.3 shows these two data sets side by side.

A cursory look at these graphs reveals a clear pattern: The decline in fatalities corresponds almost exactly with the increase in the use of seatbelts.
Needless to say, you would want to do further analysis employing other sets
of data before you claim to have demonstrated this relationship as irrefutable,
yet at this point it is beginning to appear that the actions you and your colleagues took to encourage seat belt use may well be paying dividends.

ORGANIZING DATA TO HELP ANSWER
THE THREE GENERIC QUESTIONS

When conducting a trend analysis with the data collected in response to
the three ACR research questions, it is helpful to compile and review the
data in the same order as the questions. To illustrate how this is done, we
will return to Ms. Pioneer's descriptive study of Joann Heathrow's experience in her fifth-grade class.

Figure 8.3   Reports on Seat Belts and Highway Fatalities

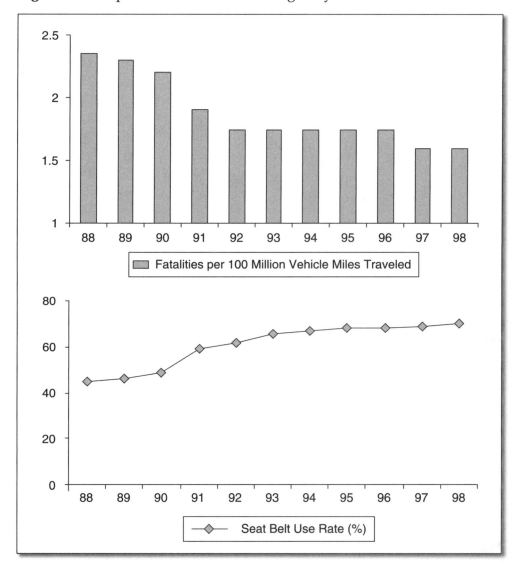

ACR QUESTION 1: WHAT DID WE DO?

Any action researchers who took the time to detail a personal theory of action will already have in their possession important historical documents with data on what they *intended to do*. The priority pies and graphic reconstructions produced during *Stage 2: Articulating Theories of Action* will provide accurate data on what you had planned and what you intended as of the date you created those documents. Therefore, the first step of this part of the analysis process is to revisit your original theory of action and then review your data on implementation for evidence of four things:

1. Was the theory of action implemented as designed?

2. In what fashion was the theory of action implemented?

3. What, if any, elements of the theory were omitted or changed?

4. What, if any, significant actions were taken that were not part of the original theory?

There are several ways we can go about answering these questions. One is to examine the sum of our actions and determine the degree to which our investments of time and energy corresponded to the percentages we had anticipated and illustrated on our priority pies (see Chapter 4). A second strategy is to see if we faithfully followed through on the theory of action as displayed on our graphic reconstructions (see Chapter 5). If you elected to use the Time Priority Tracking Form (Figure 6.2) and kept a researcher's journal or an annotated set of lesson plans (or both), you will have all the data you need to answer ACR Question 1. The following three-step process will help you synthesize this data:

Step 1: Allocating Time

Using the worksheet provided (Figure 8.4), enter the data you collected on your weekly Time Priority Tracking Forms (Figure 6.2).

The next step is to illustrate the time actually invested over the course of your study. This is done by creating a line graph. Figure 8.5 illustrates the ebb and flow of the time spent by Mr. Seeker while engaging in his action research on improving his student's writing of five-paragraph essays.

Now it is time to examine the *time allocation graph* by category to see if any notable patterns or outliers can be identified. For example, was there an extended period of time (perhaps an entire month) when nothing was done in a particular category of action, or was the time spent on each category consistent throughout the project? When we look at Figure 8.5, we can see that Mr. Seeker spent significant time early in the term on mechanics and grammar, and the time he devoted to instruction on editing increased as the term progressed.

You may want to use Figure 8.6 to plot the actual allocation of time across the categories of action identified on your original priority pie.

Another valuable use of the data on the summary sheet (Figure 8.4) is to determine if the actual expenditure of time was consistent with what you had anticipated when planning your project. This is done by producing a grand total of the hours spent working on the project and then creating subtotals for each category of action. To calculate the percentage of time invested per category, divide each subtotal by the grand total. Then, using the percentages produced, draw another pie graph; this one will be illustrating your actual expenditure of time.

By placing the priority pie, constructed prior to commencing action, next to the pie graph you just produced, you will have created a visual that clearly and succinctly contrasts your original assumptions regarding time allocation with the actual expenditure of your time. Figure 8.7 shows the two graphs produced by Mr. Seeker.

Figure 8.4 Summary Time Priority Form

Category of Action	Week 1	Week 2	Week 3	Week 4	Week 5	Week 6	Week 7	Week 8	Week 9	Totals
Totals:										

Figure 8.5 Time-Use Graph: Eighth-Grade Writing in Hours

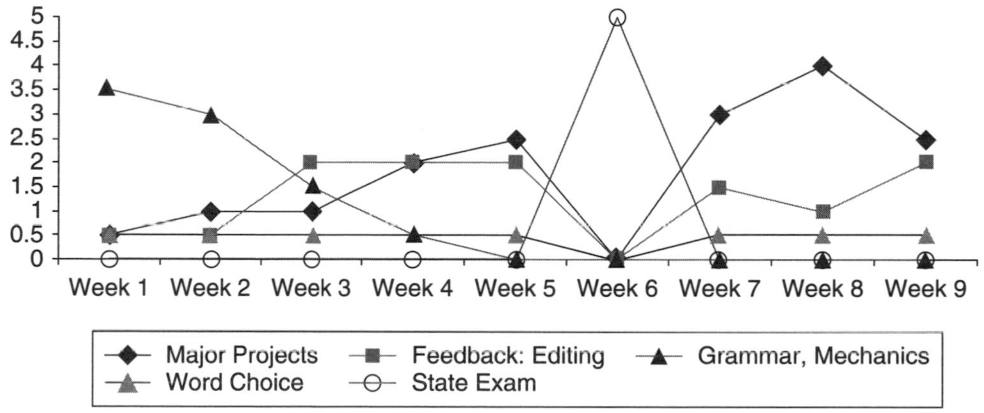

Legend:
- ◆ — Major Projects
- ■ — Feedback: Editing
- ▲ — Grammar, Mechanics
- ◐ — State Exam
- ▲ — Word Choice

Category of Action	Week 1	Week 2	Week 3	Week 4	Week 5	Week 6	Week 7	Week 8	Week 9
Major Projects	.5	1	1	2	2.5	0	3	4	2.5
Feedback: Editing	.5	.5	2	2	2	0	1.5	1	2
Grammar, Mechanics	3.5	3	1.5	.5	0	0	0	0	0
Word Choice	.5	.5	.5	.5	.5	0	.5	0	.5
State Exam Prep	0	0	0	0	0	5	0	0	0

133

134

Figure 8.6 Trends in Time Use

Project: _____

Approximate Time Spent	Week 1	Week 2	Week 3	Week 4	Week 5	Week 6	Week 7	Week 8	Week 9
5 hours									
4.5 hours									
4 hours									
3.5 hours									
3 hours									
2.5 hours									
2 hours									
1.5 hours									
1 hour									
0.5 hour									

Figure 8.7 Anticipated and Actual Time Use

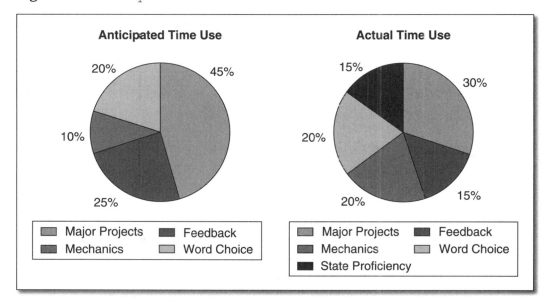

Contrasting Anticipated and Actual Energy Expended in Leadership Projects

The use of priority pies to contrast the anticipated and actual expenditure of energy across independent variables is a valuable part of data analysis regardless of the focus of the action research. On occasions when the key actions will be taking place during scheduled classes or at scheduled events such as regular faculty or PLC team meetings, the use of strategies like the "Summary Time Priority Form" will enable the action researcher to create an accurate picture of how energy was expended. This is because the "Summary Time Priority Form" process treats time and energy as if they were the same thing. But, on other occasions, for example when leaders are conducting action research on their facilitation of change, direct measures of time invested (for example entries on one's calendar) may not produce an accurate portrait of energy expended.

For this reason it is suggested that when conducting action research on leadership activities the action researcher prepare contrasting pictures of "anticipated and actual *energy* expended" (as opposed to "time expended"). To create these contrasting pictures we use a slightly modified process for generating the *actual energy expended data*. Resource C (Exhibit 8) contains instructions on how you can create contrasting priority pies of energy expended.

Now, taking all the data you just compiled to answer ACR Question 1, it is time to summarize the data in clear, unambiguous, bulleted statements. We will call these statements *findings.* For example, your data might enable you to write statements such as the following:

- The project lasted for eighteen weeks.
- Approximately sixteen percent of class time was spent each week on journal writing (thirty minutes per week).

- Overall, thirty percent of class time (an average of three hours per week) was spent engaged in work on major papers.
- Overall, five percent of class time was used for teacher feedback.
- Overall, ten percent of class time was spent on group and peer feedback.
- Overall, twenty percent of class time was spent working on mechanics and grammar.
- During six weeks (three in October, two in November, one in December), zero class time was spent on either drafting or revising major papers.

Step 2: Look for Patterns

Read through your researcher's journal, your annotated lesson plans, and/or your calendar with paper and pen in hand. Whenever you notice something that appears to be a pattern (an observation or activity that occurred three or more times), jot down a phrase that describes that pattern. For example, your list might contain items like the following:

- Class discussions about grades
- Review of previously taught material
- Use of editing groups
- Parent conferences
- PLC team meetings

Now reread the journal, annotated lesson plans, or your calendar and, using an analysis form like the one in Figure 8.8, note the date of the occurrence and tabulate the frequency of the occurrences by category.

Once again, it is time to summarize this information as bulleted findings. Examples of findings that Mr. Seeker might identify include the following:

- Class discussions were held following the return of each major writing assignment.
- On seven occasions, I made note of the need to spend an entire class period reviewing previously taught material.
- On four of the five times that peer editing was used, it took at least twice the amount of time allocated.

These are examples of the type of bulleted findings that may have emerged from Dr. Hernandez's analysis:

- I attended twenty-four meetings of faculty work groups.
- We held seven problem-solving faculty meetings.
- Four reports (October, December, February and April) were made on the status of school goals (had been scheduled monthly).
- Minutes were posted following ninety percent of team meeting sessions. Eight teams posted one hundred percent of their minutes.

Figure 8.8 Activity Analysis Form

Step 1. Read through your log, journal, or annotated lesson plans for activities or events that appear to recur. Jot down a phrase that describes the recurring event in the left-hand column.

Step 2. Reread the documents, jotting down the date for each occurrence of particular events or activities and a descriptive comment if necessary.

Event or Activity	Dates of Occurrence	Frequency	Comments
Example: Current events journal writing	9/8, 9/15, 9/22, 9/29, 10/6, 10/13, 10/20, 10/27, 11/4	Nine times; once per week	Occurs first fifteen minutes of class every Monday

Step 3: Creating a Time Line

The purpose of this step is to help you construct the equivalent of the horizontal axis of the trend graph (see Figure 8.1) by using your journal, annotated lesson plans, or calendar. First, read through the plans or journal entries for each specified period of time (generally weekly) and then write a brief summary of the key actions that occurred during that time period. Then write this out on a long sheet of chart paper. Figure 8.9 shows Ms. Pioneer's time line for second-quarter social studies.

Now review your time line as well as your sets of bulleted statements of findings and write a short narrative describing what was done by you and the participants in your project. Typically, narratives might read something like these two examples that could have been written by Mr. Seeker and Dr. Hernandez:

Mr. Seeker might have said the following:

My theory of action called for spending nearly half (forty-five percent) of class time on major projects and twenty-five percent on feedback. In practice, less than a third (thirty percent) of class time was spent on major projects and much less time than I had anticipated (fifteen percent) on feedback. Significantly, more time was spent with direct instruction on mechanics and grammar (twenty percent) than the ten percent that I had intended. Last, fifteen percent of class time was used to prepare for and take the state proficiency exam, a category of action that I hadn't even considered when planning this class.

Dr. Hernandez could have written the following:

I had intended to devote more time to compiling and sharing data with the faculty. I had committed myself to producing monthly reports (nine reports) on school goals, yet only did four. I expected this to take twenty percent of my time, yet it turned out to be a smaller percentage (ten percent). However, my journal and calendar data reveal that the total time I spent on this project was about twice what had been anticipated. I had expected that twenty percent of my time and effort would be devoted to meeting with faculty work groups and forging "limited partnerships." That work ended up consuming fifty-five percent of the total time spent on this initiative. Preparing for the problem-solving faculty meetings wasn't included in my original theory, yet I ended up spending twenty percent of my time and energy on this aspect of the project.

ACR QUESTION 2: WHAT CHANGES OCCURRED REGARDING THE ACHIEVEMENT TARGETS?

Using your grade book or whatever other records you've kept on performance on your priority achievement target over the term of the project, place the data in a chronological sequence for an individual student,

Figure 8.9 Ms. Pioneer's Instructional Time Line

Week 1	Week 2	Week 3	Week 4	Week 5	Week 6	Week 7	Week 8	Week 9
Students work in jigsaw groups. Groups brainstormed, discussed, and selected a topic. Constructed an outline. Groups assigned tasks based on the outline. Thursday spent in library. Groups organized note cards for presentations.	Groups developed presentations. Paired and did dress rehearsals of presentations with feedback. Thursday finalized the presentations. The first two groups presented their work.	Group presentations. On Friday groups met for twenty minutes to critique their own work. Class discussion on "What we learned by doing this project."	Orientation to the technology lab with Ms. Johnson, the media specialist.	Introduced the multimedia project by showing a mock-up produced by Ms. Johnson. Students regrouped. Tuesday was spent with team building. Groups selected a topic and made storyboards. Thursday and Friday in the computer lab working on group project.	No class on Monday due to the assembly. Working on the individual portions of the group project. Students could work in the classroom or computer lab.	The entire week was spent working as groups finalizing the multimedia project.	Monday and Tuesday in the auditorium: presentations of the multimedia projects. Students assessed individually and came to a group consensus on the assessment. Teams gave feedback. Class party to celebrate. Preparing for the writing assessment.	Monday and Tuesday district writing assessment. Watched a film Wednesday and Thursday, and Friday was the field trip to the courthouse.

category of students, or other group from whom data was collected. Figure 8.10 shows the grades earned during the second quarter by Joann, the hyperactive fifth-grade student in Ms. Pioneer's class. Ms. Pioneer recorded grades for homework, quizzes, journals, and group projects. She then used a line graph to ferret out any trends in this data regarding Joann's performance. Figure 8.11 reflects Joann's grades over the nine weeks of second-quarter social studies.

Figure 8.10   Joann's Grades

Week	Journals	Homework Completion	Reflection Papers	Quizzes	Group Project Grades
1	55	80		70	
2	60	60		60	
3	50	60	65	70	85
4		60		80	
5	75	80		90	
6	80	100		90	
7		80		100	
8	90	80	85	90	95
9	100	80		100	

Figure 8.11   Second-Quarter Social Studies Grades

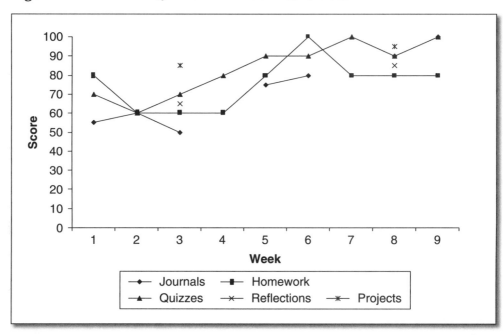

The next step in a trend analysis is comparing and contrasting trends in performance to see if they might have been influenced by variables other than your actions. With classroom research, this is easily accomplished by graphing average class (or subgroup) performance over the same time frame and comparing the achievement of individual students with overall class or subgroup performance. Figure 8.12 is an example of such a graph. It contrasts Joann's quiz grades with the average quiz grades earned by her classmates.

Another illustration of this process can be found in Figure 8.13. This contrasts Joann's grades with her classmates' on each of the five categories of performance tracked in Ms. Pioneer's grade book.

Once you have graphed or otherwise summarized all the performance data you have collected, it is time to review this data and summarize them as bulleted findings. For example, Ms. Pioneer might have generated the following list of findings:

- During the first semester, the average homework completion rate for the class was ninety-five percent, while Joann's homework completion rate was seventy-seven percent.
- Joann's homework completion rate went from sixty-five percent the first four weeks to eighty-five percent in the last four weeks.
- The class average quiz grade was eighty-seven percent; Joann's average quiz grade was eighty-three percent.
- Joann's quiz grades went from seventy percent the first four weeks to ninety-five percent in the last four weeks.

Figure 8.12   Comparison of Quiz Grades

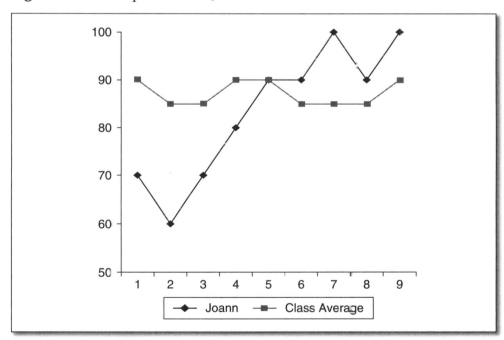

Figure 8.13 Comparison of Second-Quarter Grades

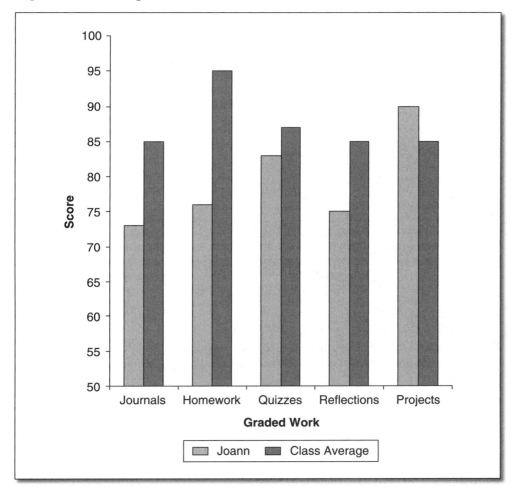

Disaggregation

Often, we want to see if our actions had a differential impact based on certain background or behavioral characteristics of the participants. This is called disaggregation and is accomplished by subdividing performance data by any categories we suspect as being potentially relevant. As a teacher, you start this process by considering the different demographic subgroups represented by your students and then asking yourself if you suspect it would be worth contrasting performance across these groups. For example, many teachers have found it valuable to disaggregate their data by categories such as the following:

- Gender
- Past level of academic performance
- Ethnic group
- Primary home language
- Years of attendance at your school

Dr. Hernandez, the principal who was working on increasing faculty collegiality at her school, might have found it valuable to disaggregate her data by grade level, departmental affiliation, years of teaching, years on the faculty, and so on. Often, schoolwide action research teams find it helpful to compare the performance of students by both their past performance (previous grades) and attendance history, for example, contrasting those who attended schools in the district for five or more consecutive years with students who had attended local schools for less than two years.

Once you have disaggregated your data, compute and graph the averages for each subgroup you deemed relevant. Compare and contrast the performance of these groups and summarize all significant patterns as bulleted statements.

Figure 8.14 is a graph that compares the average ratings on Dr. Hernandez's collegiality rating scale provided by teachers across six different departments over the course of her project.

Figure 8.15 has been provided for you to use for graphing the performance data you've collected.

Repeat the foregoing steps for each set of relevant performance data you have collected.

ACR QUESTION 3: WHAT WAS THE RELATIONSHIP BETWEEN ACTIONS TAKEN AND ANY CHANGES IN PERFORMANCE ON THE TARGETS?

You will need to do two things to answer this question. The first makes use of the findings you generated in answering the first two questions. Place the time line you developed (see Figure 8.9) when analyzing the data you collected in answer of Question 1 under the horizontal axis of the graph. Then on the vertical axis you should plot performance data collected in response to Question 2. This step is illustrated in Figure 8.16, which tracks Ms. Pioneer's weekly assessments of Joann's engagement and Joann's weekly self-assessments during the nine-week quarter.

Ms. Pioneer actually has two sets of data, both of which rightfully belong on the horizontal axis. The first is the summary of her lessons

Figure 8.14 Monthly Collegiality Ratings

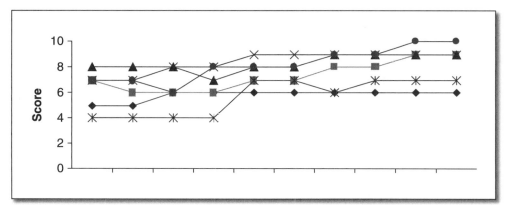

144

Figure 8.15 Performance Graph

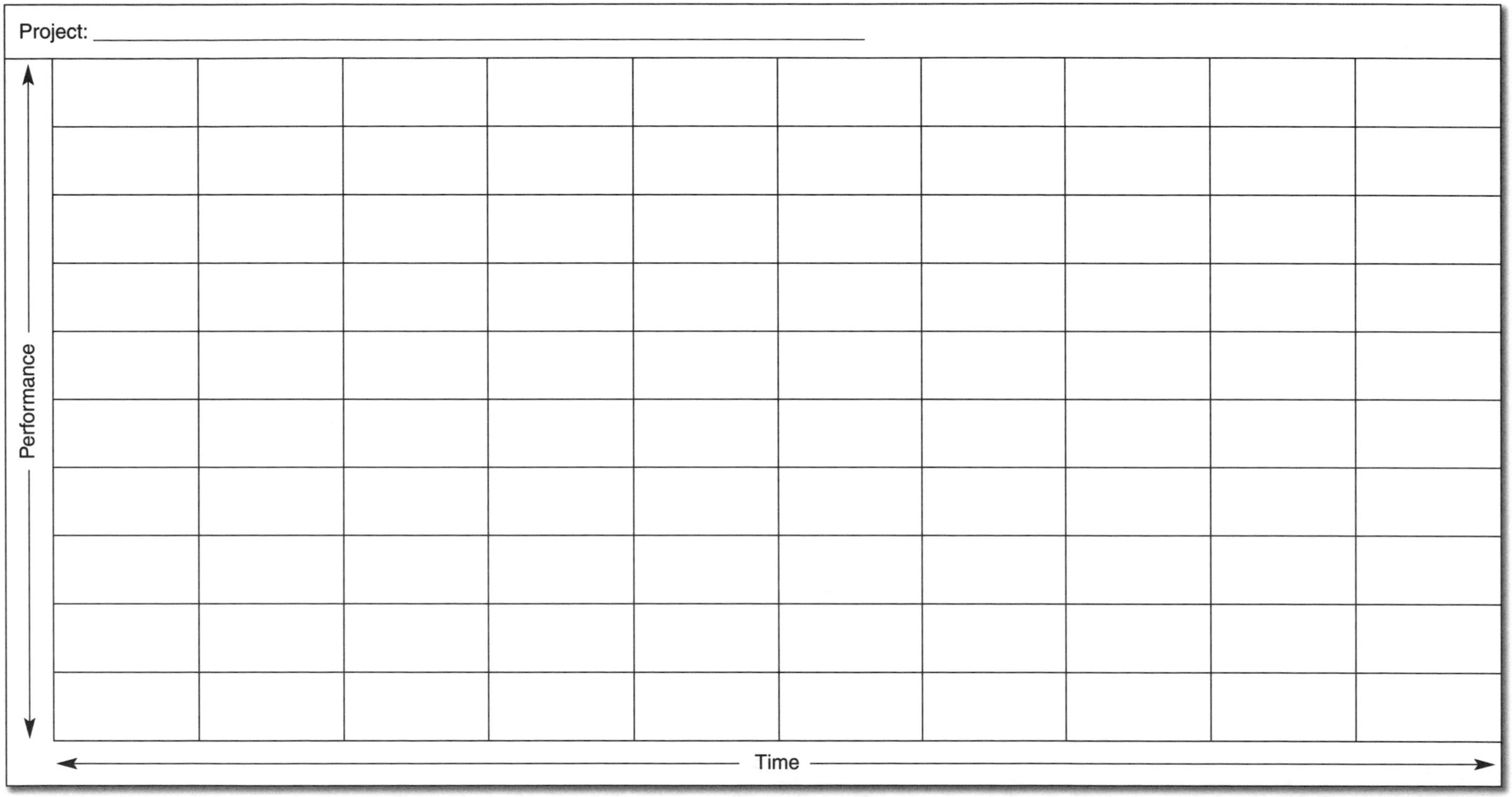

Project: _____

Performance

Time

Figure 8.16 Student and Teacher Ratings of Engagement

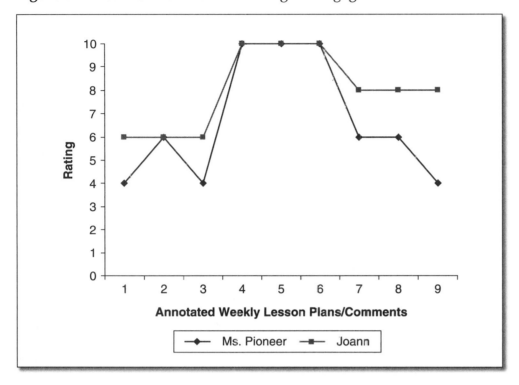

(Figure 8.7); the other is the collection of weekly narrative comments she wrote regarding Joann's behavior. Figure 8.17 incorporates both of those sets of data on the same time line.

It is at this point that Ms. Pioneer can go back and look for changes in Joann's performance, either positive or negative, and check to see if there were any particular actions or activities that corresponded to those changes. The purpose here is to see if she can identify a trend, such as the one between seat belt use and fatalities (see Figures 8.2 and 8.3) to help her explain the story of Joann's experience in class.

Let's return again to Mr. Seeker and his attempt to help his students write better five-paragraph persuasive essays. The graphs (Figures 8.18 and 8.19) reflect disaggregated data on the weekly self-report assessments by his students on the effort they had expended in class. Figure 8.18 compares those students who had been average performers (previous year's GPAs of 2.00 to 2.9) with the low performers (GPA less than 2.00) and high performers (GPA more than 3.00). Figure 8.19 contrasts this same class of Mr. Seeker's students, this time disaggregated by gender.

When Mr. Seeker examined these graphs, he could see that the effort expended by the middle and low performers began dropping during the second week of February and continued in this depressed state throughout the month of March. When he looked on the horizontal axis to see what, if any, events or actions corresponded with this drop in effort, it became apparent that his students reported putting forth less effort when his regular

Figure 8.17 Instructional Time Line

Week 1	Week 2	Week 3	Week 4	Week 5	Week 6	Week 7	Week 8	Week 9
Students work in jigsaw groups. Groups brainstormed, discussed, and selected a topic. Constructed an outline. Groups assigned tasks based on the outline. Thursday spent in library. Groups organized note cards for presentations.	Groups developed presentations. Paired and did dress rehearsals of presentations with feedback. Thursday finalized the presentations. The first two groups presented their work.	Group presentations. On Friday groups met for twenty minutes to critique their own work. Class discussion on "What we learned by doing this project."	Orientation to the technology lab with Ms. Johnson, the media specialist.	Introduced the multimedia project by showing a mock-up produced by Ms. Johnson. Students regrouped. Tuesday was spent on team building. Groups selected a topic and made storyboards. Thursday and Friday in the computer lab working on group project.	No class on Monday due to the assembly. Working on the individual portions of the group project. Students could work in the classroom or computer lab.	The entire week was spent working as groups finalizing the multimedia project.	Monday and Tuesday in the auditorium: presentations of the multi-media projects. Students assessed individually and group consensus on the assessment. Teams gave feedback. Class party to celebrate. Preparing for the writing assessment.	Monday and Tuesday district writing assessment. Watched a film Wednesday and Thursday, and Friday was the field trip to the courthouse.
Joann seemed disinterested and appeared to be off task most of the week. She appeared busy when we were in the library, but I'm not sure she was doing the assigned work. I had to stay on her all period Friday.	Joann was far more engaged this week than last. She seemed to take ownership of her group's work. She even showed some leadership. Later in the week, she needed prodding to stay on task.	I had trouble with Joann this entire week! She refused to attend when other students were presenting. Ultimately, I had her sit with me, just to keep her from disrupting.	I think the computer is Joann's thing. She was excited the moment we entered the lab. A few times I had to ask her to curb her enthusiasm, as she occasionally took over for Ms. Johnson. I had to remind her it wasn't her class.	Joann assumed the role of group leader this week. At first I thought the other kids would object to her bossy style, but they seemed to genuinely value her expertise with technology. What pleased me was that she stayed on task and focused on the assigned work!	I'm glad she was absent Monday. She would have had real trouble sitting still at the assembly. It was another good week in class. Joann acted as though she was my aide, moving between the lab and the classroom, purposefully helping her classmates and solving problems.	This week had its ups and downs for Joann. For the first time, her teammates started showing frustration with her trying to control everything. I intervened; we had a short team meeting and everything was amicably resolved.	Overall, this was an okay week for Joann. I did need to calm her down a bit on Wednesday as the party and unstructured format was a little too much stimulation for her. I don't think she liked the prep work for the writing assessment, but she stayed on task and was respectful.	Joann was cooperative during the writing assessment, although I don't know how well she did yet. She was absent for the movie and was cooperative on the field trip, but that may have been because her mom was one of the chaperons.

Figure 8.18   Student Self-Assessments of Effort by Achievement Level

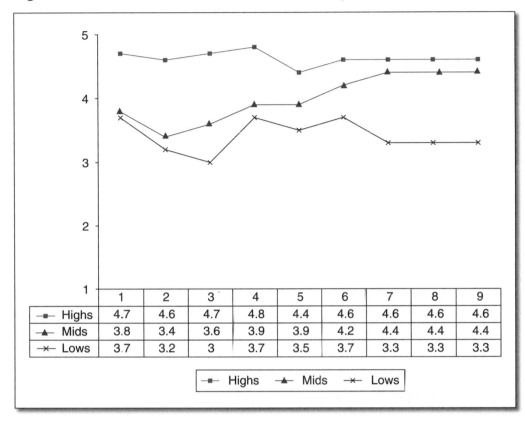

	1	2	3	4	5	6	7	8	9
Highs	4.7	4.6	4.7	4.8	4.4	4.6	4.6	4.6	4.6
Mids	3.8	3.4	3.6	3.9	3.9	4.2	4.4	4.4	4.4
Lows	3.7	3.2	3	3.7	3.5	3.7	3.3	3.3	3.3

Figure 8.19   Student Self-Assessments of Effort by Gender

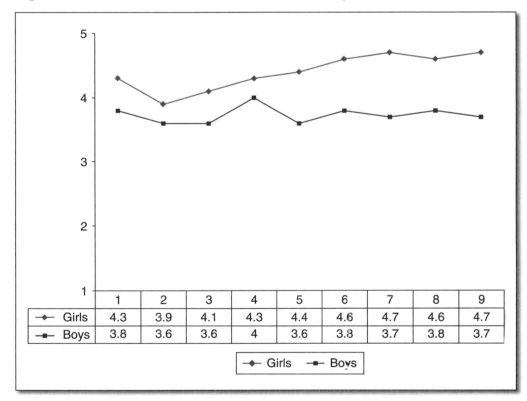

	1	2	3	4	5	6	7	8	9
Girls	4.3	3.9	4.1	4.3	4.4	4.6	4.7	4.6	4.7
Boys	3.8	3.6	3.6	4	3.6	3.8	3.7	3.8	3.7

writing program was temporarily suspended and the class focus shifted to preparation for the state test. Based on this analysis, Mr. Seeker might have noted the following regarding the achievement target of "effort":

- Average class performance declined during the period of preparation for the state exam.
- Average performance of the boys declined sharply during the period of preparation for the state exam.
- The performance of the average- and low-performing students declined during the period of preparation for the state exam.
- There was no significant change in performance of the high-achieving students during the period of preparation for the state exam.
- There was a slight improvement in performance of the girls during the period of preparation for the state exam.

It is now time for you to look for changes in performance reflected in your data and see if you can identify a pattern or patterns of corresponding actions or events that might help explain these changes. Jot down in narrative bulleted form any changes in performance and any significant corresponding events.

DRAWING TENTATIVE ASSERTIONS

At this point, review the findings (bulleted statements) you've written and reflect on how these findings might be explained. Your reflections at this stage are what action researchers call *tentative assertions*, and they combine two things:

1. Empirical data (what informed your findings)

2. Your intuition regarding the influence of actions on performance

You shouldn't be uncomfortable with the use of intuition in this context, even if you are a novice action researcher. After all, while you may be new to action research, you aren't new to the world of the classroom or the schoolhouse. You've been an active participant in the actions that you've been studying and, in all probability, this is not your first year on the job; consequently, you are an experienced and sensitive observer of the educational process. If you have a sense of why one thing impacted another and why it did so in the particular way it did, it definitely warrants being noted as an educated hypothesis.

Mr. Seeker might tentatively assert the following concerning his study of improving effort and engagement in writing:

The drop in average performance appeared to be a reflection of a decline in student motivation likely influenced by a shift of classroom focus from the writing process to review for the state exam. This observed drop in performance was most pronounced with the boys and with students with a history of moderate and low performance. I suspect the reason why there wasn't a comparable decline in the performance of the high achievers was that these kids have become so accustomed to doing what is required to receive good grades that it didn't matter to them if the work was particularly motivating or interesting. The girls in this class are a very cooperative and responsible group, and this may explain why they continued to put forth considerable effort even though their feedback made it clear they found the work to be less stimulating. My guess is that the slight improvement in the girls' performance (even though they didn't like it) was due to this fact.

As has been mentioned several times in this text, we can't prove nor should we contend to have proven causal relationships. This simply cannot be done in action research or in any other form of social science. Instead, our goal as practitioner researchers is to identify relationships and correlations that appear so strong and occur so consistently that it only makes sense to adjust our future actions in ways that are supported by those findings.

The way we build confidence in the importance of a relationship is by establishing as best we can that the relationship or correlation was more than mere coincidence. As we live out our lives, we do this all the time, and we do it intuitively. In fact, we do it the same way that scientists do: through repeated trials and attempts to accomplish the same thing in the same manner as the original researchers and see if we can replicate the results. This is nothing new to the classroom teacher; we do this routinely with our teaching. When something appears to have worked, we try it again. If it works the second time and with another group, it builds our confidence, and we probably stick with it. The more this pattern repeats itself, the more confident we become regarding the efficacy of any particular approach.

That having been said, often our action research is a first-time trial. Therefore, before we can comfortably and confidently move ahead with our answers to Question 3, we ought to consider how we might add more credibility and validity to our "tentative assertions."

USING MEMBER CHECKING TO ADD CREDIBILITY TO THE TENTATIVE ASSERTIONS

Member checking is a strategy that qualitative researchers often use to add support for and provide insight into their tentative assertions. As the name implies, this is accomplished by checking one's tentative assertions with the members of the group whose behavior or performance was documented. As action researchers we can accomplish this by following two sequential steps:

Step 1: Report the Findings

The researcher shares the *findings* with the members of the group whose work was chronicled. By findings, we mean the pertinent facts, the bulleted narrative statements, not your interpretations of those facts. For example, referring to the changes in performance Mr. Seeker observed as coinciding with time spent reviewing for the state test, the findings that he might member check with his students could be the following:

1. Average class performance declined during the period of preparation for the state exam.

2. Average performance of the boys declined sharply during the period of preparation for the state exam.

3. The performance of the average- and low-performing students declined during the period of preparation for the state exam.

4. There was no significant change in performance of the high-achieving students during the period of preparation for the state exam.

5. There was a slight improvement in performance of the girls during the period of preparation for the state exam.

6. All students reported that our class work was less fun and less stimulating during the time we were preparing for the state exam.

Step 2: Solicit Interpretations

This step can be done in either of two ways. The first is to follow your report of findings by posing an open-ended question to the members (in this case, the students in the class): *How would you interpret these findings?*

Another approach is to go further and share your interpretation of the facts, your draft statement of tentative assertions, and then ask the members, *Do you think my interpretation is correct? And if not, how would you explain these findings?*

When the perceptions of an action researcher and the members of the group whose performance was documented are in agreement, significant credibility is added to the tentative assertions.

Occasionally, when we invite member checking, we find that members disagree with us. This could mean that our tentative assertions were, in fact, incorrect. Alternatively, it might mean there are other ways reasonable people could explain the same findings. Sometimes, after considering additional data that surfaced through member checking, action researchers will change their tentative conclusions. Other times, they will feel justified sticking with their original positions. On still other occasions, the interpretations that surface though member checking are used to modify and add texture to the tentative conclusions previously drafted by the researcher. Regardless of the outcome, member checking always provides valuable insights to our understanding of the impact of action on performance.

The preceding section focused on analyzing data, much of it quantitative, collected to answer the three generic ACR action research questions. Those strategies are also applicable for many other action research questions. However, the trend analysis processes that have been reviewed so far may not help you analyze all the qualitative data you have collected. The tools in the following section will assist you in your search for the story embedded inside your qualitative and narrative data. Even if the trend analysis strategies presented thus far seem to have answered your action research questions, it is still suggested that you review the following section and consider the applicability of these qualitative analysis techniques prior to concluding your work with data analysis, as these tools may help you develop a richer and deeper understanding of the stories to be found in your data.

ADDITIONAL TOOLS FOR QUALITATIVE DATA ANALYSIS

As we continue our discussion of data analysis, it would be helpful to consider a metaphor from the world of athletics. A key element of the preparation for competition in most sports is *scouting*, a systematic process of observing the competition, reviewing statistical data on their performance, and developing a list of their tendencies. Tendencies are for athletes what correlations are for statisticians—a set of findings drawn from data on past action that are used to predict future action. A tendency reports a pattern as follows:

> When x is the *context* and y is the *action*, then z tends to be the *response*.

Having a good set of tendencies is important for an athlete or coach preparing for competition because it enables him or her to predict the consequences of an action with a certain degree of confidence. For example, let's assume I am a baseball pitcher. It is the ninth inning, there are two outs, and the batter has two strikes. I must decide where to throw my next pitch. Now, let's say I know that in this type of situation this batter has a tendency to swing at an inside fastball ninety percent of the time. If I want him to swing at my next pitch, based on my knowledge of this past tendency, I would be wise to throw an inside fastball. In this example, *the context* is the behavior of this particular batter in ninth-inning pressure situations. *The action* is the throwing of an inside fastball, and *the response* is a swing (ninety percent of the time).

Tendencies allow us to plan future action to be implemented in a given context based on a pattern of past responses to those same actions in that same context. That is precisely what most of us hope to gain from the analysis of our action research data. For this reason, as you go through the process of analyzing your data, think of what you are doing as trying to generate a reliable list of tendencies. This will necessitate sorting your data into three essential categories that will help with your final analysis:

1. Things that help you understand the *context* (especially as the context may have evolved over the period of the study)

2. Things that help you identify patterns of *actions*

3. The *response* to those actions

To illustrate the necessity of including these three things in our analyses—*context, action,* and *response*—I'll use an academic example. Figure 8.20 illustrates the average length of first drafts produced by a group of students after their teacher introduced the use of the word processor for drafting weekly written compositions. The reason this teacher started having her students create their compositions on the computer was because she theorized it would result in increased fluency.

The story told by this graph shows that the average length of compositions actually decreased after the students began using word processing. *The action* in this case was the use of the word processor, and *the response* was fewer words per composition. This data could result in a finding that use of the word processor negatively influenced the development of fluency. The problem with that finding is not that it is based on erroneous data; the data is irrefutable. The problem is that it ignores some important nuances of *context.* To illustrate, we will now add two additional bits of data:

1. This was the first time these students had been exposed to this particular word-processing program.

2. This data reflects only the papers written in the three weeks immediately following the introduction of the new software.

Figure 8.21 is a graph showing the average length of the weekly compositions, but with the data now extended over the full course of the nine-week term.

With the addition of these two bits of context, this data tells a very different story. The decrease in fluency that occurred in the first three weeks probably illustrates what Michael Fullan (2001) has called the

Figure 8.20 Weekly Papers: Fluency, Weeks 1 to 3

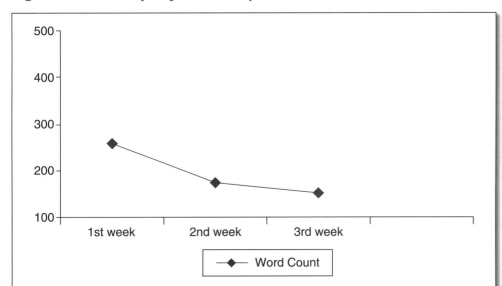

Figure 8.21   Weekly Papers: Fluency, Weeks 1 to 9

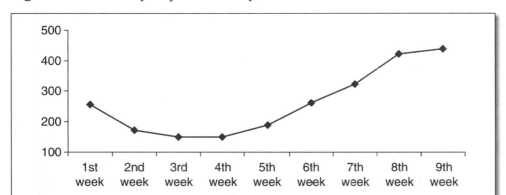

implementation dip, a temporary phenomenon that often occurs when a new skill is first being learned. Because of the awkwardness of integrating something new into old routines, performance frequently drops initially, but this is often followed by improvement once the learner has become comfortable with the newly acquired skill.

QUALITATIVE DATA ANALYSIS USING BINS AND A MATRIX

We often find ourselves analyzing *qualitative* data that appears difficult or impossible to convert into *quantitative* terms. For example, we may have collected data from interviews, from student or teacher journals, from the minutes of meetings, and so on. In those cases, it might seem difficult to effectively use a graph to illustrate how our story is unfolding. Even so, our goal for data analysis is the same: We are attempting to report on the changes and the degree of change occurring over the period of time the actions took place. Our purpose when analyzing qualitative data is the same; we still want to identify patterns and tendencies, but we use a different approach to accomplish this purpose.

The bins and matrix strategy, adapted from Miles and Huberman (1994), is a process of sorting and resorting qualitative action research data to identify and contrast tendencies and patterns as they evolve in a particular context.

Creating Bins for Your Data

I see this process as analogous to the process of preparing a family's recyclables for curbside pickup. The waste management company supplied my family with four color-coded bins. The yellow one is where we are expected to place newsprint; the blue is for glass, the green for metal objects, and the red one is where we are expected to place our non-newsprint paper products. The task we face every time we carry a load to the garage is to look at each of the recyclables in our hands and determine which bin to put it in.

When using the bins and matrix process for sorting your action research data, you will be doing the same thing. Your first task is one that was done for my family by the waste management company. Using their experience and data, they determined what categories of recyclables were likely to be collected by families in our community. This resulted in the four bins: newsprint, glass, metal, and nonnewsprint paper. Of course, each of their customers probably also had other materials that could have been recycled: for example: wood products, engine oil, scrap metal, and plastic. Apparently, it was determined (after looking at their data) that although many households possessed these other materials, they weren't present in large enough quantities to make it environmentally justifiable to send out an energy-consuming truck to collect these at the curbside.

Whenever I go to our garage with our recyclables, I sort my data into the bins that the company deemed relevant. One could look at my family's recycled items as data. In this particular case, the items accumulating in the bins in my garage constitute the raw data on our family's consumption habits.

At this stage of your analysis process, the task before you is to determine what bins or categories you deem to be most relevant and will later use for sorting your data. There are a number of things for you to consider when making this decision:

- The achievement targets your project was designed to address
- The specific phenomena that your descriptive study examined
- The significant activities you engaged in or had participants engage in

In addition to those items, you should skim through the data you collected looking for issues, ideas, and actions that reappear frequently. On a sheet of notepaper, jot down a word or phrase that captures the item being repeated. For example, if I were skimming through a set of student reading journals, I might have noticed repeated examples of students commenting on the following:

- *Genres:* Fantasy, biography, and other nonfiction
- *Relevance to their lives:* Their reasons for being attracted to the work
- *Time issues:* Finding time to engage in recreational reading
- *Family attitudes:* Family attitudes toward reading

It's now a good time to go back and review your theory of action. Take another walk through your graphic reconstruction, this time looking for the events or phenomena that you had, once upon a time (back when you developed your theory of action), thought would be particularly relevant to your ultimate success. As you take stock of these events or phenomena, add them to the list you have been building.

You are now ready to create a list of potential bins.

For example, the elementary principal, Dr Hernandez, who was studying the development of a collegial culture in her school, might have generated a list of items like the following. Each of these will become a bin for sorting her data.

- Communication
- Problem solving
- Staff morale
- The school's Intranet discussion space
- Team planning
- Role of principal
- Student performance
- Faculty meetings
- Availability of data

The next step of this process involves deliberately going through each individual piece of data you've collected and placing that piece of data into the appropriate bin. When using the bins and matrix method, it is appropriate to use all the valid and reliable data you have available, even if it came from an unanticipated source. The actual sorting procedure can be accomplished with a variety of low-tech and electronic methods. I will begin by discussing the low-tech procedure, since it is the most concrete, and then will discuss how you may accomplish the same thing with either word-processing or spreadsheet software.

Tip on Bin Creation

As was the case with my family's recyclables, there may not be a bin for each item or piece of data you collected. However, if you did a good job of choosing your bins, there should be a bin for the most important items. If you find you have a great deal of seemingly important data that can't be categorized, you should consider establishing more bins.

LOW-TECH STRATEGIES FOR BINS AND MATRIXES

Low-Tech Strategy 1: Making a Receptacle for the Data

I have implemented this procedure in two ways. The first method is to purchase a set of small plastic bins, such as the ones shown in Figure 8.22, and label them with the categories of items to be collected in each.

A second approach is to take large rolls of chart paper, tape them to the wall, and create a column for each category.

Figure 8.22 Sorting Data Into Plastic Bins

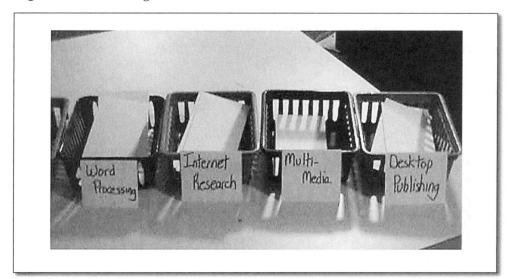

When I'm using the plastic bins, I make sure I have a large quantity of index cards on hand. When using the chart paper method, I make sure I have several colorful pads of sticky notes available.

Placing the Data Into the Bins

I now reread my data, looking for items that I believe belong in one or more of my bins. Then I write that piece of data verbatim on a sticky note or index card, indicate where it came from (such as: from Joann Heathrow's journal, a parent's comment, a note from the principal), and note the date it was obtained or the date the event took place. The card is then placed into the appropriate plastic bin or attached in the proper column on the chart paper. Keep in mind that when appropriate the same piece of data may be placed into multiple bins. Figure 8.23 shows an action research team placing their data into bins on chart paper.

This action research team was made up of master's students undertaking a descriptive study designed to identify the instructional practices most often used by local teachers with reputations for obtaining high levels of student performance. They obtained so much data from merely six classroom observations that they needed an entire classroom wall to effectively sort their data.

Other Low-Tech Strategies: Cutting and Pasting and Using Highlighters

One very efficient strategy when using data collected from surveys or written work (provided they won't have to be returned) is cutting and pasting. If you want to use this approach, it is important that your surveys or data use only one side of each sheet of paper (unfortunately, this is not an environmentally friendly strategy, however, it does make analysis easier). Then, whenever you encounter a piece of data that you feel belongs in a bin, you simply cut it out (always being sure to indicate where it came

Figure 8.23   Placing Data Into Bins

from and when it was obtained), and then physically place it into or paste it onto the appropriate bin.

A similar approach makes use of highlighting pens. When I use this strategy, I assign a color to each bin. Should I have a very large number of bins, I assign a symbol as well as a color.

USING A COMPUTER FOR BINS AND MATRIXES

Using the Sort Command

It can be a time-consuming task to retype data already collected into a computer's word-processing program or onto a spreadsheet. For this reason, using this approach will not make sense unless your data was collected electronically, you are a proficient typist, or have clerical support available. However, should you already have your data in a format where it can be pasted into a word processing program or onto a spreadsheet, then the sorting function found in virtually all word-processing and spreadsheet programs will enable you to organize your data into bins very quickly. To accomplish this just follow these four simple steps:

- **Step 1: Assign a code number to each category**. For example, with Dr. Hernandez's study of collegiality, these might be the code numbers she assigned:

  1. Communication

  2. Problem solving

3. Staff morale

4. Intranet discussion space

5. Team planning

6. Role of principal

7. Student performance

8. Faculty meetings

9. Availability of data

• **Step 2: Attach the correct code number**. Then, when typing or copying pertinent text, type the appropriate number at the beginning of the passage, and be certain to press the return key both before and after each "coded" item, thus transforming each coded item into a separate paragraph. For example, let's assume I found a quote from a teacher survey that I felt belonged in the bin for staff morale. I would make sure that item read as follows:

3. Honestly, I hated going to meetings at this school; I even dreaded reading the staff bulletin. Nothing that we ever did seemed relevant to me. But now I look forward to working together; the meetings have truly helped me enjoy my job.

• **Step 3: Sorting the data by bin**. Now by simply selecting the "sort" command (all word-processing and spreadsheet programs contain a sort function), all the items belonging in a bin with a particular number become instantly grouped together. Another nice aspect of using the computer to sort your data is that you can always resort and subsort the data inside the individual bins—a very powerful tool for purposes of disaggregating data.

• **Step 4: Disaggregating your data**. When we want to determine if there are differential trends in performance or when we want to see if certain categories of students outperform or underperform other categories of students, it is essential that we disaggregate data. This simple action can help us determine where inequities exist. Disaggregation is easily accomplished electronically. All we need to do is think through in advance each demographic subcategory we might want to sort by and consider the order in which we would want to have them sorted. For example, the order I might want to sort data I collected on elementary school reading attitudes might be

• first, by bin;
• second, by whether the item is positive or negative; and
• third, by the grade level where it originated.

Then I would assign a number to each of the subcategories (such as, 1 = positive, 2 = negative; 1 = first grade, 2 = second grade). Then, using my prearranged order of sorting, I input these numbers. Using the foregoing codes as an illustration, if the passage I quoted above had come from a second-grade teacher, the item would be prefaced by the numbers 3.1.2, meaning it is a comment on staff morale (3), it is a positive comment (1), and it is from a second-grade teacher (2).

There is virtually no limit to how many subcategories can be created. And whatever process you ultimately decide to use for sorting your data, be sure to create a coding key for easy referencing later on. What follows is an illustration of a sample key that Dr. Hernandez might have established to guide the sorting of her data into bins.

Level 1	Level 2	Level 3	Level 4
Bin 1 = Internal communication 2 = Problem solving 3 = Staff morale	Tone 1 = Positive 2 = Negative	Grade Level 1 = First 2 = Second 3 = Third 4 = Fourth	Date Obtained 1 = September 2 = October 3 = November 4 = December 5 = January

Create Factoids From the Information in the Bins

After you have sorted all the data you deemed relevant, it is time to go through the items in each bin, generating brief bulleted statements of fact that can be supported by the data contained inside that bin. Write each of these bulleted statements, which we call factoids, on a separate index card. What qualifies something as a factoid is a determination based upon your professional judgment regarding its significance. I find that I generally create two kinds of factoids:

1. *Statistical.* I will report both the quantity and percentage of items that report on the same thing (for example, I might create a factoid saying, "thirteen comments, from twenty percent of the teachers, were complimentary of the principal's leadership").

2. *Illustrative.* If a comment or a vignette helps bring a statistic to life, I write that comment verbatim on a separate card (for example, typical of the positive comments on principal leadership was this comment from a sixth-grade teacher: "It was clear that Elena [the principal] protected us from district demands on the faculty that could have drawn us away from our school goals. I really appreciate that. It showed me that she really was supportive of our priorities").

Assuming the waste management company was interested in reporting on my family's consumption habits, the factoids they might have created after reviewing the weekly data from my family's recycling bins, might read like these:

- In an average week, this family disposes of
  - forty-seven mail order catalogues,
  - sixty-four pop cans, forty percent of which are sugar free,
  - fifteen newspapers (none of which appear to have been read), and
  - no more than one tin can.

- Most weeks, the man of the household comes running out of the house in his bathrobe with additional items to be added at the last minute.

The data in the bin on staff morale in Dr. Hernandez's study might produce factoids like the following:

- Eighty percent (sixteen) of the comments on the April evaluation were positive.
- Fifty-five percent (eleven) of the comments in the September evaluation were positive.
- A typical comment from a fifth-grade teacher (April evaluation): "Honestly, I used to hate going to meetings at this school. I even dreaded reading the staff bulletin. Nothing that we ever did seemed relevant to me. But now I look forward to working together; it has truly helped me to enjoy my job."
- Eighty percent (eight) of comments made by intermediate teachers in the September evaluation were negative in nature.
- Twenty percent (two) of the comments by the intermediate teachers in the April evaluation were negative in nature.
- Twelve comments on the April evaluation referred to positive actions taken by the principal.
- There were no negative comments (regarding morale) referencing the principal.

Sift the Data Using a Matrix

Keep in mind that the main purpose of data analysis was to identify and communicate an evolving story. Every story has a context and occurs over time. To find the story, we need to see the patterns of meaningful action and identify the tendencies of the responses that followed those actions. Occasionally, this happens by the simple sorting of data into bins. However, more often, further sorting of the data is needed to enable the complete story to emerge. One good way to accomplish this is to make use of two-dimensional matrixes to further sift our data. Figure 8.24 shows the general structure of a matrix set up for analyzing the data collected in Dr. Hernandez's study of faculty collegiality.

Each bin becomes a column in the matrix, while the rows can be assigned to a variety of different values. Since I am often interested in understanding how a story unfolded over time, I usually begin by assigning time frames to the rows (fall, winter, spring or monthly, weekly, and so on). Then the factoids that I generated are placed into the appropriate cells of the matrix.

Summarize and Draw Tentative Conclusions

Once my time frame matrix has been completed, I review the rows and columns and ask myself whether this data adequately answers my

Figure 8.24 Two-Dimensional Matrix for Data Analysis

	Communication	Problem Solving	Staff Morale	Intranet	Team Planning	Principal's Actions	Student Data	Faculty Meetings
September								
October								
November								
December								
January								
February								
March								
April								
May								
June								

research questions. If it does, then I summarize the data in the form of tentative assertions.

Often, the answers to all your questions will not be apparent from one matrix, and you will need to repeat the process using different categories for the rows. Keep in mind, your purpose is always the same: identifying meaningful patterns and tendencies. The time frame matrix will highlight the relationship between changes in performance and time. Likewise, a gender matrix would highlight the relationship between gender and changes in performance. To properly answer your questions, you might want to examine other relationships; you will be able to do so relatively easily by simply changing the categories for the rows. Some of the categories that others have found helpful are as follows:

- Categories of participants
  - High achievers, middle achievers, low achievers
  - Gender
  - Ethnicity
  - English language learners, English proficient students
  - Primary teachers, intermediate teachers, middle school teachers, high school teachers
- Type of data
  - Interviews
  - Surveys
  - Portfolios
  - Teachers' journals
- Source of data
  - Students
  - Parents
  - School staff

Use Member Checking to Add Credibility to Your Findings

Once you have generated a set of tentative conclusions that you feel adequately respond to your research questions, it is time to test your perceptions against those of other participant observers of the same process. This is done by using the process of member checking that was discussed earlier in this chapter.

This concludes our discussion regarding the analysis of action research data. Analysis ends with our acknowledging what we've learned through our actions. In the next chapter, our focus shifts to the second part of our Stage 4 work where we will deal with the bottom-line question for all action researchers,

Now that we know what we know, what do we plan to do about it?

9

Turning Findings Into Action Plans

I n Chapter 8, we began working through the final stage of the action
research process—*Stage 4: Reflecting on the Data and Planning Informed
Action.* This stage has three parts: analysis, action planning, and reporting.
In the last chapter, we covered data analysis where our purpose was dis-
covering the story embedded in our action research data. The analysis portion of this stage concluded with the generation of a list of findings and
tentative conclusions backed up with data.

Whether your action research was descriptive or quasi-experimental,
the analysis process should have resulted in greater clarity on what had
occurred as you endeavored to realize your achievement targets.
Hopefully, the insights generated through analysis were meaningful for
you on a number of levels.

The greatest value of what we learn from our action research lies in the
power of the new knowledge and the insights we gained for informing our
future actions and consequently benefiting our students. This value is fully
realized as we make use of our findings and conclusions to adjust our
practice and generate new operative theories of action.

MODIFYING YOUR THEORY OF ACTION

If we are to become truly reflective practitioners, the thing we must always
do before commencing action is to reflect deeply on what we already know
about the challenges before us and use that thinking to design thoughtful

theories of action to guide our future work. The processes you employed to accomplish this when you began your project involved two visual aids, the priority pie, and the graphic reconstruction. Now that you have concluded your action and analyzed your data, it is time to return to those two documents and modify them based on what you have learned.

A classic way to illustrate change over time is by contrasting *before* and *after* pictures. A graphic reconstruction is a type of before picture; it is a sketch of your best thinking before you initiated action and conducted your investigation. The after picture will be a portrait of your best thinking after completing your study. In Chapter 5, I shared my revisionist history, asserting that Christopher Columbus was one of the earliest educational action researchers, and I suggested that a map by Henricus Martellus, circa 1489 (Figure 5.1), was the type of graphic reconstruction that likely guided Columbus on his first voyage—his before picture. For a comparison after picture, we could use Figure 9.1. This is a map drawn by John Speed in 1627, 138 years after Columbus's first voyage.

The difference between these maps illustrates the increased understanding of planet earth by Western European geographers as they integrated the action research findings of Columbus, Magellan, Cabot, Cook, and others.

When we initially articulated our theories of action, we constructed a priority pie and produced a graphic reconstruction. At this point you would be wise to redo both of these documents based on what you've learned through your analysis of the data collected on your actions

Figure 9.1   John Speed's 1627 Map

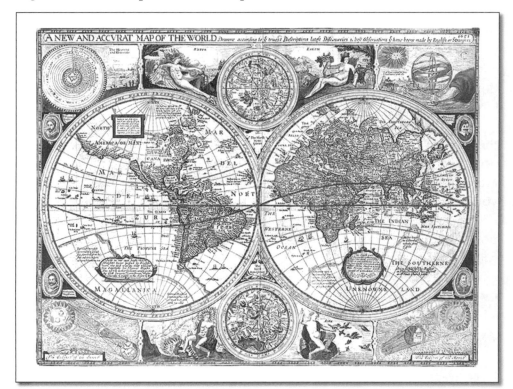

Source: http://www.henry-davis.com/MAPS/Ren/Ren1/464.html

(Chapter 8). However, this time I suggest that you prepare these two visuals in reverse order: draw your graphic first and then bake your pie.

Step 1: Taking Stock of What You Have Learned

Review your list of findings and the tentative assertions you drafted (see Chapter 8). Then take out the graphic reconstruction, the implementation road map you had designed prior to implementation (Chapters 5). Now, one last time, take a slow and deliberate walk through your graphic reconstruction, asking a set of questions of every event. activity, relationship, or cluster of relationships you encounter along the way.

For every activity or event, ask, *Based on what I've learned, do I now think that*

1. there were other critical events or activities that should have occurred prior to this activity?

2. this activity is still essential for success with this target?

3. there are additional activities that ought to be included to improve performance on this target?

For each relationship or cluster (arrows, linking lines, and groups of events), ask, *Based on what I've learned, do I now think that*

1. this relationship is still important?

2. these activities or events influence each other in the manner illustrated?

3. there are other relationships that should be added to this theory?

Based on your answers to those questions, make any additions, deletions, and alterations to your graphic reconstruction that you now deem necessary.

Once you have made the changes you feel are warranted, proof your new theory of action, just as you did in Chapter 5 (walk through it in the shoes of different categories of participants). Once you are satisfied that your new graphic reconstruction illustrates a theory of action with real promise for producing universal success on your priority achievement targets, you will have created your "after" picture.

Now place your before and after pictures side by side. Figure 9.2 contains Ms. Pioneer's two graphic reconstructions, before and after her action research on cooperative team learning.

On close examination of Figure 9.2, one can see that Ms. Pioneer made two significant changes in her theory of action regarding this unit based on the analysis of her data:

1. Strategic Grouping. Prior to conducting her research, she felt it was a good idea to randomly group and regroup her students for each project. But her data revealed a significant disparity between the functioning of the

Figure 9.2 Before and After Graphic Reconstructions

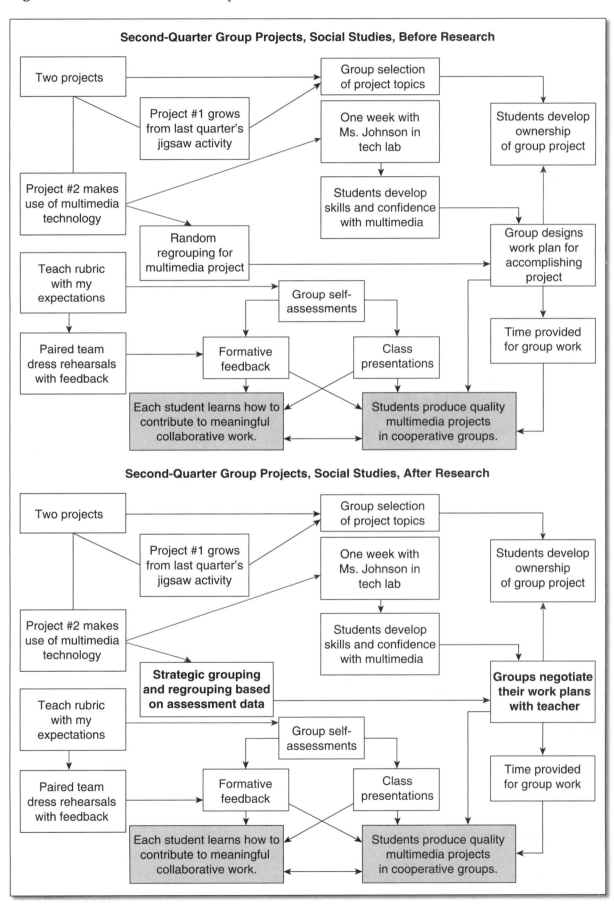

groups. It seemed that random assignments didn't always result in groups with a productive chemistry. Based on this data, she now believes that student groups would function better if she strategically assigned students based on her analysis of their strengths and needs.

2. Negotiated Work Plans. In her earlier theory, she had left the development of work plans completely to the members of each group, with no teacher input. She did this because she felt this would contribute to student ownership of the final projects. But her data told a different story. Several groups stumbled along and wasted valuable time that could have been used for developing their plans, causing some students to become frustrated and force their ideas on other group members, which actually undermined group cohesiveness. Furthermore, two of the groups' work plans were so inadequate that it made the creation of a quality product very difficult. As a result of these findings, she now plans to have the groups negotiate their work plans directly with her, prior to executing them.

Step 2: Reconsider the Time Issue

To begin this step, locate your original priority pie, which represents how you had thought your time and energy should be allocated to achieve universal success on your priority achievement target. If you completed the Time Priority Tracking Form (Figure 8.4) and constructed a second pie that reflected actual time usage, this is a good time to review those two graphs. Now take a good look at the graphic reconstruction you just developed (your "after" picture), and, considering the theory of action depicted on this visual, conduct another intuitive regression analysis by using Figure 9.3 (this is the same form that was used earlier in the text as Figure 4.1) and create a third pie graph. This graph will illustrate how you now believe time (after conducting your research) *should* be allocated in the future.

Figure 9.4 shows the before and after pies created by Ms. Pioneer. You can see that based on her experience, she has created an entirely new category of action (a brand new slice of pie): *coaching students on the development of work plans*. She found the time for this new activity by reducing the time she had previously devoted to team building and group work.

Now place your original priority pie next to the one you just produced. A comparison of these two pie graphs should visually illustrate some of the insights gained through your research and help you better plan for the allocation of your finite time and energy next time you attack this target.

DATA-BASED DECISION MAKING

The Use of Ed Specs

Frequently, when organizations such as schools begin planning for a major purchase or enter into a long-term contract, they start the decision-making process by developing a set of bid specifications. In the case of school architecture and school facility development, those specifications

Figure 9.3 Intuitive Regression Analysis

Using the following form, make a judgment regarding the relative importance of each of the factors you identified as critical to success on this achievement target. Use a separate form for each target you are pursuing.

Achievement Target: _____

List Each Factor Deemed Critical to Fostering Success With This Achievement Target	Importance of This Factor (%)
	Total: 100%

Figure 9.4 Comparison of Priority Pies

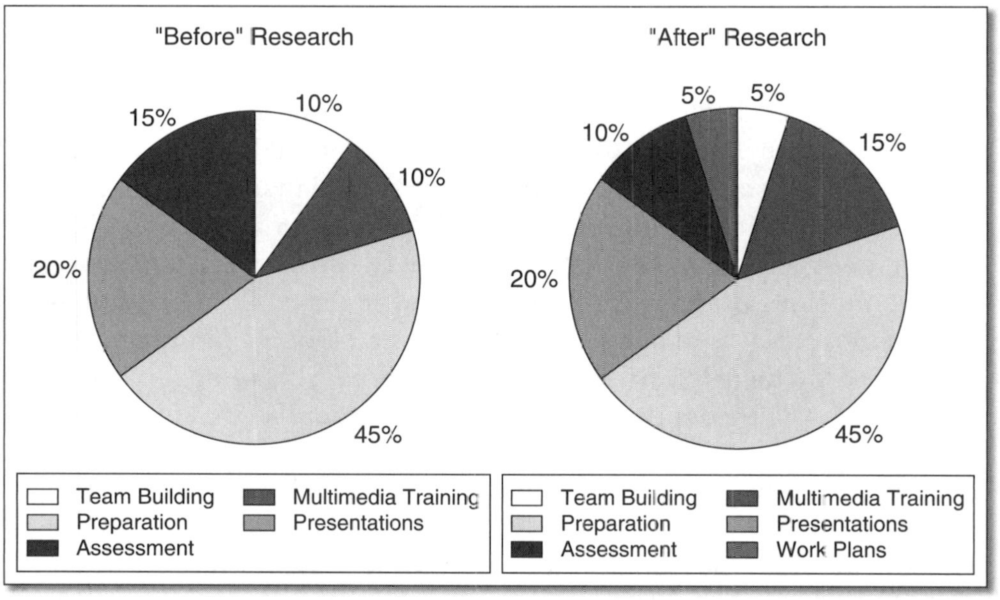

are generally called educational specifications (ed specs), which later become the criteria used to assess competing proposals. Using a quality set of ed specs can go a long way toward ensuring that the decisions that are ultimately made are sound.

As you plan future action in your focus area, you will have many programs and alternative strategies to consider and consequently would be well served to have a sound set of criteria (ed specs) to guide you toward wise decisions. One very good place to find such criteria is in the insights gained from the action research you just conducted and any related research that was conducted in the recent past by you and your colleagues.

To understand precisely how selection criteria can be used to inform decision making, it would be instructive to review how it is often applied in other educational arenas (such as school facility development and purchasing) and then adapt it for our work with performance, program, and process targets.

Ed Specs and School Facilities

Generally the process begins by convening a meeting of individuals with the most up-to-date knowledge of the situation. At this meeting these key individuals are asked to take stock of the context and the operative theories of action. Then they use that information to develop a list of specific things that they want to see accomplished by the new facility or equipment.

A few years ago, I was working for a school district that was about to commence construction on a number of new elementary schools. A staff committee had reviewed everything they knew about best practices for elementary education and theorized that in future decades, children would be spending nearly equal portions of their time at school engaged in individual, small-group, and large-group learning. Therefore, they wanted their new elementary schools to be designed to effectively accommodate all three types of learning.

There were also several givens (what we might call contextual issues) that needed to be taken into account. One was the state funding formula, which established the maximum square footage of the buildings and the amount of money available for construction. This meant that the designs produced by the district's architect would have to fit within the state's cost and size restrictions. It was important that the architect provide for district consideration several alternative designs; however, each of the alternatives had to accommodate the future needs of staff and students. Consequently, every design proposal was required to meet the demands of the future program as developed by the ed specs committee (specifically: equal opportunities for individual, small-group, and large-group instruction) as well as to conform to state regulations.

By considering only designs that addressed both categories of considerations, the district was able to ensure that whatever design they ultimately adopted, the new facilities would meet their educational needs. Before we translate this process to your action planning, it will be helpful to look at one other educational application of criteria-based decision making, one that is a little closer to the issues you may be facing.

Ed Specs for Purchasing Computers

This second example of ed specs involves what at first may seem like a routine purchasing decision. In all likelihood, you work in a school system that regularly purchases significant numbers of computers for student and teacher use. Since there are a number of manufacturers that produce and market computers for schools and there are several different operating systems to choose from, there are always many proposals to consider. As a great deal of money is at stake, and since, for budgetary reasons, schools must live with the computers they purchase for several years, it is important that wise decisions be made. Therefore, prior to soliciting bids, most school systems create a set of purchasing criteria for use in evaluating the alternative proposals submitted by perspective vendors. Usually those criteria cover a multitude of factors, including the following examples:

Cost and Reliability

- The purchase price per computer
- The past defect record of these computers

Service

- Availability of onsite personnel for routine repairs
- Turnaround time for repairs

Versatility

- The ability of the computers to run needed software
- Ease of use
- Availability of inservice and technical support
- Quality of documentation/user manuals

Those charged with making the final decision on which computers should be purchased will insist that every bid address each one of these criteria and will ultimately choose the vender whose proposal scores best on the criteria. Inevitably, some proposals will score better on certain elements than others. This is why it is crucial that each of the assessment criterion be weighed based on importance.

Weighing Assessment Criteria

When you look at the above list of criteria that might be considered when purchasing computers, you can easily see that they are not of equal importance. For instance, although having high-quality user manuals would be nice, even the most well-written documentation won't make up for computers that turn out to be unreliable, break down, and take forever to get fixed.

This is why, when developing ed specs, one needs to take care to determine, in advance, which factors are deemed the *most critical*—so important that going ahead with a plan that does not satisfy these criteria is simply foolhardy. Other criteria, while not absolutely essential, might be deemed *highly desirable*. Last, there are criteria that are *valuable*, involving things we would like to have but which, like superlative user manuals, are not absolutely crucial to program success. When we are making data-based decisions, those distinctions need to be made *prior* to evaluating competing proposals.

Now we will return to concerns more central to the life of the classroom teacher and school leader, the type of program-planning decisions that you are asked to make on a regular basis and that ultimately determine the success of the actions taken in our schools and classrooms. You will see how the same principles of data-based decision making can be applied to instructional and program planning.

TURNING YOUR FINDINGS INTO ED SPECS

The list of findings you generated in Chapter 8 will now become your first draft of ed specs for assessing the proposals and ideas for new programs or the design of novel innovations for use in your school or classroom. The form shown in Figure 9.5 was designed to help you convert your action research findings into ed specs.

In the left-hand column, write all of the bulleted findings that emerged from your data. Then convert these into ed specs; this is done in the middle column of the worksheet. Once you have listed all the findings as ed specs, it is time to ask of each item,

How important is this particular ed spec to the decisions I must make on my future actions?

Based on your answer to that question, rate each item using the following scale:

5 = *Essential Factor.* (Programs that do not address this ed spec aren't appropriate for use here.)

3 = *Important Factor.* (Programs or actions that address this ed spec should be of significant help in improving performance with this priority achievement target.)

1 = *Worthy Factor.* (Programs or actions that address this ed spec are better suited for use than those that do not.)

Tip on Formulating Ed Specs

When using action research findings for ed specs, you needn't limit yourself to the findings from your most recent study. Findings from studies conducted by other teachers or other relevant data on the needs of your program can also be added to your list of specifications.

SOLICIT AND BRAINSTORM ACTION ALTERNATIVES

At this point, it is time to return to the graphic reconstruction you completed at the end of the data analysis process. This is the graphic that illustrated your *revised* theory of action. Take a look at the changes you made to your original theory and ask yourself (or your teammates) what strategies we are aware of that have been implemented elsewhere in an effort to achieve success with our achievement targets. To illustrate how this might be done, let's return once again to the case of Ms. Pioneer.

In her revised theory of action (Figure 9.2), she noted two significant changes in the way this particular unit should be implemented next year:

1. Strategically assigning students to cooperative groups

2. Having the groups negotiate their work plans with the teacher

Figure 9.5 Turning Research Findings Into Ed Specs

Step 1. List all the pertinent findings from your and other relevant research in this focus area.	
Step 2. Write the essence of each finding in the form of an educational specification.	
Step 3. Determine the weight to be assigned to each ed spec, with 5 indicating the highest effectiveness:	

Pertinent Action Research Finding	Finding Rewritten as an Ed Spec	Weighting: 5, 3, or 1
Example: Time for writing was limited due to preparation for the state assessment.	The need for additional time for use with the writing process.	5 = Essential factor

For dealing with the issue of strategic grouping, she quickly came up with a list of possible approaches:

1. My students could submit a "most wanted to work with" list and I could use this data to make group assignments.

2. I could rank the students by past performance and select groups to maximize heterogeneity (to increase diversity).

3. I could rank the students by past performance and assign groups to maximize homogeneity (to reduce diversity).

4. I could assign the students to single-gender groups.

5. I could use random assignments modified by my personal perceptions of student compatibility.

The different strategies on her list are called action alternatives. Each one is an approach that, on the surface, appears to have promise for fulfilling Ms. Pioneer's needs. What she now needs to do is to choose which one of these action alternatives will likely work best for her students and her program.

Tip on Surfacing Action Alternatives

If the list you have generated seems adequate, it is okay to proceed with that list. However, if you sense that you are unable to find strategies that hold real promise to solve your problem, it is a good idea to conduct another literature review (see Chapter 3 if needed).

USING ED SPECS TO EVALUATE ACTION ALTERNATIVES

Having collected a comprehensive set of action alternatives, it is time to evaluate each one using the weighted ed specs you developed from the relevant findings. One way of doing this is by constructing a chart for each action alternative like the one shown in Figure 9.6. I usually do this by creating posters on large sheets of chart paper for each action alternative.

Now you need to review the elements of each action alternative through the lens of your ed specs (Figure 9.5). This is done by standing in front of each action alternative with your ed specs in hand and asking the following question regarding each one of your ed specs:

Is the implementation of this action alternative likely to have a positive influence, negative influence, or no influence on this criterion?

Whenever your answer is *positive*, that ed spec and its weighted score should be placed on the top portion of the chart. If the answer is *negative*,

Figure 9.6   Sample Action Alternative Poster

Action Alternative: _____	
Ed Specs in Support of AA	*Points*
Total Points Supporting:	

Ed Specs in Opposition of AA	*Points*
Total Points Opposing:	

then that ed spec and its number should be placed on the lower portion of the chart. If the answer to your question is *no influence,* then nothing is written on the chart.

Repeat this process with each of the action alternatives. Once each action alternative has been assessed using your set of ed specs, total the positive points (top portion of the chart) and subtract any negative points that have been assigned (the lower portion) to produce a score for that action alternative. Then list the action alternatives in rank order based on the point totals awarded.

At this point, your decision-making process will differ from the bid procedure used by school business offices. Frequently, state or provincial laws require the awarding of contracts to the lowest bidder. This is a reasonable requirement that ensures fiscal accountability. However, as professionals who are using action research findings to improve their teaching and their students' learning, it makes no sense to bind yourself to a decision simply because a particular strategy achieved a marginally higher score than a competing one.

When using this approach to data-based decision making, you will generally find that your action alternatives fall neatly into three groups:

Group 1: Weak Proposals. Some action alternatives may, in fact, have obtained a negative score. This means that this particular approach would likely make things worse than the current situation.

Group 2: Adequate Proposals. A second group of alternatives will have received positive scores but a significant number of negative ones as well. Consequently, the total score is rather low. It probably is not worth the effort to alter your current approach and go through all the work and possible expense of implementing a new program that, at best, will turn out to be only marginally superior to the approach you've been using.

Group 3: Strong Proposals. There will be some action alternatives that received many positive scores from your ed specs and attracted very few, if any, negative ones. These are proposals that appear to hold real potential for making a difference in your efforts to produce universal success on your priority achievement targets.

Making a Final Decision on Action

It is now time to consider the applicability of each of the action alternatives in Group 3, the strong proposals. This is another point in the process where it is appropriate to use intuition. For each alternative, ask yourself these three questions:

1. How well do these strategies fit my or our teaching style?

2. How might the students in our school respond to this program or approach?

3. What, if any, additional problems or expenses would this program entail?

Facilitating collaborative decision making is one of the most challenging issues for school leaders. Many times leaders feel torn between two equally unpleasant alternatives. They could invite faculty to propose ideas they are passionate about, but by doing so they might risk a vote that could split the faculty into opposing camps. Alternatively, they could try to broker a compromise that no one disagrees with, yet no one is particularly passionate about either. Neither approach is very helpful for a school that wishes to collegially and energetically pursue universal student success.

USING ED SPECS TO EVALUATE ACTION ALTERNATIVES FOR SCHOOLWIDE PROJECTS

If the project you are working on is a collaborative effort, it is well worth taking some meeting time to discuss these issues and employ a group decision-making process to decide on the particular action alternative that best fits your situation. In my experience, this is rarely a contentious decision. While I might hold a preference for one of the high-scoring alternatives and some of my teammates might find themselves more attracted to another, it is unlikely that I would have a strong objection to going along with their choice, since every proposal receiving final consideration was one that scored well on criteria drawn from "our" research findings.

The open collaborative assessment of action alternatives with the use of ed specs built from locally generated data is an ideal way to minimize conflict. When decisions are made in this manner, it is rarely contentious. This is because the decision is being made by data, not by personalities. Furthermore, the data that is being used to inform decision making is deemed credible because it was generated by and for the people making the decisions. We often hear school leaders express a desire to see their workplaces transformed into professional learning communities. There is no better way for a school community to assume ownership of decisions than to have those decisions informed by ed specs derived from their own professional learning.

COMPLETING THE CYCLE: REVISED THEORY OF ACTION 2

Unless you discovered the magic elixir that succeeded in getting every single student or every participant in your project to excellent performance on your target, your work as a reflective practitioner and action researcher can't be considered complete.

What you have accomplished, however, is the completion of one full lap around the action research cycle. (Reporting, which will be discussed in the next chapter, does not necessarily need to occur prior to beginning another cycle of action research.)

Figure 9.7 illustrates the relationship between the steps of repeated cycles of action research when done on the same targets by the same researchers. You are now nearly ready to restart the process. However, this

Figure 9.7 Action Research Cycle

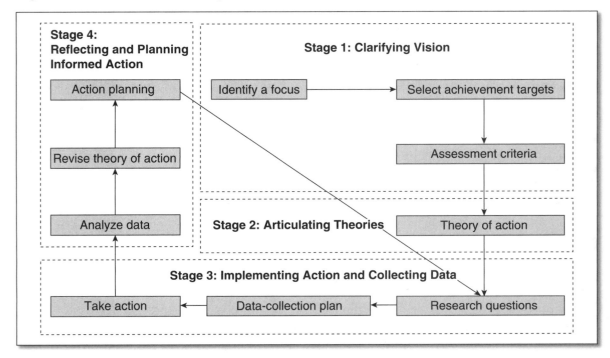

time you can jump ahead and begin your work at *Stage 3: Implementing Action and Collecting Data* by developing a new set of research questions (see Chapter 6).

As you may recall, the process of developing meaningful action research questions required having a clear and unambiguous theory of action that you were committed to implementing. Therefore, the only thing left for you to do before commencing your second round of research is to do one final review of your revised theory.

It is now time to examine the revised theory of action you developed earlier in this chapter and ask if it requires any further modification in light of the action alternatives you have just adopted, considered, or rejected for your program. If it does, you should insert those changes into your graphic and alter your priority pie indicating any necessary revisions to the proposed allocation of time and energy.

Once you are satisfied that you have a revised theory of action that captures your best current thinking, is consistent with the findings of your research, and incorporates any action alternatives you will be adding, you are ready to select a new set of research questions and rejoin the action phase of the process.

Hopefully, you aren't in too great a rush because in the next chapter we will discuss the very important topic of *reporting and sharing action research findings*. Many action researchers, myself among them, have found that whenever our findings are presented to colleagues, a great deal is learned from their reactions and comments. Consequently, I generally like to share my findings with my peers and solicit their ideas before I jump into my next round of action.

10

Reporting and Sharing Action Research

There is nothing in the world of scholarship and science less controversial than the need for faithful and accurate reporting of results. From our earliest experiences studying science in school, to our professional endeavors, and even in our lives as consumers, we have all learned how important it is to be able to access accurate summaries of the experience of others to inform our own future actions and decisions.

In science class we learned that it isn't enough to conduct an experiment correctly; the results of that experiment must also be presented competently in a lab report. These are reasonable expectations for the science student because they parallel the real world of scientific practice. Reporting is so crucial to advancements in science that the scientific community has institutionalized processes for the sharing of findings, and these processes are rigorously followed throughout the world.

Presentations of findings are made at professional meetings, and studies are reported in widely circulated journals. Papers are only accepted for publication or presentation after careful peer reviews for comprehensiveness, clarity, and accuracy. After initial review, research reports are publicly presented to knowledgeable and skeptical audiences who are expected to examine the findings as much to identify fatal flaws as to validate the accuracy of the findings. Scholarly debates are publicly reported in conference proceedings as well as in the pages of refereed journals and throughout the halls of academe.

As much as these processes are an esteemed part of the culture of the world of science, and as much as citizens have come to depend on the results of scientific sharing for the development of the products and services we consume, being an active participant in the scholarly presentation of research while simultaneously working as a full-time educator probably appears daunting at best.

However, if we overlook the crucial importance of the reporting process and choose not to engage in it, we do so at our own and at our sacred profession's peril. When we don't share what we've learned through our experience, we are forcing every other educator and every other faculty to be required to reinvent the same wheel all by themselves. Furthermore, as sound as our analysis may have been, when we have additional eyes and ears considering and debating our findings, it inevitably leads to deeper and sharper understanding. All of our students suffer when those who are guiding their education aren't in possession of the very best information when making instructional decisions. Finally, when educators don't share what they're learning, it perpetuates professional isolation and reinforces the myth that this amazingly complex work is actually rather simple and can be mastered by people working alone in their own cubicles.

The good news is that while self-interest—as well as our professional interests—requires the reporting of our action research, the process for sharing need not be onerous. There are as many ways and as many formats for reporting and sharing action research as there are educators conducting these studies. In this chapter, we take a look at a few reporting processes and formats, ranging from the simple to the complex, and discuss the circumstances that call for using different approaches. But first, we examine a set of common issues that should be considered whenever you are planning a report on your action research.

COMMON ISSUES

Common Issue 1: Consider the Audience

As stated at the outset of this book, the primary reason for any of us to engage in action research is to help *us* learn from *our* practice to inform *our* future actions. Defined this way, every action research study already had an audience before it ever began, even if a small one: the actor himself or herself. But even when working in a remote and isolated location, this is likely not the only potential audience for our work. Even if we are working in a one-room schoolhouse, our students, their parents, and the community will have a keen interest in the results of our inquiries. And if there is at least one other professional working in our school, there will be someone else who is trying to teach a similar curriculum to similar students. It is a fair guess that our immediate colleagues will have at least a passing interest in hearing about the story told through our data. Last, since we are all part of the larger community of educators who are collectively engaged in a search for best practices, we can be certain that there are other educators in other places who are grappling with the same issues and consequently will find our insights of particular interest.

One way to conceptualize the different potential audiences for our action research is to look at them as nested circles, as illustrated in Figure 10.1.

The first consideration when preparing for sharing and reporting one's action research is determining who the principal audience (or audiences) will be for your report. Your answer will help you determine both the form and format that will work best for reporting on your work. Frequently, we are able to use our action research to kill multiple birds with a single stone. For example, I might be studying the use of problem-based learning (PBL) in my science class. I am doing this primarily to improve my own skills. In addition, my school's annual school improvement plan is focused on making the science curriculum more relevant, and the implementation of PBL is an integral part of the school's plan. Coincidently, I am enrolled in a master's program and am expected to complete an action research project to fulfill the research requirement for my degree. In a circumstance like this, the same piece of research—looking at the implementation of PBL

Figure 10.1 Audiences for Action Research

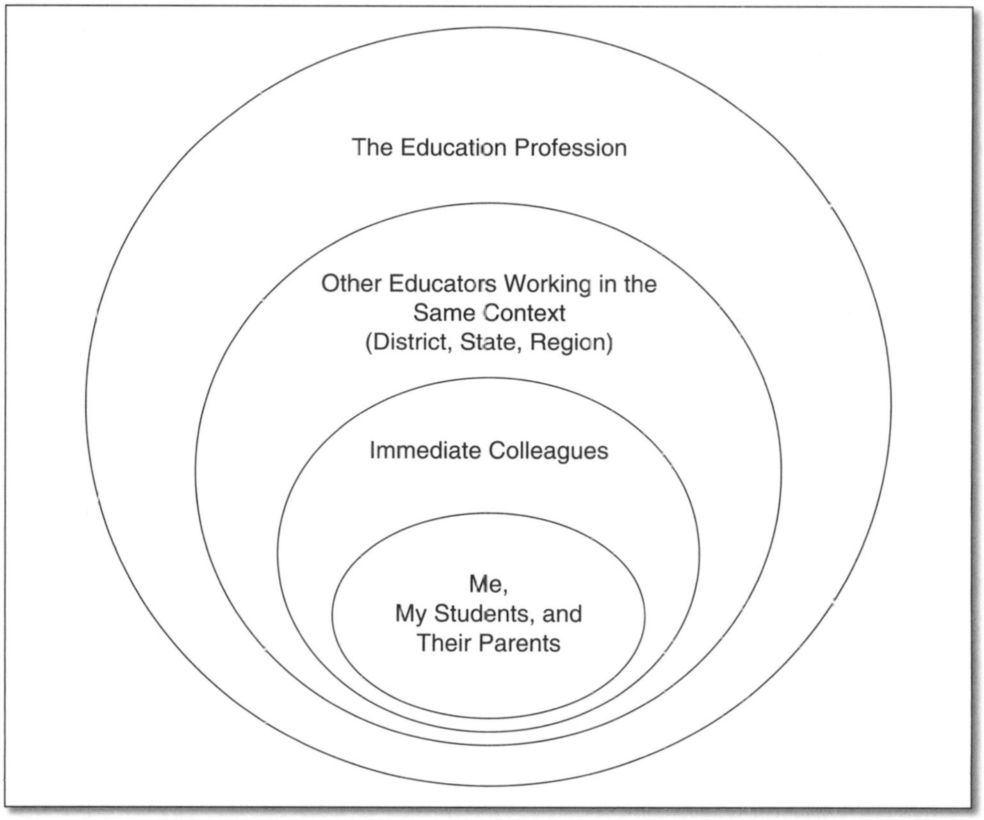

with my fifth-period science class—could become the subject of three different research reports. However, each of these reports will need to satisfy different criteria.

Consider the levels displayed in Figure 10.1 and ask yourself which audience or audiences you will be aiming your report at:

- *Immediate Audience:* Only those people with a direct interest in me, my students, and this class
- *Immediate Colleagues:* The other teachers and educators with the responsibility for teaching this subject or these students: my grade level or department
- *Other Educators in the Same Context:* Others in my district, region, state, or province
- *The Larger Educational Community:* All K–12 educators and policy makers with an interest in educational settings similar to mine

Common Issue 2: Purpose—What Decisions Need to Be Made?

All action research reports share one purpose: to help inform decisions on future action. In some cases there is only one decision to be made. However, there are occasions when a number of different decisions are influenced by the reports of our action research results. For example, if you were planning to submit your action research project as part of a master's program, in addition to providing you with information to inform your instructional decision making, your report will also help your professor make a decision on your grade.

Many times, action research is used as part of the evaluation of an externally funded project. In such cases, the report is likely to influence decisions on whether this work should be continued and encouraged elsewhere. On occasion, educators are also interested in developing their own scholarly publication record. These levels of decision making that can be influenced by action research reports can be illustrated by another series of nested circles, as illustrated in Figure 10.2.

Common Issue 3: Degree of Detail

Every consumer of an action research report won't need or want the same degree of detail. The superintendent might have a keen interest in the efficacy of the new "standards-focused homework hotline" program and whether the three goals established by the school board for the program were being achieved:

1. Enhanced parent-school communication

2. Continuous improvement on the state standards

3. More effective use of homework for learning

Figure 10.2 Purposes of an Action Research Report

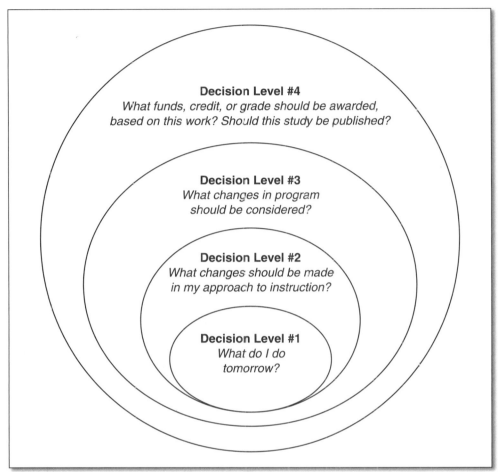

Decision Level #4
*What funds, credit, or grade should be awarded,
based on this work? Should this study be published?*

Decision Level #3
*What changes in program
should be considered?*

Decision Level #2
*What changes should be made
in my approach to instruction?*

Decision Level #1
*What do I do
tomorrow?*

However, reports on other aspects of the study may be more than he or she needs or wants—for example, the specific nature of the homework assigned, how homework grades were determined, and the patterns in homework assessments across individual teachers.

Here's another example: When presenting my research to my Language Arts Department colleagues, it might be enough to describe the context by saying, "This research was conducted with the three sections of sophomore basic writing I taught last semester." But if I were presenting the same research study at a national conference for English teachers, I would need to provide significantly more detail on the nature of our school, its curriculum, and the type of students who take basic writing as sophomores.

As you prepare for sharing, it is important to realize that you probably have already generated a great many documents and artifacts as you conducted your research:

- Your reflective writing
- Your priority pies
- Your graphic reconstructions
- Your data-collection matrix
- Any graphs or charts you made while analyzing data

All of these documents are items that you might choose to include in a report on your research.

Occasionally, an action researcher will use the series of activities engaged in and the documents prepared as the *outline* for the report. By doing it this way, all that remains is for you to add a few transitions and explain the rationale for your actions and the connections between those actions so that your professional decisions are clear to your audience.

The Report Planning Form (Figure 10.3) is a good place to begin the planning for your report. It should help you focus on the three common issues discussed earlier: audience, purpose, and detail.

FORMATS FOR REPORTING

I have seen compelling reports of action research projects in a wide range of formats. I've read articles written by teacher researchers in refereed journals, and I've seen action research shared informally in a teachers' lounge with a few colleagues sitting in a circle. I've watched teacher-produced videos that visually told the story of a research project, and I've seen research teams presenting their work on stage at a large national convention. I've attended poster sessions held in school libraries with audience members moving from display table to display table, informally discussing the projects with the researchers.

At action research presentations, I've been given one-page handouts summarizing the findings, and at others I've received colorful, bound, fifty-page written reports. Determining the appropriate format is a decision for you to make, based on your needs and those of your audience. While formats may differ, I have found that there is a general flow and sequence that ensures that attendees will benefit from what was presented. This is a good time to once again remind ourselves that a completed action research report is basically a story. And just as there are infinite ways to write or tell a story, every story still contains a plot, starts from a beginning, and moves through a middle on the way to its end.

The report on your action research is the story of your trip through the four stages that framed this book:

Stage 1: Clarifying Vision and Targets

Stage 2: Articulating Theories of Action

Stage 3: Implementing Action and Collecting Data

Stage 4: Reflecting on Data and Planning Informed Action

As an audience member, I have found it particularly helpful when the person, video, or paper led me through the story of the researcher's inquiry in the same sequence as the four stages. Even when I'm unfamiliar

Figure 10.3 Report Planning Form

Step 1. Determine who your audience will be.

Step 2. Reflect on the reason for their interest in your inquiry.

Step 3. Using the following table, review each of the steps you took in conducting your research, the activities you engaged in, and the documents you produced.

Step 4. Based on your determination of the audience's need (Step 1), decide which documents to share and which activities to describe.

Stage or Process	Documents, Events	What Will You Share?
Identify focus	Reflective writing, journaling, reflective interview	
Select achievement targets	List of priority achievement targets	
Literature review	Information gathered	
Develop assessment criteria	Rating scales for targets	
Develop theory of action	Priority pies and graphic reconstructions	
Research questions	List of questions	
Create data-collection plan	Triangulation matrix	
Action, collection of data	Raw data, vignettes	
Analysis of data	Revised graphic reconstruction and revised priority pie	
Action planning	Review of action alternatives	

Step 5. Using the following table, make a determination on both the detail called for and the presentation technique you will use for presenting the information you have decided to share.

Thing to Be Shared (from the right-hand column in the foregoing table)	Detail Needed (summarized or with specifics)	Method for Sharing (handouts, displays, graphs, discussion, and so on)

with the focus area, I find it easy to follow a story that begins with this foundation:

- This is the context where I work (where my action takes place).
- This is what I was trying to accomplish (the vision I was pursuing and my targets).
- This is how I thought I could best accomplish it (my theory of action).

Once I have heard that background information, I am prepared to learn what happened next:

- This is what I did (the implementation of my theory of action).
- This is what data I collected along the way.

When I know what they were trying to accomplish and how they went about it, my appetite has been whetted to find out the ending:

- This is what I learned (my reflection on the data).
- This is what I intend to do about it (my action plan).

The Action Research Report Checklist (Figure 10.4) contains items that are often (although not always) addressed in an action research report. It is a good idea to go through this checklist prior to preparing your report. It should help alert you to items that you may want to consider including in your final product.

CREATING A BANK OF ABSTRACTS

Much has been written about the current knowledge explosion. In virtually every field, more and more information is being produced every single day. Finding efficient ways to access this information is becoming a necessity for people who want to stay current on their fields' knowledge base. The increased sophistication and ease of use of information technology, including publicly available Internet search engines, are making locating information much easier and will continue to do so. But there are other, more low-tech techniques that you and your colleagues might wish to consider.

One low-tech strategy for sharing, which many school systems have had success with, is the production of a readily accessible book of abstracts of locally conducted action research. For example, in the Madison (Wisconsin) Metropolitan School District, the books of action research abstracts now contain virtually hundreds of projects, spanning all grades and every academic discipline. In many districts, each teacher is given a personal copy of the district's action research catalogue (in hard copy or on a disk), or catalogues are made available in faculty rooms, through the district's media centers, or on the district's website. These action research compilations are made user

Figure 10.4 Action Research Report Checklist

Characteristic 1: Explanation of Context, Problem. Issue		Include? Yes or No
Elements	Significance of issue for other educators and students	
	Unique or general factors impacting issue	
	Potential for change/improvement	
Characteristic 2: Theoretical Perspective		Include? Yes or No
Elements	Summarize applicable literature	
	Logic behind this particular approach	
	Why not another approach?	
Characteristic 3: Research Design		Include? Yes or No
Elements	Why is it valid?	
	Why is it reliable?	
	How does it deal with extraneous or intervening variables?	
Characteristic 4: Analysis of Data		Include? Yes or No
Elements	The support and logic of the conclusions	
	Alternative explanations of data	
	Limitations explained	
Characteristic 5: Action Planning		Include? Yes or No
Elements	How is the plan supported by findings?	
	Is the potential for improvement theoretically sound?	
	Plans for further action research	
	Outline of potential value for self and others	

friendly through cross-referencing by focus area, school subject, grade level, and program. Short abstracts provide enough information to enable a prospective user to get an idea of what has been investigated, without having to wade through a great many details. Then, if and when more information is desired, contact addresses, phone numbers, and e-mail addresses are provided. A particularly nice aspect of this approach is that writing a brief abstract doesn't take very long.

It is helpful to limit the length of an abstract. I have found the guideline of five paragraphs and 300 words works quite well. It can be accomplished by writing a straightforward paragraph in response to each of the following five prompts:

1. State the problem or the challenge that was being addressed by this research.

2. Provide a brief description of the setting of the research and the researchers (the context).

3. Briefly describe the methodology used to collect data for this study.

4. Summarize the principal findings.

5. State the conclusions, action plans, or additional research that resulted from this research.

Figure 10.5 provides an example of an action research abstract written in response to the five prompts.

Figure 10.5   Sample 300-Word Action Research Abstract

Begin with a statement of the problem or the challenge being addressed by the research.	The faculty at Sagor Elementary has been impressed with the affective and academic benefits of cooperative learning. However, significant concern was expressed about the variance of productive engagement when cooperative activities are used. The purpose of this study was to help us understand the relationship of specific strategies with the level of engagement of our diverse learners. (fifty-seven words)
Then provide a brief description of the context of the research and the researchers.	Sagor Elementary School is a Title 1 school. Forty-two percent of Sagor students are English language learners. The study team consisted of two primary teachers and two intermediate teachers. (twenty-eight words)
Briefly describe the methodology of the study.	A teacher survey was used to determine the array of cooperative strategies being used at the school. A rating scale was developed to assess the degree of student engagement. During a nine-week period, four observations were made in each classroom where cooperative learning was used. The observers (ten teacher volunteers) used an engagement rating scale to assess the performance of nine students in each room (three low, three middle, three high achievers). (seventy-three words)

Summarize the principal findings.	The data reflected a direct relationship between structure and both the amount of and variations observed in productive engagement. The four principal findings were as follows:
	1. The more structured the activity, the higher the average level of engagement.
	2. Average engagement dropped as the structures became more ambiguous.
	3. In less-structured classrooms, the high achievers demonstrated slightly higher degrees of engagement.
	4. In less-structured classrooms, middle and low achievers were significantly less engaged. (seventy-four words)
State the conclusions, action plans, or additional research that resulted from this research.	After a presentation of the research, the faculty developed a continuum of cooperative strategies based on degree of structure. We are currently investigating strategic interventions designed to provide extra guidance and support for the middle- and low-achieving students with the use of the less-structured approaches. (forty-seven words)

Now it's your turn. Try writing a 300-word abstract describing the study you just completed, using Figure 10.6.

CREATING A DISTRICT ARCHIVE

For several years, the Killeen (Texas) Independent School District has been building the professional development capacity of their district by providing two-year grants to teachers who volunteer to document their work on innovative projects while working with a network of colleagues in the same focus area. At the end of the two years, participants prepare a written report for presentation to their colleagues, and that report then becomes part of a district-maintained knowledge base. The reports prepared by the Killeen teachers focus on the five characteristics found in Figure 10.4. Resource B contains a rubric that the Killeen teachers have used as a guide when preparing their written reports.

Tip on Evaluation Criteria

It is strongly recommend that whenever one of the purposes of your action research report is to satisfy a requirement, mandate, or external expectation, you *request in advance the criteria by which it will be evaluated*. In most cases, the college, funder, or agency requiring the report will have established criteria that will help guide you through report preparation. If no criteria are available, you may want to consider using the rubric provided in Resource B as you develop your report.

Figure 10.6 300-Word Action Research Abstract Worksheet

Topic	Response
Begin with a statement of the problem or the challenge being addressed by the research.	
Then provide a brief description of the context of the research and the researchers.	
Briefly describe the methodology of the study.	
Summarize the principal findings.	
State the conclusions, action plans, or additional research that resulted from this research.	

11

Conclusion

The School as a Learning Organization

Dickens began *A Tale of Two Cities* with the line, "It was the best of times, it was the worst of times." The same thing could be said for the situation in which most of us K–12 educators currently find ourselves. I began this book discussing the context confronting the modern educator. The expectations have never been higher, and it has never been more important that our graduates be well educated.

Becoming adults in our society without adequate language, reasoning, and learning skills places young people at risk of not being able to support themselves or their families. Students who leave school without a moral compass, an ability to appreciate beauty, and an adequate supply of self-confidence and self-esteem will find living a fulfilling life difficult at best. And modern democratic societies need citizens who are well grounded in the natural, social, and behavioral sciences.

Beyond the moral imperative of achieving universal success, increasingly punitive public policies are subjecting students, teachers, and the public schools to high-stakes sanctions if arbitrary benchmarks aren't met on a preordained schedule. None of this would be problematic if only we knew how to make universal success a reality. If it were possible that a fix for every teaching and learning problem could one day surface like a cure for a terrible disease, we could simply support the scientists working on these breakthroughs and eagerly await their great discoveries. But alas, the solution to education's challenges isn't likely to be found that easily.

As was discussed at the opening of this book, the acts of teaching and learning present problems that are among the most complex endeavors any professional ever has to deal with. And the front line workers in the education enterprise, the teachers and administrators working in schools, are the only people in a position to design adequate solutions to these challenges. Recruiting the best and brightest people to educate our children is arguably the most important issue facing modern society, and the future of public education rests solely on our ability to do so. Meanwhile, securing adequate funding for our schools and providing support for the people working in them is more tenuous than ever.

But there is also ample reason for optimism. Bright and capable people choose their careers based on an assessment of how rewarding the work will likely be. There are few things in the world of work more rewarding than working with colleagues trying to solve complex and important problems. It wasn't hard to persuade the rocket scientists at NASA and the medical researchers at the Salk Institute to work on their monumental breakthroughs. Likewise, nothing provides more joy for educators than seeing evidence of our students' growth and development. The best and most reinforcing thing about action research is that it creates a system for providing regular, credible data on student development while simultaneously enabling us to appreciate the role we have played in nurturing and facilitating that growth.

Educators who integrate the four sequential stages of action research into their professional routines tend to be happy and satisfied professionals. Who wouldn't be happy when they possess credible data on the success they are achieving in overcoming problems that have perplexed others for generations?

Anyone who has been involved in public education in recent years has been inundated with the surface trappings of modern organizational theory. It is a rare school or district that hasn't developed a vision and mission statement, backed up by a strategic plan. Those things are important, but inspiring words and elaborate plans are not what make organizations successful; rather, what makes a real difference in school performance are the routine habits of adult behavior that are consistent with an organization's core values.

THE TWO KEYS: COHERENCE AND CONGRUENCE

Nobody needs a mission statement to know what the core value of schools should be in a democratic society. Surely, the business of public schools is maximizing the human potential of the next generation through growth, development, and mastery of a wide array of knowledge and skills. Accomplishing this requires organizational behavior that is consistent with the belief that everyone can learn, grow, and accomplish more than they had ever been able to do in the past. The two critical factors that determine whether an organization is staying true to its core values (behaving in accordance with its theory of action) are captured by the words *coherence* and *congruence.* Deliberate attention to the essence of the four stages of the action research process is one way for educators to ensure that the schools they work in manifest both of these elements.

Coherence

Schools are busy places. The typical teacher makes more decisions in one hour than most other people make in a day. Yet the question so often heard in the schoolhouse is, "Why are we doing this?" Principals ask this of the central office, teachers ask it of the curriculum department, and students ask it of their teachers. When people are busy and are asked to do something but they are not sure why they are asked to do it and why they are required to do it a particular way, it is more than frustrating. It should be no surprise that a lack of clarity on goals and methods generally leads to increased alienation and a decrease in organizational effectiveness.

Fortunately, coherence is never lacking where teachers, schools, and students have integrated into their routines the first two stages of the action research process—*clarifying the vision and targets and articulating a rationale for pursuing a specific plan of action.* Publicly sharing the rationale behind what they are doing further builds coherence for those who are affected by their work.

Congruence

The educational process is about learning, and most every school's mission statement includes a recitation of the school's commitment to life-long learning. But unfortunately, the behavior at many schools is far from consistent with that belief. The reality is that behavior is a more powerful teacher than words. When schools behave as though the authorities (teachers, administrators, professors, and so on) know all that one needs to know and have all the answers to the issues of practice, they are modeling a very different set of beliefs. The best way to convince our students of the value of lifelong learning is to let them see us cast in the role of learners. When students see the significant adults in their lives being curious, goal-driven people, trying to gain insight and knowledge from each experience they engage in, they will come to believe that we mean it when we say that learning is forever.

PUTTING THE PIECES TOGETHER

Jane Stickney, the former principal at Willamette Primary School in West Linn, Oregon, uses the phrase *the ethic of action research* to refer to the norms of collaboration and experimentation that prevailed at Willamette as she and her colleagues helped that school affect a remarkable turnaround in academic performance (Sagor, 1995). In schools such as Willamette, where the ethic of action research has taken hold, the system itself transmits many powerful lessons: First, it teaches that it is okay to dream, to create, and to believe in the achievement of visions and targets. Second, it teaches that through action research and thoughtful reflection, it is possible to design strategies that can help us realize those dreams. Most important, it teaches that the die is never completely cast. We can always learn from experience and get better at whatever it is we truly care about and value.

Institutionalizing the Ethic of Action Research

The Washoe County School District is a large school system serving the city of Reno, Nevada, and its surrounding communities. For several years, the district embraced action research as part of its strategy to foster continuous improvement, collaboration, and professional development.

A few years ago, the staff in the district began carrying cards in their wallets that captured the essence of what they were working to accomplish (see Figure 11.1). On one side of the card it says, "*Washoe County School District—Our Goal: Continuous improvement in student performance based upon disciplined use of data.*" On the reverse side it says, "*What Constitutes Sound Decision Making: 'The Big Five.'*"

1. What do you want to accomplish? (Vision, Target)

2. What criteria will determine success? (Assessment Criteria)

3. What do you think it will take to achieve success? (Theory of Action)

4. What data will you collect? (Data to Inform Decisions)

5. How will you share your learning? (Community of Learners)

In Washoe County, they dream of a day when The Big Five becomes a mantra chanted by everyone, to everyone, over and over, throughout the schoolhouse.

Those questions can frame discussions with students, helping them to visualize and strategize achieving their goals. They can structure discussions between classroom teachers and, in doing so, reinforce the experience that colleagues are interested and excited to be working alongside one another and want to learn from each other. And finally, the Big Five forms the outline of a process for school improvement and provides a structure for ongoing discussions with parents and the community.

I truly hope that while reading this book, your participation and involvement with the four stages of action research has made you a believer in the power of the process. Chanting the Big Five mantra or finding other ways to share your belief in the empowerment that can flow from practicing the action research process can become your personal way of sharing your enthusiasm for an approach to problem solving that you have found to be professionally satisfying and have consequently made a

Figure 11.1 Washoe County School Goals and Endeavors Card

WASHOE COUNTY SCHOOL DISTRICT

OUR GOAL:

Continuous improvement in student performance based upon disciplined use of data

WHAT CONSTITUTES SOUND DECISION MAKING: "The Big Five"

1. What do you want to accomplish? (Vision, Target)
2. What criteria will determine success? (Assessment Criteria)
3. What do you think it will take to achieve success? (Theory of Action)
4. What data will you collect? (Data to Inform Decisions)
5. How will you share your learning? (Community of Learners)

Source: Used with permission of Washoe County School District.

routine part of your practice. When you discuss *your* vision, *your* theory, *your* data, and *your* action plans, you are providing public testimony to the empowerment and satisfaction that one receives by engagement in the role of learner.

Building learners is more than noble work. When one believes in the innate human capacity to learn, then anything seems possible. Paraphrasing Christa McAuliffe, when you chose teaching for your career, in no small way, you were choosing immortality. When your students and the educators you work with learn from you how good it is to be a learner, they will have gained something that will stay with them a lifetime. Through the model you are providing, they will get to see their own future: one filled with excitement, curiosity, and unlimited possibilities, and one where they, like you, can use their own learning to help others grow and develop, thereby making this a better world for us all.

Good luck and a heartfelt thank you for all that you do.

Resource A

How to Use the Feedback Forms and Summary Reports

FEEDBACK FORMS

- These forms were designed for use with a class in order to efficiently collect regular feedback on students' perceptions on things of interest to their teacher. Carbonless paper is used so the students can maintain a record of their responses over time.

- When using this process, it is important to think through the nature of the student perceptions you wish to collect—there are infinite possibilities. In the past, teachers have used these forms to collect data on such things as *enjoyment of the class, engagement in activities, how much students felt they learned, how difficult they found the material, how they felt during class,* and so on.

- After selecting the nature of the perceptions you want to collect, develop a rating scale for the students to use. Provide them with a copy of the scale or post it on the wall of your classroom or both. When doing this with students who aren't able to comprehend the meaning of a number scale, you might choose to build a scale with a sequence of smiling or frowning faces.

- It is often a good idea to have the students look at their previous feedback reports prior to filling out new ones. This makes it more likely that they will apply the scale consistently and it will reduce the chance that changes in ratings are influenced by temporary changes in mood.

- Encourage students to provide comments to explain their ratings since often there can be several different explanations for the same score. This enables you to know the specific justification for a student's choice of score. Also, these comments will later assist the students in recalling what they were thinking when they provided the feedback.

• Be sure the students date their feedback forms. This will prove important when you and they attempt to interpret any trends found in the ratings (for example, a relationship between their reactions and the teaching technique being used).

SUMMARY REPORTS

• These carbonless forms serve two purposes. They save you, the teacher researcher, the time required to ascertain patterns of changes as you look for trends with individual students or within particular classes. Second, they cause your students to reflect on the changes that occurred in their perspectives over the course of the class or the term of your study, which enables them to develop a deeper understanding of themselves as learners.

• Another value of the summary form is that it provides you with an additional and important piece of triangulated data: the students' personal explanations of the reasons behind changes that occurred in their perspectives. Later you will be able to compare and contrast their explanations with your own observations.

• When having students fill out the summary reports, use the following steps:

1. Have the students plot their numerical ratings on the two graphs. If you are doing this with students who don't yet understand how to plot scores on a graph, have a parent volunteer or older student plot the scores for the student.

2. Ask the students to look for changes in the direction and slope of the lines on their graphs and make tentative conclusions about the trends. For example, a student might conclude something like, "I enjoyed this project more and more as time went on," or "I got frustrated in the middle of last week."

3. Ask the students to sequentially review the written comments they provided on the feedback forms and reflect on the reasons for changes in perceptions. The student should then record those explanations or thoughts in the space provided below the graphs on the summary form. Should you be doing this with students who are unable to write their own responses, ask an adult or older student to pose the questions to the students and then write down their responses.

Resource B

Five Characteristics of a Quality Action Research Project

CHARACTERISTIC 1: EXPLANATION OF CONTEXT, PROBLEM, ISSUE

Elements

- Significance of issue for teachers and learners
- Unique or general factors impacting issue
- Potential for change or improvement

Basic	*Developing*	*Proficient*	*Strong*
Declares the hope for change and improvement	Demonstrates awareness of possible benefits for teaching and learning	Adequately explains the benefits for the researcher's teaching or the student's learning	Makes strong case for the need and desirability for improvement
Doesn't address applicability beyond the case at hand	Seems unsure or unclear about relevance beyond the case at hand	Recognizes and explains the applicability of this inquiry to other educators	Perceives and explores a broad range of implications beyond the case at hand
Reports on context but leaves out several critical details	Provides accurate but incomplete report on research context	Recognizes and addresses the relevant and unique characteristics of the researcher's context	Provides readers with enough contextual data to take into account the uniqueness of the context

CHARACTERISTIC 2: THEORETICAL PERSPECTIVE

Elements

- Understanding or awareness of applicable literature
- Logic behind and reasonableness of approach
- Clarity of expression

Basic	Developing	Proficient	Strong
Demonstrates awareness of the procedures recommended by developers of an intervention	Shows a basic understanding of major premises behind intervention	Demonstrates an understanding of key research findings or commentaries on the issue or problem	Provides a thorough literature review presented in a logical, clear, and concise manner
Explains how the researcher intends to implement the intervention	Explains the rationale behind proposed intervention	Provides a logical and clear explanation of the researcher's theory	Detailed, logical, and clear explanation for the theory informing the proposed intervention
		The proposed intervention is justified based on the researcher's theoretical stance	The proposed intervention logically follows from the findings of others and the researcher's own theory

CHARACTERISTIC 3: RESEARCH DESIGN

Elements

- Potential for yielding valid findings
- Potential for yielding reliable findings
- Consideration of extraneous or intervening variables

Basic	Developing	Proficient	Strong
A technique or techniques are proposed to demonstrate impact	The research design uses authentic or recognized techniques to determine impact	The research design makes appropriate use of triangulation to corroborate and support findings	The research design takes into account and adequately controls for most apparent and possible extraneous or intervening variables
The techniques have the potential for accurately reflecting performance	The research design reflects an awareness of the risk of inaccuracy	The research design makes use of multiple data points to increase accuracy	The research design uses sampling techniques that make accurate findings highly likely

CHARACTERISTIC 4: ANALYSIS OF DATA

Elements

- Supportable and logical conclusions
- Alternative explanations addressed
- Limitations explained

Basic	Developing	Proficient	Strong
Conclusions are not contradicted by the available data	The conclusions are logical and generally supported by the available data	All findings are supported by credible pieces of data	All reported findings and conclusions are supported by multiple and credible pieces of data
	The potential for alternative interpretation is recognized	Reasonable alternative interpretations of data are reported	Reasonable alternative interpretations of the data are recognized and discussed
	The researcher shows an awareness that possible limitations exist	Reasonable limitations are addressed	Reasonable limitations are recognized and addressed along with suggestions for overcoming them

CHARACTERISTIC 5: ACTION PLANNING

Elements

- Supported by findings
- Potential for improvement theoretically sound
- Contains an action research assessment design
- Outlines potential value for self and others

Basic	Developing	Proficient	Strong
The plan is consistent with a theory	The plan has reasonable face validity	The plan is consistent with the data and conclusions	The plan is a direct and logical extension of the findings and conclusions
The plan is not contradicted by available data	The available data appears supportive of the plan	The findings suggest that the plan will make a difference in student performance	Based on the available data, it appears likely that student performance will improve if and when the plan is followed
	The plan seems logical	The theory behind the plan is addressed	The theory behind the plan is clearly outlined and addressed
		The action plan contains a viable assessment strategy	The assessment plan should provide valuable evidence of the effectiveness of the plan
		The researcher should benefit from data on the implementation of the action plan	The researcher and other educators are likely to benefit from data on the eventual implementation of the plan

Resource C

Applications
for Leadership Projects

Exhibit 1: Target Identification Form for Leaders

Exhibit 2: Post-Hoc Analysis of Leadership Form

Exhibit 3: Rating Scale for a Collegial School

Exhibit 4: Rate of Growth Charting With Leadership Projects

Exhibit 5: Using the Two-Step Walk-Through With a Leadership Project

Exhibit 6: Data-Collection Planning Matrix

Exhibit 7: Data-Collection Planning Matrix (ACR Questions)

Exhibit 8: Creating a Comparison Graph of Actual Energy Expended

EXHIBIT 1: TARGET IDENTIFICATION FORM FOR LEADERS

Reread your report, your journal, or your interview, asking the following questions (write your responses under each one):

What were the specific accomplishments (such as improved climate, improved morale, greater collaboration, improved behavior)? These are *performance targets*.

_____
_____
_____
_____
_____
_____
_____

What specific changes did you observe in your leadership skills (better facilitation of discussions, improved questioning skills, greater delegation)? These are *process targets*.

_____
_____
_____
_____
_____
_____
_____

What specific changes did you observe in your school or program (greater sense of community, improved behavior, greater proficiency with state standards)? These are *program targets*.

_____
_____
_____
_____
_____
_____
_____

EXHIBIT 2: POST-HOC ANALYSIS OF LEADERSHIP FORM

Briefly describe the goal of this initiative:

_____

_____

_____

_____

State the way you had hoped things would change or evolve as a result of this initiative:

_____

_____

_____

If this initiative had been completely successful what would a colleague (or a staff member responsible for carrying out this initiative) be saying about this project?

_____

_____

_____

What is this colleague (or staff member) now saying about this initiative?

_____

_____

_____

Using the table provided, list in sequence all the significant activities and facilitation you provided during the implementation of this initiative and this colleague's (staff member's) reaction to that activity:

Date	Activity	Colleague's Reaction

Use additional space if necessary.

EXHIBIT 3: RATING
SCALE FOR A COLLEGIAL SCHOOL

Trait	Emerging (1)	Basic (2)	Developing (3)	Proficient (4)	Fluent (5)
1. Universal excellence in student performance	There is at least one arena (academic or behavioral) where more than ninety percent of the students demonstrate proficiency.	There are arenas (both academic and behavioral) where more than ninety percent of the students demonstrate proficiency.	The mean performance of students in every demographic category are at or above proficiency in reading, math, and writing.	Sixty-seven percent of students in every demographic category are at or above proficiency in reading, math, and writing.	More than ninety percent of students are proficient in every subject and arena of importance. Performance is equally excellent across demographic groups.
2. Excellent staff morale	There are staff members who report being personally and/or professionally satisfied with their work at this school.	Many staff report enjoying their work at this school and being personally and professionally satisfied with their work.	Most staff report enjoying their work at this school and being personally and professionally satisfied with their work.	More than ninety percent of the staff report being personally and professionally satisfied with their work at this school.	Everyone reports loving their work at this school.
3. Team Culture	Some people work regularly with colleagues.	Some people work regularly with their colleagues. Collegial work is thought of in a positive way.	Every staff member is engaged in at least one significant collaborative endeavor. The staff reports enjoying collegial work.	Every staff member is engaged in multiple collaborative endeavors. Collegial work is cited by most staff as characteristic of the school.	Every staff member is repeatedly engaged in numerous collaborative endeavors. Collegial work is cited by all staff as characteristic of the school.

(Continued)

(Continued)

Trait	Emerging (1)	Basic (2)	Developing (3)	Proficient (4)	Fluent (5)
4. Staff as skilled problem solvers	Teachers identify and articulate educational problems	Teachers bring educational problems to the attention of other professionals.	Teachers routinely seek the input of colleagues when dealing with educational problems.	Teachers routinely seek the input of colleagues and collaboratively develop alternative approaches when dealing with educational problems.	Solutions to complex problems always involve solicitation of input, action research, and the collaborative development of alternatives.
5. Alignment of curriculum, instruction, and assessment	Teachers choose instructional strategies in consideration of the content being taught and monitor student performance.	In several disciplines the faculty follows a common curriculum, chooses instructional strategies based on that curriculum, and uses common assessments for student evaluation.	In every core subject the faculty follows a common curriculum, chooses instructional strategies based on that curriculum, and uses common assessments for student evaluation.	In every subject the faculty adapts the common curriculum, chooses instructional strategies based on that curriculum, and uses common assessments for student evaluation.	In every subject the faculty collaboratively adapts the common curriculum, chooses instructional strategies based on that curriculum, and creates common assessments for student evaluation.

EXHIBIT 4: RATE OF GROWTH CHARTING WITH LEADERSHIP PROJECTS

1. Generate a two-column table set up like the one below.

Key Activities/Accomplishments:	*Anticipated Date:*
A:	
B:	
C:	

2. In the left-hand column, list all the key activities/accomplishments that you believe will need to occur for your initiative to realize its full potential. This list should not be considered final until after you have completed the development of your theory of action (Chapter 5).

3. In the right-hand column, place the date when each key activity/accomplishment should occur if your initiative to realize its full potential in the allocated time.

4. Create a rate-of-growth chart. The horizontal axis is for plotting the elapsed time between the initiation of your project and the expected end date. On the vertical axis you should list each of the key activities/accomplishments from your table.

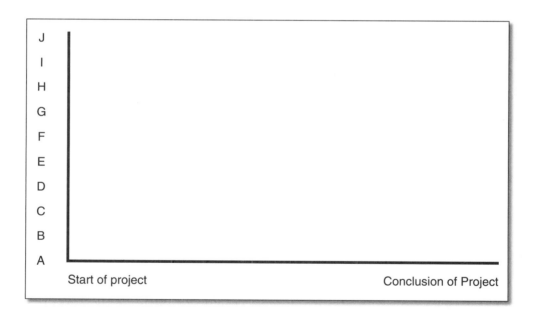

5. Draw a line graph reflecting the anticipated completion date for each key activity/accomplishment as assigned on the table.

6. Periodically check in with key participants in your project regarding the status of each key activity/accomplishment and indicate the date that activity actually occurred on the rate-of-growth chart below.

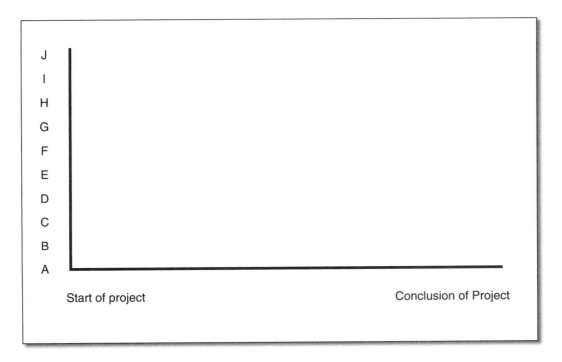

7. Connect the points indicating the actual dates of completion for the key activities/ accomplishments of your project. That line represents your actual "rate of growth." When the actual rate of growth line is above your anticipated line (step 5), it represents faster than the expected rate of growth. When and if the "actual" line falls below the "anticipation" line, it reflects slower than expected rate of growth.

EXHIBIT 5: USING THE TWO-STEP WALK-THROUGH WITH A LEADERSHIP PROJECT

Below is Dr. Hernandez's graphic reconstruction of her plan to increase faculty collegiality by applying the two-step walk-through for the creation of research questions.

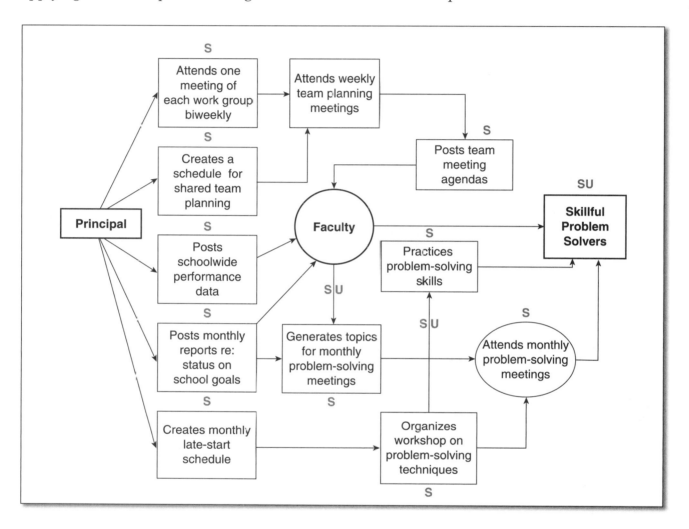

The two questions she asked of each assumption in a graphic reconstruction are as follows:

1. Is this factor, issue, variable, or relationship significant?

2. How confident am I regarding the workings of this factor, issue, variable, or relationship?

A yes answer to the first question is indicated with the letter "S" for *significance* and a yes to the second question is indicated by a "U" for *uncertain*.

After taking her two-step walk-through, Dr. Hernandez listed all the significant aspects of her theory, emphasizing in bold those aspects about which she had considerable uncertainty.

Significant Aspects of Theory

1. The principal attends meetings of each group biweekly.

2. The principal creates a schedule for shared team planning.

3. The principal posts schoolwide performance data.

4. The principal posts monthly reports on school goals.

5. The principal creates a monthly late-start schedule.

6. The principal organizes a workshop on problem solving.

7. The principal attends monthly problem-solving meeting.

8. The faculty generates topics for monthly problem-solving meetings.

9. Everyone attends monthly problem-solving meetings.

10. The faculty practices problem solving.

11. **The faculty becomes skillful problem solvers.**

Significant Relationships

1. **The relationship between team meetings informed by data and the faculty's ability to generate meaningful topics for problem solving.**

2. **The relationship between problem-solving professional development and actual use of the skills.**

3. **The relationship between practicing problem solving and becoming skillful problem solvers.**

Based upon this assessment, Dr. Hernandez generated the following three action research questions:

1. What was the nature of faculty development with problem-solving skills?

2. What factors influenced the faculty's decisions on topics for group problem solving?

3. In what ways did the principal's actions and professional development contribute to the development of faculty skills with problem solving?

EXHIBIT 6: DATA-COLLECTION PLANNING MATRIX

Project Focus: Enhancing Faculty Collaboration

Research Question	Data Source #1	Data Source #2	Data Source #3
What was the nature of faculty development with problem-solving skills?	Faculty survey	Focus-group interviews with each faculty work team	Video transcripts from problem-solving meetings
What factors influenced the faculty's decisions on topics for group problem solving?	Faculty survey	Focus-group interviews with each faculty work team	Journal
In what ways did the principal's actions and professional development contribute to the development of faculty skills with problem solving?	Faculty survey	Focus-group interviews with each faculty work team	Faculty response to the researcher's tentative assertions (member checking)

EXHIBIT 7: DATA-COLLECTION PLANNING MATRIX (ACR QUESTIONS)

Project Focus: Enhancing Faculty Collaboration

Research Question	Data Source #1	Data Source #2	Data Source #3
What did I/we actually do?	Daily journal	Minutes from team meetings and faculty meetings	Materials produced as part of project
What improvements occurred on our/my achievement targets?	Faculty survey	Focus-group interviews with each faculty work team	Contrast student performance data before and after each problem-solving session (pertaining to the problem focus)
How did our/my actions influence the changes in performance on the achievement targets?	Faculty survey	Focus-group interviews with each faculty work team	Faculty response to my tentative assertions (member checking)

EXHIBIT 8: CREATING A COMPARISON GRAPH OF ACTUAL ENERGY EXPENDED

1. Consider the percentage of your (or your group's) total attention that you had expected (before the work started) this project would command.

2. Review your calendar, meeting agendas and minutes, and any other artifacts you have available regarding the work and energy that was ultimately expended on this project.

3. Based on your review of the data (#2 above) make a subjective judgment on the energy consumed by the project. Was it approximately what you had anticipated? Did you end up spending twice as much energy on this than you had anticipated? Did it garner only half the attention you thought it would? Or, something else?

4. Make a list of all the significant *categories of action* that consumed attention from you or your group during the project.

5. If the total attention devoted to the project was less than anticipated, add an item to the list of *categories of action* (#4 above) titled "other priorities." If the attention devoted was approximately the same or more than you had anticipated (#1 above) do not add the "other priorities" category.

6. Assign percentages to the items on your list of *categories of action*. If you have a category for "other priorities," the percentage you should assign to that category should equal the loss of attention noted in Step 5 above. (For example, if you felt this project had only received half the attention you anticipated, then the category "other priorities" should be assigned fifty percent.) The percentage you assign to the remaining categories on your list should be based on your subjective judgment after a careful review of your calendar and other artifacts.

7. Using the percentages assigned (Step 6), draw a pie graph illustrating your perception of the actual energy expended.

8. If you had determined that the total energy expended on this project was significantly in excess of what was anticipated (Step 5), that fact should be noted in the narrative comments you write explaining your two priority pies.

Glossary

This is a listing of terms used throughout this book, many of which have more than one meaning even within the field of action research. This glossary defines these words and phrases as they are used in this book.

academic postmortem   A comprehensive review of the educational and instructional activities that preceded and likely contributed to a particular educational outcome

achievement target   A performance or outcome that one believes can be influenced by the actions of educators

adequate yearly progress (AYP)   The rate of growth expected of a student or group of students over the course of a school year

analytic discourse   The process of being interviewed by a group of colleagues to assist in articulating, clarifying, and deepening one's perspective on an issue

boundaries   Limits placed on the scope of an inquiry or activity to assist in maintaining focus

cause and effect   A supposition that a particular action is responsible for producing a specified result

context   Factors found in an environment that may have an influence on what works or doesn't work in that environment

dependent variable   The behavior, outcome, or performance that one expects to see changed as a result of targeted action

descriptive research   An inquiry or study that seeks to answer the question of what is currently going on in a specified arena

educated hypothesis   An assumption or prediction regarding what will result from a particular action based upon past experience

emergent theory of action   The beginnings of a theory of action that is still under development

extraneous variable   A factor that has nothing to do with the phenomenon under study (the relationships between the dependent and independent variables) and exerts its own separate effect on the dependent variable

face validity Something that seems obvious or true based on simply looking at it

hypothesis A prediction of what will result from an action or set of actions

intervening variable A phenomenon that has its own relationship with the independent variable and has a separate influence on the dependent variable

literature review A systematic examination of what has been written or reported on a phenomenon

operative theory of action The approach currently in use and the rationale behind that approach

performance targets Particular skills, outcomes, or performances that one would like to see improved

principal investigator (PI) The person with primary leadership responsibility for a research project. This individual sets the focus, articulates the theory, and establishes the research design that guides the study

process targets Professional techniques, actions, or procedures that one would like to see improved

qualitative data Material that is collected or assembled pertaining to a phenomenon being studied, made up of descriptions, opinions, artifacts, or some combination of these—frequently subjective in nature

quantitative data Material that is collected or assembled pertaining to the phenomenon being studied that is made up of objective ratings or scores that can be expressed mathematically

quasi-experimental research An inquiry or investigation that infers a relationship between an action or set of actions and a defined target (dependent variable)

rate of growth The speed at which progress is being made on an achievement target

rating scale A pre-established continuum of performance that can be used to reliably determine a level of performance or an achievement target (also referred to as a rubric)

reflective interview A discourse with a colleague designed to identify and explore a potential action research focus

relationship A pattern of consistent influence between factors, variables, programs, or actions

reliability The accuracy of the data

research assistant (RA) An individual who assists in carrying out an investigation or study as a subordinate to the principal investigator (PI)

researcher's journal Notes kept by an action researcher for the purpose of tracking events that transpire during the course of research, especially any deviations from a pre-established theory of action

spreadsheet An expandable record-keeping matrix (either paper or electronic) that enables a researcher to assemble data on numerous variables across a large number of subjects

team reflection A process for a work group to deliberate in an effort to arrive at a collective research focus

tentative assertions Statements regarding patterns or trends that surfaced during the analysis of action research data

theory of action The rationale behind the actions to be taken by a practitioner and the particular inferences that back up that rationale

trend analysis A search for patterns in data over time to identify any relationships between changes in performance and specific actions and events

universal student success All students meeting academic expectations without gaps in performance due to demographic or socioeconomic factors

validity The truthfulness of data; whether the data does, in fact, represent what it purports to represent

vision The overall picture of what one would like to see accomplished as a result of action

References

Aronson, J., Zimmerman, J., & Carlos, L. (1999). *Improving student achievement by extending school: Is it just a matter of time?* San Francisco: WestED. Retrieved September 12, 2010, from http://www.wested.org/cs/we/view/rs/95

Brown, M., & Macatangay, A. (2002). The impact of action research for professional development: Case studies in two Manchester schools. *Westminster Studies in Education, 25*(1), 35–45.

Caro-Bruce, C., & Zeichner, K. (1988). The *nature and impact of an action research professional development program in one urban school district.* Madison, WI: Madison Metropolitan School District.

Century, J., Freeman, C., Rudnick, M., & Leslie, D. (2008). *Rigorous measurement of fidelity of implementation of instructional materials.* Baltimore, MD: National Association for Research in Science Teaching.

Deming, W. E. (2000). *Out of crisis.* Cambridge: MIT Press. (Original work published 1986)

Depree, M. (1998). *Leading without power.* San Francisco: Jossey-Bass.

Fishman, B., Marx, R., Best, S., & Tal, R. (2003). Linking teacher and student learning to improve professional development in systemic reform. *Teaching and Teacher Education: An International Journal of Research and Studies, 19,* 643–658.

Fullan, M. (2001). *Leading in a culture of change.* San Francisco: Jossey-Bass.

Hale, J. A. (2008). *A guide to curriculum mapping: Planning, implementing, and sustaining the process.* Thousand Oaks, CA: Corwin.

Hargreaves, A. (1991). Teaching and guilt: Exploring the emotions of teaching. *Teaching and Teacher Education, 7*(5/6), 491–505.

Hattie, J. (2008). *Visible learning: A synthesis of over 800 meta-analyses relating to achievement.* New York: Rutledge.

Hersey, P., & Blanchard, K. H. (1993). *Management of organizational behavior: Utilizing human resources* (6th ed.). Englewood Cliffs, NJ: Prentice Hall.

Hord, S. (1997). *Professional learning communities: Communities of continuous inquiry and improvement.* Austin, TX: Southwest Educational Development Laboratory.

Hubbard, R., & Powers, B. (1999). *Living the questions: A guide for teacher researchers.* Portland, ME: Stenhouse.

Jacobs, H. H. (1997). *Mapping the big picture integrating curriculum and assessment K-12.* Alexandria, VA: Association for Supervision and Curriculum Development.

Joyce, B., & Calhoun, E. (1996). *Learning experiences in school renewal: An exploration of five successful programs.* Eugene, OR: ERIC Clearinghouse on Educational Management.

Kemmis, S., & McTaggart, R. (Eds.). (1988). *The action research planner.* Victoria, BC: Deakin University Press.

Little, J. W. (1982). Norms of collegiality and experimentation: Workplace conditions of school success. *American Educational Research Journal, 19,* 325–340.

Los Angeles Unified School District. (2010). *Fidelity of implementation.* Retrieved September 10, 2010, from http://www.lausd.k12.ca.us/lausd/offices/hep/news/fidelity.html

Miles, M., & Huberman, A. M. (1994). *Qualitative data analysis* (2nd ed.). Thousand Oaks, CA: Sage.

Nir, A. E., & Bogler, R. (2008). The antecedents of teacher satisfaction with professional development programs. *Teaching and Teacher Education: An International Journal of Research and Studies, 24*(2), 377–386.

No Child Left Behind Act of 2001, Pub. Law No. 107-110 (2002).

O'Donnell, C. (2006). Fidelity of implementation in scaling up highly rated science curriculum units. In A. Benbow (Ed.), *NSF K-12 mathematics, science, and technology curriculum developers' conference 2005: Dealing with challenges to effective and widespread implementation of IMD curricula.* Alexandria, VA: American Geological Institute.

Reeves, D. (2008). *Reframing teacher leadership to improve your school.* Arlington, VA: Association for Supervision and Curriculum Development.

Reeves, D. (2010). *Transforming professional development into student results.* Alexandria, VA: Association for Supervision and Curriculum Development.

Rosenholtz, S. J. (1985). *Teachers' workplace: A study of social organization of schools.* New York: Longman.

Sagor, R. (1995). Overcoming the one solution syndrome. *Educational Leadership, 52*(7), 24–27.

Sagor, R. (1996). *Local control and accountability: How to get it, keep it, and improve school performance.* Thousand Oaks, CA: Corwin.

Sagor, R. (2000). *Guiding school improvement with action research.* Alexandria, VA: Association for Supervision and Curriculum Development.

Sagor, R. (2010). *Collaborative action research for professional learning communities.* Bloomington, IN: Solution Tree.

Sagor, R., & Curley, J. (1991, April). *Can collaborative action research improve school effectiveness?* (ERIC Document Reproduction Services Nos. ED 336 864 & EA 023 349). Paper presented at the American Educational Research Association annual meeting, Chicago, IL.

Schlecty, P. C., & Vance, V. (1983). Recruitment, selection, and retention: The shape of the teaching force. *Elementary School Journal, 83,* 469–487.

Senge, P. M. (1990). *The fifth discipline: The art and practice of the learning organization.* New York: Doubleday Currency.

Sizer, T. R. (1984). *Horace's compromise: The dilemma of the American high school.* New York: Houghton Mifflin.

Stanley, K. R., Spradlin, T. E., & Plucker, J. A. (2007). The daily schedule: A look at the relationship between time and academic achievement. *CEEP Education Policy Brief, 5*(6), 1–7.

Index

Note: In page references, e indicates exhibits, and f indicates figures.

Abstracts, 186, 188–189f, 190f
Academic postmortem, 76, 214
Achievement targets, 214
  action research questions and, 91, 94
  data analyzing and, 154
  intuitive regression analysis and, 66f
  performance rating scales and, 45
  rate of growth and, 50
  success and, 31, 168f, 172
  team reflection and, 27, 29
  See also Dependent variables; Priority
    achievement targets
ACR questions, 88–91, 94–96
  data analyzing and, 129, 130–131
  data collection and, 112–114, 113f,
    115, 212e
  data collection planning matrix for, 212
  See also Action research questions
Action alternatives, 172, 174
  educational specifications and, 174–176,
    175f, 177–178
Action plans:
  abstracts and, 188
  formats for reporting action research
    projects and, 186
  turning finding into, 163
  See also Planning
Action research, 5–6
  abstracts and, 186, 188–189, 188–189f,
    190f
  archiving, 186
  audiences for, 180–182, 181f, 185f
  formats for reporting, 184, 186
  four stages of, 4, 6–7, 61, 192–193
  principal categories of, xii–xiv
  reporting/sharing, 178–181
  theory of action and, 57, 77f
  two categories of, 7–8
  See also Descriptive research
Action research cycle, 8f, 177–178, 178f
Action Research Journal, 22, 23f. *See also*
  Journaling

Action research questions, 87–88
  drafting, 101–104
  generic, 88–91, 94–96, 127, 150
  See also ACR questions; Research
    questions
Action Research Report Checklist,
  186, 187f
Action research reports, 182, 183f
Activity Analysis Form, 137f
Adequate Yearly Progress (AYP), 50–52,
  52f, 53f, 214
  rate-of-growth charts and, 53–55
Analytic discourse, 13, 26–27, 214
Analyzing data. *See* Data analyzing
Anthropology, 107
Articulating theory, viii, 4, 6–7, 10f, 184
Assumptions:
  lesson-planning and, 86
  theory of action and, 96–97, 97–98,
    99–100

Barth, R., viii
Boundaries, 14, 21, 214

Carbonless paper, 117, 118f, 122f
  feedback forms and, 196–197
Causal relationships, 82, 149
Coherence, 193
Collaboration, ix–x, xi
  enhancing faculty, 104, 211, 212
Colleague Interview Guide, 36, 37–38f
Computers:
  educational specifications and, 170–171
  literature reviews and, 39
  spreadsheet software for, 124–125, 155,
    157–158, 216
Congruence, 193
Context, 191, 198, 214
  data analyzing and, 151, 152
  stories and, 160
Cooperative teaming, 99, 112
Curriculum maps, 89

Data:
  action alternatives/educational
    specifications and, 177
  action research and, 4
  action research questions and, 88–90, 91,
    94, 95, 96
  actual energy expended, 135, 213
  analysis of, 165, 200
  creating bins for, 153–162, 156f, 157f
  definition of, 107
  drafting action research questions
    and, 103
  empirical, 148
  feedback forms and, 196–197
  fluency of, 152f, 153f
  formats for reporting action research
    projects and, 186
  keeping file copies of, 117, 118f
  proven practices programs and, 59
  quasi-experimental/descriptive research
    and, 10f
  reporting findings and, 180–181. *See also*
    Findings
  research questions and, 87, 88
  sorting, 159, 160
  student development and, 192
  student performance and, 91, 94
  summary reports and, 197
  theory of action and, 7
Data analyzing, 126–127
  achievement targets and, 154
  ACR research questions and, 129,
    130–131
  bins and matrix process for, 153–162,
    156f, 157f
  context and, 151, 152
  disaggregation and, 142–143, 158
  factoids and, 159–160
  findings and, 135–136, 149–150
  fluency and, 152f
  implementation dip and, 152–153
  journaling and, 131, 135, 136, 138
  leadership projects and, 135–136, 138
  lesson plans and, 131, 136, 138
  member checking and, 149, 162
  narratives and, 126–127, 160
  patterns and, 136, 143, 149, 151, 153,
    160, 162
  planning and, 126, 131
  PLC teams and, 135, 136
  priority achievement targets and, 127,
    128, 138, 140–141
  priority pies and, 131
  qualitative data and, 151–155
  success and, 127, 154
  tendencies and, 151, 153, 160, 162
  tentative assertions and, 149–151,
    160, 162
  theory of action and, 131, 154
  time line and, 138, 139f, 143, 146t

trend analysis and, 127–129, 128f, 129f
two-dimensional matrix for, 161f
Data collection, 105
  behavioral ratings and, 117, 119
  descriptive research and, 107
  feedback forms for, 119, 121f, 122–123f,
    196–197
  fishing for, 110
  journaling and, 22, 111, 113, 124
  leadership projects and, 115
  planning matrix for, 211, 212
  precision and, 108–110
  quasi-experimental research and, 108
  research assistants and, 110–111, 115, 119
  supervisors and, 106–107
  technology and, 115, 124–125
  triangulated plan for, 112–114, 113f, 114f
  triangulation worksheet for, 116
Data collection plans, 115, 211e, 212e
Decision making:
  complexity of, 2–3
  data collection and, 108, 109, 177.
    See also Data collection
  educational specifications and, 167,
    169–172
  educators and, 57, 171, 193
  future actions and, 182
  school leaders and, 177
  See also Planning; Problem solving
Deming, W. E., 56
Dependent variables, 61, 62, 214
  drafting action research questions
    and, 103
  human behavior/social interactions
    and, 94–95
  See also Achievement targets
Descriptive research, xiv, 7, 8–11, 10f, 214
  data collection and, 107
  graphic reconstructions and, 76,
    78–85, 86
  priority pie and, 68–69
  See also Action research
Direct instruction, 3, 65, 67f, 73, 106
Disaggregation, 124, 142–143, 158

Educated hypothesis, 148, 214
Educational specifications:
  action alternatives and, 174–176,
    175f, 177
  computers and, 170–171
  decision making and, 167, 169–172
  research findings and, 171, 173f
Extraneous variables, 95, 96, 214

Face validity, 71, 115, 215
Facilitators, 106
Factoids, 159–160
Feedback, xiv
  data analyzing and, 136
  data collection and, 121f, 122f

drafting action research questions and, 102, 103, 104
performance targets and, 20
teaching and, 106
Feedback forms, 196–197
data collection and, 119, 121f, 122–123f
Findings, 163
data analyzing and, 135–136, 149–150
reporting, 178, 179–186
Fluency, 152f, 153f
Focus form, 27, 28f
Fullan, M., 152
Funding, 170, 192
Future actions, 5, 6
data analyzing and, 149, 151
decision making and, 182
reporting findings and, 180

Geographic maps, 71. *See also* Maps
Goals:
action research and, 6
educational policies and, 58
long-range, 49–50, 54
reflective writing and, 16
schools and, 193
supervisors and, 107
Grading:
decision making and, 182
spreadsheet software and, 124
Graphic reconstruction, 63, 69
building, 73–74
data analyzing and, 154
descriptive research and, 76, 78–85
finalizing, 86
proofing, 84–85, 86
quasi-experimental research and, 74–76
revised theory of action and, 172
time issues and, 167
using findings and, 164–165, 166f
walk-through process for, 97–101, 99f, 101f

Hargreaves, A., 2
Huberman, A. M., 153
Hypothesis, 7, 51, 71, 148, 215

Implementation dip, 152–153
Improvement team, 6
Independent variables, 61–62, 62–63
descriptive research and, 68
drafting action research questions and, 103
human behavior/social interactions and, 94–95
priority pie and, 63–68
summarizing, 65, 69
Informed action, 4
action research cycle and, 8f
journaling and, 125
planning, 7, 8f, 10f, 126, 163, 184
Instructional postmortem, 32

form for, 33–34f, 35
Instructional Timeline, 146t. *See also* Time issues
Internet, 39. *See also* Computers
Intervening variables, 95, 187f, 215
Interview Guide, 37–38f
Intuitive Regression Analysis, 65–66, 66f, 168f
descriptive research and, 69

Journal Analysis Form, 22, 24f
Journaling, 20–24
data analyzing and, 131, 135, 136, 138
data collection and, 111, 113, 124
reporting findings and, 179, 180

Kemmis, S., 5
Knowledge workers, 106

Leadership, xi
form for, 35, 204
target identification form and, 20
Leadership Form, 35, 204
Leadership projects, xi
applications for, 202–213
ascertaining rate of growth in, 54–55
data analyzing and, 135–136, 138
data collection and, 115
surfacing research questions for, 104
two step walk-through with, 209–210
Lesson planning, 92f
action research questions and, 90–91
assumptions and, 86
data analyzing and, 131, 136, 138
data collection and, 114f
decision-making and, 3
Literacy development, 20
Literature review, 36, 58, 72, 79, 100, 215
planning form for, 39, 40f

Maps, 71–73
curriculum, 89
geographic, 71
using findings and, 164
McAuliffe, C., 195
McTaggart, R., 5
Member checking, 150, 211e, 212e
data analyzing and, 149, 162
Miles, M., 153
Motivated learners, 80f, 82f, 83f, 85f

Narratives, 16, 18
data analyzing and, 126–127, 160
formats for reporting action research projects and, 184, 186
See also Reflective writing
No Child Left Behind (NCLB), 50, 60

Operative theory of action, 9, 10f, 58, 215
descriptive research and, 9, 68, 69

Past actions, 5, 151
Patterns:
    data analyzing and, 136, 143, 149, 151,
        153, 160, 162
    data collection and, 114, 117, 119
    homework assessments and, 183
    running records of behavioral ratings
        and, 117
Performance Graph, 144f
Performance rating scales, 43–47
    worksheet for, 46f
Performance targets, ix, 18, 20, 42, 44, 215
Planning:
    action research and, 31–32
    data analyzing and, 126, 131
    data collection and, 105, 112–114, 115,
        211, 212. *See also* Data collection
    educational specifications and, 167,
        169–172
    educators and, 171
    gathering insights from colleagues
        and, 36
    reporting findings and, 180
    researcher's journals and, 125
    research projects and, 200–201
    success and, 30–31
    supervisors and, 106
    time, 4. *See also* Time issues
    See also Action plans; Decision making
Plan of action, 68, 76, 126, 193
PLC teams:
    collaboration and, ix–x
    data analyzing and, 135, 136
Post-Hoc Analysis of Leadership
    Form, 35, 204
Present action, 5
Prewriting exercises, 14
Principal Investigator (PI), 111, 215
Priority achievement targets, 20f
    data analyzing and, 127, 128, 138,
        140–141
    data collection and, 113
    data collection/quasi-experimental
        research and, 108
    dependent variables and, 61, 62. *See also*
        Dependent variables
    developing criteria to measure changes
        with, 41–43
    success and, 165, 167, 176
    See also Achievement targets
Priority pies:
    actual energy expended and, 135, 213
    comparison of, 169f
    data analyzing and, 131
    descriptive research and, 68–69
    independent variables and, 63–68
    revised theory of action and, 178
    success and, 98
    time issues and, 167
    using findings and, 164–165

Priority targets, 108, 119
Problem solving, 67f, 79f, 194
    priority pie strategy and, 64
    See also Decision making
Process targets, ix, 18, 20, 42, 215
    decision making and, 169
    success and, 31
Professional learning communities, viii,
    xvii, 177
Program action research, 47–48
Program targets, ix, 18, 20, 31, 32, 44
Prompts:
    journaling and, 21
    reflective writing and, 14–15

Qualitative data, 151–155, 215
    member checking and, 149
    quasi-experimental studies and, 9, 11
    trend analysis processes and, 150
Quantitative data, 153, 215
    quasi-experimental studies and,
        9, 11, 108
Quasi-experimental research, 7–8, 10f, 215
    data collection and, 108, 113–114
    graphic reconstruction and, 74–76

Rate of growth:
    academic achievement and, 50
    charts, 53–55, 207, 208
    expectations for, 52f, 53f
Rating scales, 43–47, 120f, 205–206
    adequate yearly progress and, 51
    data collection and, 113–114
    dependent variables and, 62
    feedback forms and, 196
    program action research and, 47–48
    reading proficiency and, 48f
    running records of behavioral ratings
        and, 117, 119
    worksheet for, 45, 46f
    See also Performance rating scales
Record keeping, 91
Reflection:
    lesson plans and, 91
    researcher's journals and, 125
Reflective interviews, 25, 27, 29
Reflective writing, 13–16, 18
    journaling and, 20–21
    worksheet for, 16, 17f
Regression Analysis Worksheet, 65, 66f, 69
Reliability, 215
    data collection and, 109–110
    data collection/leadership projects
        and, 115
Report Planning Form, 184, 185f
Research Assistants (RA), 215
    data collection and, 110–111, 115, 119
Researcher's journals, 125. *See also*
    Journaling
Research projects, xiii, 198–201

Research questions, 87–88
  achievement targets and, 91, 94
  data and, 94, 95, 96, 129, 130–131
  dependent variables and, 103
  developing, 96–97
  feedback and, 102, 103, 104
  generic, 88–91, 94–96
  independent variables and, 103
  leadership projects and, 104
  lesson-planning and, 90–91
  student performance and, 103
  success and, 103
  time issues and, 104
  See also Action research questions
Results *See* Findings
Revised theory of action, 7, 61, 172,
  177–178. *See also* Theory of action
Rubrics, 43, 47. *See also* Performance rating
  scales

Sagor, R., x, 1
Schools, 191–195
  data collection and, 110
  educators and, 2, 57, 171, 193
Scientifically proven practices, xi, 58, 59–60
Sizer, T., 106
Spreadsheet software, 124–125, 155,
  157–158, 216
Standards, xi–xii
  educational policies and, 58
  program targets and, 18
  success and, 2
Stickney, J., 193
Student performance:
  cultural norms/organizational practices
    and, 4–5
  data and, 91, 94
  drafting action research questions
    and, 103
  graphing of trends in, 124
  programs to improve, 89–90
  rating scales and, 47–48
Success, ix
  achievement targets and, 168f, 172
  action research and, 4–5
  data analyzing and, 127, 154
  drafting action research questions
    and, 103
  educational knowledge base and, 58
  educators and, 171
  educators/students and, 2
  experience and, 35–36
  gathering insights from colleagues
    and, 36
  independent variables and, 64
  long-range goals and, 49–50, 52
  organizational, 56
  planning and, 30–31. *See also* Planning
  priority achievement targets and, 165,
    167, 176

priority pies and, 98
proven practices programs and, 59–60
schools and, 191–192
theory of action and, 61, 66, 68, 86
universal student, ix, 1, 2, 4, 11, 58, 60,
  177, 216
visualizing, 31
Summary reports, 197
Support staff, 4, 125

Target identification forms, 18, 19f, 20,
  25, 203
Team reflection, 13, 27, 29, 216
Technology, 186
  data collection and, 115, 124–125
Tendencies, 151, 153, 160, 162
Tentative assertions, 148, 162, 165, 216
  data analyzing and, 149–151, 160, 162
Testing:
  adequate yearly progress and, 50–51
  rate-of-growth charts and, 54–55
Theory development, 54, 56, 57, 68
Theory of action, 216
  action research and, 57
  action research cycle and, 8f
  action research/inquiry and, 77f
  articulating, 55, 56–57
  assumptions and, 96–97, 97–98, 99–100
  building, 62–63
  commercial programs and, 39, 41
  data and, 7, 151, 154
  descriptive research and, 9, 68
  educational specifications and, 169
  flawed, 75
  formats for reporting action research
    projects and, 186
  graphic reconstructions and, 78
  implementing, 97
  implementing/exploring, 87
  modifying, 163–167
  proofing, 165
  quasi-experimental research and, 8
  researcher's journals and, 125
  revised, 7, 61, 172, 177–178
  significant aspects of, 102f
  success and, 61, 66, 68, 86
  time issues and, 167
  walk-through process for, 97–101,
    99f, 101f
Time issues:
  data analyzing and, 131, 132f, 133f, 134f,
    135f, 136
  data collection and, 105, 106, 119
  data collection/leadership projects
    and, 115
  data collection/technology and, 124
  drafting action research questions
    and, 104
  educators and, 13
  independent variables and, 65

learning and, 63
lesson plans and, 91
literature reviews and, 36
reflective writing and, 13, 14
research assistants and, 110–111
researcher's journals and, 125
revised theory of action and, 178
using findings and, 167
Time priority sheets, 91, 93f, 131, 132f, 135, 167
Time-Use Graph, 133f
Traits, 45, 62
Trend analysis, 128f, 129f, 141, 150, 151, 216
data analyzing and, 127–129

Triangulated data-collection plan, 112–114, 113f, 114f
Triangulation, 94, 109, 109f

Universal student success, ix, 1, 2, 4, 11, 58, 60, 177, 216. *See also* Success

Validity, 6, 43, 94, 103, 108, 149, 216
data collection and, 109–110
data collection/leadership projects and, 115

Writing prompts, 14–15, 21
Writing skills, 78f

CORWIN
A SAGE Company

The Corwin logo—a raven striding across an open book—represents the union of courage and learning. Corwin is committed to improving education for all learners by publishing books and other professional development resources for those serving the field of PreK–12 education. By providing practical, hands-on materials, Corwin continues to carry out the promise of its motto: **"Helping Educators Do Their Work Better."**